Yellowstone

AND

Grand Teton National Parks

2nd Edition

by Geoff O'Gara

IDG Books Worldwide, Inc.
An International Data Group Company
Foster City, CA • Chicago, IL • Indianapolis, IN • New York, NY

S0-AYB-413

ABOUT THE AUTHOR

Geoff O'Gara writes travel guides, fiction, and non-fiction on natural resource issues from his home in Lander, Wyoming, where he also works for Wyoming Public Television. His next book is *What You See in Clear Water* (Knopf).

IDG BOOKS WORLDWIDE, INC.

An International Data Group Company
919 E. Hillsdale Blvd.
Suite 400
Foster City, CA 94404

Find us online at **www.frommers.com**

ISBN 0-02-863698-8
ISSN 1093-9792

Editor: Margot Weiss
Production Editor: Scott Barnes
Production Team: John Bitter, Eric Brinkman, and Heather Pope
Design by Michele Laseau
Digital Cartography by Ortelius Design & Roberta Stockwell
Illustrations in chapter 9 by Jasper Burns

SPECIAL SALES

For general information on IDG Books Worldwide's books in the U.S., please call our Consumer Customer Service department at 1-800-762-2974. For reseller information, including discounts, bulk sales, customized editions, and premium sales, please call our Reseller Customer Service Department at 1-800-434-3422.

Manufactured in the United States of America

5 4 3 2 1

Contents

List of Maps

AN INVITATION TO THE READER

In researching this book, we discovered many wonderful places—hotels, restaurants, shops, and more. We're sure you'll find others. Please tell us about them, so we can share the information with your fellow travelers in upcoming editions. If you were disappointed with a recommendation, we'd love to know that, too. Please write to:

Frommer's Yellowstone & Grand Teton
National Parks, 2nd Edition
IDG Travel
1633 Broadway
New York, NY 10019

AN ADDITIONAL NOTE

Please be advised that travel information is subject to change at any time—this is especially true of prices. Every effort has been made to ensure the accuracy of the information provided in this book, but we suggest that you write or call ahead for confirmation when making your travel plans. The authors, editors, and publisher cannot be held responsible for the experiences of readers while traveling. National parks are, by their very nature, potentially hazardous places. In doing any of the activities described herein, readers assume all risk of injury or loss that may accompany such activities. The publisher disavows all responsibility for injury, death, loss, or property damage that may arise from a reader's participation in any of the activities described herein, and the publisher makes no warranties regarding the competence, safety, and reliability of outfitters, tour companies, or training centers described in this book.

WHAT THE SYMBOLS MEAN
✪ Frommer's Favorites

Hotels, restaurants, attractions, and entertainment you should not miss.

The following abbreviations are used for credit cards:

AE	American Express	JCB	Japan Credit Bank
CB	Carte Blanche	MC	MasterCard
DC	Diners Club	V	Visa
DISC	Discover		

FIND FROMMER'S ONLINE

www.frommers.com offers up-to-the-minute listings on almost 200 cities around the globe—including the latest bargains and candid, personal articles updated daily by Arthur Frommer himself. No other Web site offers such comprehensive and timely coverage of the world of travel.

Introducing Yellowstone & Grand Teton National Parks

*L*ong before you reach the entrance to Grand Teton National Park your vision will be filled with the towering spires of the Teton Range—those signature hornlike peaks made famous through photographs. Yellowstone's geography is not as dramatic; much of the parkland is comprised of heavily forested mountains and arid, high-country plateaus. However, Yellowstone's natural marvels are world famous: hundreds of geysers including Old Faithful, inspiring waterfalls, and river gorges that rival the Grand Canyon. Both parks command the imagination and will envelop your senses from the moment you arrive.

Creatures both great and small thrive in Yellowstone and Grand Teton national parks. In the wilderness of Yellowstone's southern corners, grizzlies feed on cutthroat trout during their spawning run to the Yellowstone headwaters. In the soft blue depths of Octopus Pond, microbes of enormous scientific value are incubated and born, and in the mountain ridges coyotes make their dens and mountain lions hunt bighorn sheep. The Snake River in Grand Teton is a haven for bald eagles and osprey, moose munch their way through meadows of native foliage, and elk and buffalo lazily traverse the park on the same roads as visitors.

When John Colter, a scout for Lewis and Clark, first wandered this way in 1807, his descriptions of geysers and sulfurous hot pools and towering waterfalls were scoffed at. No one doubts him now, but this is still a place you should see for yourself. The explorers of today come in minivans and on bicycles, aboard snowmobiles and telemark skis, and in such numbers that the parks sometimes groan under the strain.

In the early days of the park, visitors were few, so few that the things they did—catching a string of 100 trout, washing their underwear in the hot pools—left no noticeable scars. Now, with millions of people visiting the parks annually, the strain on everything from sewer systems to fish population is immense.

The Yellowstone/Grand Teton Area

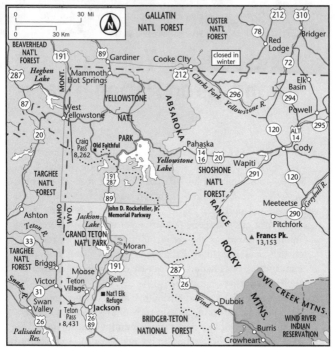

But while there are problems, these parks retain the extraordinary beauty of their landforms: The jagged Tetons, the glass surface of Jenny Lake, the Grand Canyon of the Yellowstone, the towering Obsidian Cliff, the steaming meanders of the Firehole River. Wild-life most Americans see only in zoos wanders unfettered here, from the grizzly to the river otter, the trumpeter swan to the rufous hummingbird. Aspen groves, fields of lupine, the howl of reintroduced wolves—all these testify to the resilience and vitality of the Yellowstone ecosystem, which extends beyond the borders of the park to include Grand Teton, and much more.

This is not just a paradise for sightseers—it's a scientific preserve as well. The hot pools have produced unique microbes useful in everything from gene splicing to laundry detergents; studies of the elk herds and grizzly have yielded crucial information on habitat needs and animal behavior; and the rocks of Yellowstone are like the earth turned inside out, a treasure trove for geologists.

Most of the parks' visitors will see or know little of this. They park in a pullout on U.S. Highway 191/89/26 to pose in front of Grand Teton, or sit on the crowded benches to watch Old Faithful—which is less faithfully on time these days—erupt. However, if you have more time, I suggest that you take little sections of these parks—just the Jackson Lake area, say, or Yellowstone's northeast corner, the Lamar Valley—and savor them in all their fine detail, rather than race to see every highlight.

Try to get out of your car and away from the road—into the wild heart of this wilderness. These parks embody our country's beginnings: a nation of wilderness, of challenging and rugged extremes, and a landscape of extraordinary bounty and beauty. Use this guide as a set of footprints to help you find your way there.

1 The Best of Yellowstone & Grand Teton National Parks

A "best of" list could never do justice to Yellowstone and Grand Teton. These are just starting points, the best of the excellent accommodations and food the parks offer, as well as of the virtually unique sightseeing and recreational opportunities. Some involve back-country expeditions, others can be enjoyed from behind the steering wheel. In the wildly diverse environments of these two parks, there are always choices to make about how adventurous you're willing to be.

THE BEST VIEWS

You'll never get it all in a camera lens, but you'll undoubtedly try. Don't let that viewfinder get attached to your face; take a few shots, or run a little videotape, and then put it down so you can enjoy this place with all your senses.

- **Grand Canyon of the Yellowstone River** (Yellowstone): The waterfalls are spectacular, dropping 1,000 feet (farther than Niagara Falls) and the steeply cut canyon walls are colorful. Take the short, easy hikes to **Inspiration Point** or **Artist Point,** and you'll see the falls that stimulated Thomas Moran's creativity. If you're in reasonable shape, hike down the short but steep trail to the **Brink of the Lower Falls.** (Be careful of ice or mud in the spring, or after an afternoon thundershower.) See chapter 3.
- **Lamar Valley** (Yellowstone): Bring your telephoto lens or binoculars to the northeast corner of the park, one of the best spots to spot wildlife—**bison** and **elk** grazing along the Lamar River,

or **wolves** up Slough Creek and among the big ungulates, plus, it's less crowded than the rest of the park. See chapter 3.

- **Yellowstone Lake** (Yellowstone): Sunrise over Yellowstone Lake is stunningly beautiful, especially if there's fog on the lake, whether you watch it from the sunroom at the Lake Hotel or (better) from a campsite along the southern wilderness shore. See chapter 3.

- **Cathedral Group** (Grand Teton): The three central mountains in the Teton range rarely disappoint, except on the rare occasions when weather gets in the way—more often, clouds accent rather than obscure their majesty. You'll need a wide-angle lens to get it all in from the valley floor (there are pullouts along the highway between Moran Junction and Jackson), but if you want a bigger shot, drive east on U.S. Highway 287/26 toward Togwotee Pass. See chapter 5.

- **Elk** (Grand Teton): Visiting the Jackson/Grand Teton area during the winter, take the opportunity to ride a horse-drawn sleigh out among thousands of elk on the **National Elk Refuge.** You'll get close-up shots of some of the biggest antler racks in the world, and you'll probably see coyotes, and sometimes wolves. See chapter 8.

THE BEST THERMAL DISPLAYS

Yellowstone has more thermal features—geysers, mud pots, steam vents—than the rest of the world combined. When you're angling for a good shot of a colorful pool or a belching mud pot, obey the signs—otherwise, you could find yourself, literally, on shaky ground.

- **Old Faithful Geyser** (Yellowstone): Not quite as faithful as it used to be—the intervals stretch as long as 80 minutes—but its powerful blast rises 130 feet and higher. How could you skip this one? See chapter 3.

- **Echinus Geyser** (Yellowstone): This is about the best-looking, liveliest spouting tub of water in the Norris Geyser Basin, which gets fewer visitors than other thermal areas but has a great variety of hot spring activity. See chapter 3.

- The **Riverside Geyser** (Yellowstone): This one sits on the bank of the Firehole River and sends 75-foot columns of water arching over the river. See chapter 3.

THE BEST DAY HIKES

Just a few hundred yards off the road things get a lot less crowded, and you'll have the views and the wildlife (almost) to yourself. The hikes described have an easy rating—you'll find more challenging options later in the book.

- The **Mt. Washburn Trail** (Yellowstone): Starting at Dunraven Pass south of Tower Junction, this walk offers unsurpassed views of both parks, plus the opportunity to see mountain wildlife like bighorn sheep. See chapter 4.
- The **Lonestar Geyser Trail** (Yellowstone): This gentle, 5-mile hike along the Firehole River presents several places to stop and take in the scenery, fish, and view this medium-size geyser. In the winter, this is a popular ski trail. See chapter 4.
- **Cascade Canyon** (Grand Teton): This hike can be short and sweet or long and rewarding. Make a day of it, or simply take a boat ride across the lake and hike to Hidden Falls, and you'll barely break a sweat. See chapter 6.
- **Signal Mountain Summit Trail** (Grand Teton): The hike from Signal Mountain to the Summit is rewarding for its solitude. While everyone else drives to the top, you'll have the same views and be closer to the greenery and wildlife. See chapter 6.

THE BEST BACKCOUNTRY TRAILS

- **The Thorofare Trail** (Yellowstone): This hike will take you deeper into roadless wilderness than you can get anywhere else in the Lower 48 states. You'll spend a few nights on the trail, climbing up to the park's southern border and beyond to the Yellowstone River's headwaters, a high valley bursting with wildlife. The cutthroat spawning run early in the summer attracts grizzlies and fishers if the snow has melted. It's not for the faint of heart. See chapter 4.
- **Cascade Canyon Loop** (Grand Teton): Perhaps the most popular trail in Grand Teton, the Cascade Canyon loop, which starts on the west side of Jenny Lake, winds northwest 7.2 miles on the Cascade Canyon Trail to Lake Solitude and the Paintbrush Divide, then returns past Holly Lake on the 10.3-mile Paintbrush Canyon trail. The payoff comes at the highest point, Paintbrush Divide, with marvelous views of the Jackson Hole Valley and Leigh Lake. See chapter 6.

THE BEST CAMPGROUNDS

If you stay in developed campgrounds in the parks, the outdoor life is pretty civilized. You'll have running water and, in most cases, flush toilets, plus, there are opportunities to meet fellow campers. All of these are detailed in chapter 7.

- **Canyon Campground** (Yellowstone): Though it's crowded, the Canyon Campground has excellent sites with a little elbow room, as well as well-maintained flush toilets. The site of numerous ranger talks, the campground is close to the Grand Canyon of the Yellowstone River and just a stone's throw from Canyon Village (especially handy when you crave an ice-cream cone.)
- **Slough Creek Campground** (Yellowstone): Another favorite is out in the Lamar Valley. The campground is smaller, but it's away from the crowds (and other services) yet close to fishing and wolf-viewing.
- **Signal Mountain** (Grand Teton): Camping slots are landscaped for privacy near the edge of Jackson Lake with great views of the mountains on the other side. The perfect place to spend the night if you plan to launch your canoe or Hobie Cat the next morning. The only problem is, there are no site reservations, and sites are all taken early in the morning.

THE BEST PLACES TO EAT IN THE PARKS

Don't expect five-star dining (with one exception) or a great variety, but the food is well prepared, the servers are cheerful, and the dining rooms are mostly big, convivial gathering places. All of these are detailed in chapter 7.

- The **Old Faithful Inn,** Yellowstone (☎ **307/545-4999**): Can't beat the ambience: a grand stone-and-timber lodge perched next to the most famous geyser in the world. The food's not bad either.
- The **Lake Yellowstone Hotel,** Yellowstone (☎ **307/344-7901**). Enjoy a bit of Victorian-era hospitality (without dressing up) in the Wyoming wilderness. There are views of the lake from the dining room and the comfortable lounge area off the lobby.
- **Jenny Lake Lodge,** Grand Teton (☎ **307/543-3300**): This place gets my five-star award: Dine where presidents have dined on six-course meals with such delicacies as smoked sturgeon ravioli. Breakfast and dinner are included in the price of a room, nonguests can call for reservations.
- **Signal Mountain Resort,** Grand Teton (☎ **307/543-2831**): Not everyone wants a fancy, sit-down meal, and the **Cottonwood Café** or appetizers in the bar here make great snacks, with a view of Jackson Lake or, in the lounge, a view of several sports-tuned televisions.

THE BEST PLACES TO SLEEP IN THE PARKS

Our Yellowstone favorites are both grand hotels, but very different. In Grand Teton, we lean toward the rustic option. All of these are detailed in chapter 7.

- The **Lake Yellowstone Hotel,** Yellowstone (☎ **307/344-7311**): Try this recipe for a great vacation: A quiet drink in the sunroom overlooking the lake, a friendly meal in the big dining room, a walk by the lake, and then a comfortable bed in one of the big wings.

- The **Old Faithful Inn,** Yellowstone (☎ **307/344-7311**): As if the wonders outside aren't enough, this is an architectural gem, a huge open ceiling 85 feet high with lodgepole balconies inside and out. Get a room in the old lodge, not the wings, even if the bathrooms are down the hall.

- **Jenny Lake Lodge** (☎ **800/628-9988**): Solitude, great food, and beautifully appointed cabins with porches have one downside: the high prices.

- **Colter Bay Village,** Grand Teton (☎ **800/628-9988** or 307/ 543-2855): Rough it in a roomy canvas tent with a stove and bunk beds and firewood delivered to your door (or flap)—the tent is inexpensive, the fresh air is free. For a step up, try the rustic cabins.

THE BEST PLACES TO EAT OUTSIDE THE PARKS

This is food so good you won't mind spending $15 to $30 for entrees. Both of these are detailed see chapter 8.

- **In Jackson, Wyoming: Nani's Genuine Pasta House** (☎ **307/ 733-3888**) offers fare from a featured region of Italy, as well as a menu featuring traditional pasta favorites, and it's all good. Mornings, though, you'll find me at **Nora's Fish Creek Inn** (☎ **307/733-8288**) at nearby Wilson with a bottomless cup of coffee and a huge plate of huevos rancheros.

- **In Cody, Wyoming: Franca's Italian Dining** (☎ **307/ 587-5354**) is yet another example of how good Italian cooking has taken root in Wyoming. Note that they close for lengthy periods during the off-season.

THE BEST PLACES TO SLEEP OUTSIDE THE PARKS

All of these are detailed in chapter 8.

- **In Jackson, Wyoming: Rusty Parrot Lodge** (☎ **307/ 733-2000**) brings luxurious country inn charm to a downtown location; it's new and expensive, like most things in Jackson.

- **In Gardiner, Montana:** The **Absaroka Lodge** (☎ 800/ 755-7414) has modern rooms and decks overlooking the Yellowstone River, near the center of town.
- **In West Yellowstone, Montana:** The **Stage Coach Inn** (☎ toll free **800/842-2882** or 406/646-7381). Come here for the Western charm and ambience, well-furnished rooms, and a popular sports bar and restaurant.
- **In Cody, Wyoming: Cody's Guest Houses** (☎ 307/ 587-6000). These nicely restored, older properties feel homey, and afternoon tea is served at the Mayor's Inn.

THE BEST THINGS TO SEE & DO OUTSIDE THE PARKS

Don't assume all the best scenery, best snow, or best fishing waters are in the parks. Here are a few attractions worth highlighting in the area. See chapter 8 for more information.

- **In Cody, Wyoming:** The Buffalo Bill Historical Center is the best museum in the region; don't miss its art, gun and Indian artifact collections.
- **In Jackson, Wyoming:** Take a wild ride—in rafts or kayaks— on the Snake River as it courses through Snake River Canyon.
- **In West Yellowstone, Montana:** For a postmodern approach to visiting Yellowstone, sit in a dark room and watch the film *Yellowstone* in IMAX format on a 57-foot-high screen at the National Geographic Theater.

THE BEST SCENIC DRIVES

Roll down the windows, crank up your favorite music, and take time to relax as you travel these byways.

- Every stretch along the figure eight of roads at the center of Yellowstone has some scenic allure, but my favorite is the part along the western and northern shore of **Lake Yellowstone.** There's less traffic than around Old Faithful or the Grand Canyon of the Yellowstone, and a good chance of seeing wildlife east of **Fishing Bridge,** as well as steaming geothermal features near **West Thumb.** The drive is best in the morning, when the sun is rising over the steaming lake. See chapter 3.
- From the northeast entrance of Yellowstone head across the **Beartooth Highway** (U.S. 212) to Red Lodge, Montana; at Red Lodge, head southeast toward Cody (MT 308 to WY 120), then catch the **Chief Joseph Highway** (WY 296) and return to the park. Imagine this: dramatic mountain peaks, river valleys,

painted landscapes, and two Old West towns, all on this 155-mile drive. See chapter 3.

- A twisting, narrow road climbs **Signal Mountain** to a fine 360° view of the valley and the mountains. On the way up you'll see wildflowers and birds, and from the top you can study the moraines and potholes left by retreating glaciers. See chapter 5.

2 A Look at Yellowstone

Think about this: What other national park boasts such an assortment of thermal geysers and hot springs? Even when the rest of North America was largely a wilderness, Yellowstone was unique. The geothermal area is greater than any other in the world, with mud pots, geysers, and hot springs of all colors, sizes, and performances. Plus, there's a waterfall that's twice as tall as Niagara Falls, and a canyon deep and colorful enough to fall into the "grand" category. Sure, other parks have great hiking trails and beautiful geologic formations—Grand Teton is pretty spectacular in its own right, as is Yosemite—but virtually all of the geology in Yellowstone is reachable by anyone in average shape.

Wildlife? Ever focus your telephoto lens on a wild, untamed grizzly bear? Or a bald eagle? What about a wolf? Thousands of visitors have these experiences here every year. Protected by the national park and surrounding forests from development, Yellowstone is home to herds of bison, elk, grizzly bears, trumpeter swans, Yellowstone cutthroat trout, and more subtle beauties like wildflowers and hummingbirds.

And the park doesn't appeal solely to the visual senses; you'll smell it, too. By one biologist's estimate, Yellowstone has more than 1,100 species of plants. When wildflowers cover the meadows in spring, their fragrances are overpowering. The mud pots and fumaroles have their own set of odors, though many are less pleasing than a wild lily.

Your ears will be filled with the sounds of geysers noisily spewing forth thousands of gallons of boiling water into the blue Wyoming sky. After sunset, coyotes break the silence of the night with their high-pitched yips.

You can spend weeks hiking its backcountry or fishing its streams—or the park is easy to see in a day or two from behind the windshield.

Yes, *really.* It's possible to see the highlights of Yellowstone without ever leaving your car. Park roads lead past most of the key attractions and are filled with wildlife commuting from one grazing area to another. There's no doubt you will return home with vivid memories if you take this approach to your visit of the park, but you'll be shortchanging yourself.

Yellowstone is just as active when summer ends, when the park is open for snowmobiling and skiing for 3 months during the winter.

3   A Look at the Grand Tetons & Jackson Hole

Because the Grand Tetons stand so tall, with the park curling snugly at their feet, visitors sometimes fail to appreciate this surrounding environment of rivers and high valley floor. The Tetons are a young range of old pre-Cambrian granite, abrupt and sharp-edged as they knife up from the Snake River valley, sliding upward long a 40-mile-long fault sculpted 15,000 years ago by retreating glaciers and erosion. The result is a masterpiece. With its shimmering lakes, thickly carpeted forests, and towering peaks blanketed with snow throughout most of the year, Grand Teton National Park is regarded by many visitors as more dramatically scenic than its northern neighbor.

It's also an accessible park. You can appreciate its breathtaking beauty on a quick drive-by, or take to the trails and waterways in search of lakes and waterfalls. The Tetons are especially popular with mountain climbers, who scale them year-round.

There's a dynamic relationship between the Tetons and the valley. The elk and other wildlife migrate from the high country down to the open grasslands to forage during the winter; the snowmelt curls across the valley floor and west through a gap in the mountains; and the moraines and alluvial soils slough off the mountains and provide rich soils for the pastures below.

Visitors can float and fish the lively Snake River, visit the National Elk Refuge in the winter, hike in nearby ranges like the Wind Rivers or the Gros Ventre, or play cowboy at one of the dude and guest ranches that dot the valley. Skiers and snowboarders have a blast at the resorts here, as well as at Grand Targhee on the other side of Teton Pass. And the snug town of Jackson, with its antler-arched town square and its busy shops, offers everything from classy art galleries to noisy two-step cowboy bars.

4   Making the Most of Your Trip

Yellowstone Superintendent Michael Finley suggests, "Get out of your car or bus, and go find a safe location to sit and absorb the scenery. Allow the nonmotorized sounds to dominate the scene. Bask in the wind and sun."

We think you should do more than that. Yellowstone and Grand Teton are more than photo ops and zoos where the animals roam free. Nor are they museums, where magnificent scenery is merely on display. Both parks, unlike a picture hanging lifelessly on the wall of a museum, are works in progress; they are living, breathing wilderness areas. Plant your feet in a comfortable pair of walking or hiking shoes, find a trailhead, and head into the woods with a sack lunch and bottle of your favorite beverage. Better yet, if you can afford the time, plan an excursion around Shoshone Lake or to the south end of Yellowstone Lake by boat to areas few visitors ever see. There are isolated areas in Grand Teton, too—even on the far shore of popular Jenny Lake—where, with a little hiking, you'll be rewarded by a pristine, forested glade with nothing to distract your attention but an awe-inspiring mountaintop.

If you're more adventurous, take a white-water trip down the canyon, or let a guide take you up to Grand Teton's summit. Sleep under the stars and listen to the wolves howl at Slough Creek Campground or backpack for a week on the Thorofare Trail.

You will never plumb the absolute depths of these parks—no one ever will. You can spend your whole life trying, though, and have a great and illuminating time doing it.

5 Some Historical Background

YELLOWSTONE NATIONAL PARK

Before the arrival of European settlers, the only residents on the plateau were small bands of Shoshone Indians known as "Sheepeaters," who lived on the southern fringe. Three other Indian tribes came and went: the Crows (Absaroka), who were friendly to the settlers; the Blackfeet, who lived in the Missouri Valley drainage and were hostile to both whites and other Indians; and the Bannocks, who largely kept to themselves. The nomadic Bannocks traveled an east-west route in their search for bison, from Idaho past Mammoth Hot Springs to Tower Fall, and then across the Lamar Valley to the Bighorn Valley, which is outside the park's current boundaries. Called the Bannock Trail, it was so deeply furrowed that evidence of it still exists today on the Blacktail Plateau near the Tower Junction. (You'll be able to see remnants of the trail if you take Blacktail Plateau Drive, described in chapter 3.)

The first non-Indian to lay eyes on Yellowstone's geothermal wonders was probably John Colter, who broke away from the Lewis and Clark expedition in 1806 and spent 3 years wandering a surreal landscape of mud pots and mountains and geysers. When he described his discovery on his return to St. Louis, no one believed him. Miners and fur trappers followed in his footsteps, reducing the plentiful beaver of the region to almost nothing, and occasionally making curious reports of a sulfurous world still sometimes called "Colter's Hell."

The first significant exploration of what would become the park took place in 1869, when a band of Montanans led by David Folsom completed a 36-day expedition. Folsom and his group traveled up the Missouri River, then into the heart of the park, where they discovered the falls of the Yellowstone, mud pots, Yellowstone Lake, and the Fountain Geyser. But it was an expedition led by the director of the U.S. Geological Survey, Ferdinand Hayden, that brought back convincing evidence of Yellowstone's wonders, in the form of astonishing photographs by William H. Jackson and drawings by famed Western artist Thomas Moran.

A debate began over the potential for commercial development and exploitation of the region, as crude hot tubs and "hotels" went up near the hot springs. There are various claimants to the idea of a national park—members of the Folsom party later told a story about thinking it up around a campfire in the Upper Geyser Basin—but in any case the idea caught on as Yellowstone explorers hit the lecture circuit back East. In March 1872, Pres. Ulysses S. Grant signed legislation declaring Yellowstone the nation's first national park.

The Department of Interior got the job of managing the new park. There was no budget for it, and no clear idea how to take care of a wilderness preserve, so many mistakes were made. Inept superintendents granted favorable leases to friends with commercial interests in the tourism industry; poachers ran amok, and the wildlife population was decimated; a laundry business near Mammoth cleaned linens in the hot pool.

By 1886, things were so bad that the U.S. Army took over control of the park; their iron-fisted management practices resulted in new order and protected the park from those intent upon exploiting it. (However, the military did participate in the eradication of the plateau's wolf population.) By 1916, efforts to make the park more visitor-friendly had begun to show results: Construction of the first roads had been completed, guest housing was available in the area, and order had been restored. Stewardship of the park was then transferred to the newly created National Park Service.

GRAND TETON NATIONAL PARK

Unlike Yellowstone, Grand Teton can't boast of being the nation's first park, and a model for parks the world over. This smaller, southerly neighbor was created in a way more typical of parks in the modern world.

The first sign of human habitation in the Grand Teton region points to people being here around 12,000 years ago. Among the tribes who hunted here in the warmer seasons were the Blackfeet, Crow, Gros Ventre, and Shoshone, who came over the mountains from the Great Basin to the west. Summers were spent here hunting and raising crops, before heading to warmer climes.

The trappers and explorers who followed them into the valley were equally distressed by the harsh winters and short growing season, which made Jackson Hole a marginal place for growing crops or ranching. Among these early visitors were artist Thomas Moran and photographer Henry Jackson, whose images awoke the country to the Tetons' grandeur. Early homesteaders quickly realized that their best hope was to market the beauty of the area, which they began doing in earnest as early as a century ago.

The danger of haphazard development soon became apparent. There was a dance hall at Jenny Lake, hot dog stands along the roads, and buildings going up on some prime habitat. In the 1920s, Yellowstone park officials and conservationists met to discuss how the Grand Teton area might be protected, and then went to Congress. Led by local Maude Noble and Yellowstone superintendent Horace Albright, the group was able to protect only the mountains and foothills, leaving out Jackson Lake and the valley, but Wyoming's congressional delegation, and many locals, were violently opposed to enclosing the valley in park boundaries.

Then, in the 1920s, something called the Snake River Land Company started buying up ranches along the base of the Tetons. It was a front for John D. Rockefeller Jr., one of the richest men in the world, working in cahoots with the conservationists. He planned to give the land to the federal government, while keeping a few choice parcels for himself. But Congress wouldn't have it, and Rockefeller made noises about selling the land, about 35,000 acres, to the highest bidder. In the 1940s, Pres. Franklin D. Roosevelt created the Jackson Hole National Monument out of Forest Service lands east of the Snake River. That paved the way for Rockefeller's donation, and in 1950 Grand Teton National Park was expanded to its present form.

6   Issues Facing the Parks Today

BISON, BEARS & WOLVES

In the frontier West, where bison seemed to be everywhere, grizzly bears were fearsome, and wolves regularly raided livestock, wildlife was treated with a certain carelessness. Eventually, the bison and grizzly populations around Yellowstone and Grand Teton were whittled down to near extinction, and wolves were gone completely by the 1930s.

It took some intensive management to bring grizzlies and bison back to reasonably healthy numbers in the area, and now a similar effort is underway for wolves, which were reintroduced from Canada in 1995. But these high-profile species—called "charismatic megafauna" by biologists—are not out of the woods yet. Given the pressures of development around the parks, they may never be secure again.

There are now thousands of bison in Yellowstone and Grand Teton, and, naturally, they are entirely disrespectful of the park's invisible boundary line. In the winter, when snows are deep, they leave the park to forage at lower elevations, sometime in ranch pastures shared with domestic cattle. The ranchers fear the bison will spread brucelosis, a virus that can be transmitted to cattle. If infected, cows will abort their unborn calves. While park officials try to entice the bison back into the park, Montana officials allow them to be shot. Animal rights activists are outraged, and park and state officials, as well as some Indian tribal representatives, are negotiating.

Wolves are another sore point with area ranchers. The reintroduction has been astonishingly successful—rapidly reproducing, feeding on abundant elk in the park's Lamar Valley, there are now more than 100 wolves, and the packs have spread as far south as Grand Teton, where several have denned and produced pups. Though the Defenders of Wildlife have set up programs to compensate ranchers for livestock lost to wolves, the ranchers have gone to court seeking to have the wolves removed. The wolves have indeed been implicated in the deaths of sheep and cattle, and a federal judge in Wyoming has decided they have to go (at press time his decision had been stayed pending appeal).

Grizzly bears once teetered on the brink of extinction in the parks, but they've made a slow comeback to a healthier population of around 400. Unfortunately, the habitat they need so much of keeps shrinking, as more and more development takes place around the plateau.

A MULTIPLE USE PARK

Grand Teton National Park is much more than just a preserve of mountains and lakes and wildlife. Its land is used for all sorts of things that most people don't expect of a national park. There's a big dam holding irrigation water for potato farmers in Idaho; commercial climbing businesses that charge big bucks to take climbers up the peaks; cattle grazing on seeded, irrigated pastures; and even a commercial airport with big jets flying in and out daily.

Each year, one of these conflicting uses makes headlines. Lately, it's the cattle, which graze in the fall only a short lope from a den of young wolves. What's the purpose of this park, critics ask, to feed a rancher's cattle or to protect wildlife?

As park spokesperson Joan Anselmo points out, these are the sort of public lands conflicts that will arise more often in modern times. With its private holdings of land, uses that pre-date the creation of the park, and heightened debate between park purists and multiple-use advocates, Grand Teton is a prime example of the difficulty of modern park management.

A BURNING ISSUE

Yellowstone's park managers faced the ultimate test of their non-interference philosophy of fire management in 1988, when nearly one-third of Yellowstone was burned by a series of uncontrollable wildfires. These violent conflagrations scorched more than 700,000 acres, leaving behind dead wildlife, damaged buildings, injured firefighters, and ghostly forests of stripped, blackened tree trunks.

The debate over park and public land fire policies still rages, though things have quieted down some. After years of suppressing every fire in the park, Yellowstone in 1988 was operating under a new "let it burn" policy, based on scientific evidence that fires were regular occurrences in nature, part of the natural cycle of a forest.

What you will see as you travel Yellowstone today is a park that may be healthier than it was before. Saplings have sprouted from the long-dormant seeds of the lodgepole pine (fires stimulate the pine cones to release their seeds), and the old, tinder-dry forest understory is being replaced with new green shrubs and grass more tempting to herbivores. Visitors who want to better understand the effects of the fires of 1988 should visit the exhibit *Yellowstone and Fire* at the Grant Village visitor center; its coverage is the best in the park.

2

Planning Your Trip to Yellowstone & Grand Teton National Parks

*I*t's no one's idea of a fun vacation to end up sucking exhaust behind a long line of cars waiting for a break in construction at Yellowstone's east entrance, or wearing a T-shirt in a Montana snowstorm. Few things can ruin a much-anticipated vacation more than poor planning. So look over some of the crucial information in this chapter before you hit the road—it might be the difference between a trip you'll never forget and one you'd rather not remember.

1 Getting Started: Information & Reservations

The primary entries to Yellowstone and Grand Teton are through Montana and Wyoming, so if you want information about the surrounding areas, contact these states' travel services: **Travel Montana,** P.O. Box 200533, 1424 9th Ave., Helena, MT 59620-0533 (☎ **800/VISIT-MT** or 406/444-2654; www.visitmt.com), and the **Wyoming Business Council Tourism Division,** I-25 at College Drive, Cheyenne, WY 82002 (☎ **800/225-5996** or 307/777-7777; www.wyomingtourism.org).

YELLOWSTONE NATIONAL PARK   To receive maps and information prior to your arrival, contact Visitors Services, Box 168, **Yellowstone National Park,** WY 82190 (☎ **307/344-7381;** www.nps.gov/yell).

   Information regarding lodging, tours, boating, and horseback riding is available from **Yellowstone National Park Lodges,** P.O. Box 165, Yellowstone National Park, WY 82190, (☎ **307/ 344-7311;** www.amfac.com). You'll find complete information about lodging both inside the park and in the surrounding communities in chapters 7 and 8.

For information about educational programs at the Yellowstone Institute, contact **The Yellowstone Association,** P.O. Box 117, Yellowstone National Park, WY 82190 (☎ **307/344-2293;** www.YellowstoneAssociation.org). The association also operates bookstores in park visitor centers, museums, and information stations; contact them for catalog of the books they offer.

GRAND TETON NATIONAL PARK   To receive park maps and information before your arrival, contact **Grand Teton National Park,** P.O. Drawer 170, Moose, WY 83012 (☎ **307/739-3600;** www.nps.gov/grte).

Lodging information is available from three park concessionaires: **Grand Teton Lodge Company,** P.O. Box 240, Moran, WY 83013 (☎ **800/628-9988**); **Signal Mountain Lodge Co.,** P.O. Box 50, Moran, WY 83013 (☎ **307/543-2831**); and **Flagg Ranch Village,** Box 187, Moran, WY 83013 (☎ **800/443-2311**). You'll find complete information about lodging both inside the park and in the surrounding gateway communities in chapters 7 and 8.

Educational and field trips are offered by several organizations based in Jackson Hole: **Great Plains Wildlife Institute,** P.O. Box 7580, Jackson, WY 83002 (☎ **307/773-2623;** www.wildlifesafari. com); and the **Teton Science School,** P.O. Box 68, Kelly, WY 83011 (☎ **307/733-4765;** e-mail: tss@wyoming.com).

The **Grand Teton Natural History Association** is a not-for-profit organization that provides information about the park, through retail book sales at park visitor centers; you can also buy books about the park from them by mail. Contact the association at P.O. Drawer 170, Moose, WY 83012 (☎ **307/739-3403;** www.grandteton.com/gtnha/).

National forests and other public lands surround the parks. For information about national forests and wilderness areas in Montana, as well as **Bridger-Teton National Forest** in Wyoming, contact the **U.S. Forest Service Northern Region Office,** Federal Building, 200 E. Broadway, Box 7669, Missoula, MT 59807 (☎ **406/329-3511;** www.fs.fed.us/r1). The rest of Wyoming's forests, including the **Shoshone National Forest** east of the Tetons over Togwotee Pass, are covered by the **Rocky Mountain Region Office,** P.O. Box 25127, Lakewood, CO 80225 (☎ **303/275-5350;** www.fs.fed.us/r2).

The federal **Bureau of Land Management** also manages millions of acres of recreational lands and can be reached at its Wyoming state office, 5353 Yellowstone Rd., Cheyenne, WY 82003 (☎ **307/ 775-6256**), or its Montana state office, 222 N. 32nd St., Billings, MT 59101 (☎ **406/255-2888**).

GENERAL TOURIST INFORMATION   Other sources of information include **Yellowstone Country,** P.O. Box 1107, Red Lodge, MT 59068 (☎ 800/736-5276); **Gardiner Chamber of Commerce,** 222 Park St., P.O. Box 81, Gardiner, MT 59030 (☎ 406/848-7971); **Colter Pass/Cooke City/Silver Gate Chamber of Commerce,** Box 1071, Cooke City, MT 59020 (☎ 406/838-2395); **West Yellowstone Chamber of Commerce,** 100 Yellowstone Ave., West Yellowstone, MT 59758 (☎ 406/ 646-7701); **Jackson Chamber of Commerce,** P.O. Box E, Jackson, WY 83001, (☎ 307/733-3316); **Jackson Hole Central Reservations** (☎ 800/443-6931); **Travel Wizard of Jackson Hole** (☎ 800/606-0011); **Cody Country Chamber of Commerce,** P.O. Box 2777, Cody, WY 82414 (☎ 307/587-2777).

USEFUL PUBLICATIONS   The following books are interesting, informative, and easy to find: *Yellowstone, A Visitor's Companion,* by George Wuerthner, Stackpole Books, Harrisburg, PA; *The Yellowstone Story* (2 Volumes), by Aubrey Haines, Colorado Associated University Press; *The Yellowstone National Park,* Hiram Chittenden, University of Oklahoma Press, Norman, Oklahoma; *Yellowstone Trails: A Hiking Guide,* by Mark C. Marschall, Yellowstone Association, Yellowstone National Park; *Exploring the Yellowstone Backcountry,* by Orville Bach Jr., Sierra Club Books, San Francisco; *Grand Teton National Park,* available from the Grand Teton Natural History Association; *A Guide to Exploring Grand Teton National Park,* Linda L Olson/Tim Bywater, RNM Press, Salt Lake City, Utah; *An Outdoor Family Guide to Yellowstone and Grand Teton National Parks,* Lisa Gollin Evans, The Mountaineers, 1001 SW Klickitat Way, Seattle, Washington; *Teton Trails: A Guide to the Trails of Grand Teton National Park,* Katy Duffy and Darwin Wile, Grand Teton Natural History Association; Falcon Press (Helena, Montana) also publishes a long list of hiking, fishing, climbing and other guides to the Yellowstone/ Grand Teton region.

If you cannot find these publications in your local bookstore, many can be ordered from either the **Yellowstone Association** or the **Grand Teton Natural History Association** (see above for addresses and telephone numbers).

What Things Cost in Yellowstone & Grand Teton National Parks	U.S. $
Double motel room in or around the parks, peak season	$52–$225
Double motel room, winter season	$48–$95
A cabin with bed and bathroom	$45–$77
Dinner in a full-service hotel restaurant	$12–$28
Dinner in a coffee shop	$6–$15
Horseback riding for 1 hour	$18
A stagecoach ride	$6
A 1-hour lake cruise	$9
1-day audio tour cassette rental	$25
Bus sightseeing tour (Yellowstone)	$29-$33
1-day snowmobile rental	$115–$130
Snowcoach round-trip to Old Faithful	$88

2 When to Go

Summer, autumn, and winter are the best times to visit the Northern Rockies. The days are sunny, the nights are clear, and the humidity is low. A popular song once romanticized "Springtime in the Rockies," but that season lasts about 2 days in early June. The rest of the season formally known as spring is likely to be chilly and spitting snow or rain. Trails are still clogged with snow and mud.

From mid-June on you can hike, fish, camp, and watch wildlife, and if you come before July 4, or after Labor Day, you won't have to share the view much. The great wildflower season? The flowers actually bloom at these elevations in early summer—beginning in May in the lower valleys and plains, while in the higher elevations they open up in July.

Autumn is not just the time when the aspen turn gold—it's also the time when gateway motel and restaurant rates are lower, and the roads are less crowded. That allows you to pay attention to the wildlife, which is busy fattening up for the winter.

Winter is a glorious season here, though not for everyone. It can be very cold. But the air is crystalline, the snow is powdery, the skiing is fantastic. If you drive in the parks' vicinity in the winter

always carry sleeping bags, extra food, flashlights, and other safety gear. Every resident has a horror story about being caught unprepared in the weather.

THE CLIMATE   The region is characterized by long, cold winters and short, though usually warm, summers. There is not a lot of moisture, winter or summer, and the air is dry, except for the brief wet season in March and April.

We've already warned you about the brief glimpse we get of spring in these parts. Cold and snow may linger into April and May, though temperatures are generally warming. The average daytime readings are in the 40s to 50s (F), gradually increasing into the 60s to 70s (F) by early June. So, during **spring** a warm jacket, raingear, and water-resistant walking shoes may be welcome traveling companions.

The area is never balmy, but temperatures during the middle of the **summer** are typically 70° to 80°F in the lower elevations and are especially comfortable because of the lack of humidity. Remember, too, that the atmosphere is thin at this altitude, and sunscreen is a must. Nights, even during the warmest months, will be cool, with temperatures dropping into the low 40s, so you'll want to include a light jacket in your wardrobe. Since summer thunderstorms are common, you'll probably be glad you've included a waterproof shell or umbrella.

As **fall** approaches you'll want to have an additional layer of clothing, since temperatures remain mild but begin to cool. The first heavy snows typically fall in the Valley by November 1 (much earlier in the mountains) and continue through March or April. Aspen turn bright yellow, cottonwoods a deeper gold.

During **winter** months you'll want long johns, heavy shirts, vests, coats, warm gloves, and thick socks since temperatures hover in single digits, and subzero overnight temperatures are common. Supercold air can cause lots of health problems, so drink fluids, keep an extra layer of clothing handy, and don't overwork.

AVOIDING THE CROWDS   Between the Fourth of July and Labor Day, the Northern Rockies come to life. Flowers bloom, fish jump, bison calves frolic—and tourists tour. The park roads are crowded with trailers, the well-known spots jammed with a significant portion of the millions who make their treks to Montana and Wyoming every year. Your best bet: Travel before June 15, if possible, or after Labor Day. If you can't arrange that, then visit the major attractions off-peak hours when others are eating or sleeping,

Road Openings & Closings

In Yellowstone   Traveling Yellowstone's roads during spring months can be a roll of the dice, since openings can be delayed for days (sometimes weeks) at a time, especially at higher altitudes. There is always some section of road in Yellowstone under reconstruction, most recently the East Entrance, so call ahead and get a road report (☎ **307/344-7381**). It's irritating, but don't take it out on the road workers: They often labor through the night to cause as little inconvenience as possible.

The only road open year-round is the north entrance to **Mammoth Hot Springs.** From Mammoth, a winter access road to the northeast entrance and **Cooke City** is plowed throughout the winter. This service for Cooke City residents gives visitors a great opportunity to watch wildlife in winter in the Lamar Valley. Just be watchful of the weather; the road is often icy.

Snowplowing begins in early March. In Yellowstone, the first roads open to motor vehicles usually include **Mammoth–Norris, Norris–Canyon, Madison–Old Faithful,** and **West Yellowstone–Madison.** These roads may open by the end of April. If the weather cooperates, the East and South entrances, as well as roads on the east and south sides of the park, will open early in May. Opening of the **Tower-Roosevelt** to **Canyon Junction** road, however, may be delayed by late season snowfall on Dunraven Pass.

The **Sunlight Basin Road** (which is also called the **Chief Joseph Highway**), connecting the entrance at Cooke City, Montana, with Cody, Wyoming, often opens by early May. The **Beartooth Highway** between Cooke City and Red Lodge, Montana, is generally open by Memorial Day weekend.

Road closures begin in mid-October, when the Beartooth Highway closes. Depending upon weather, most other park roads remain open until the park season ends on the first Sunday in November.

In Grand Teton   Since Grand Teton has fewer roads and they're at lower elevations, openings and closings are more predictable. **Teton Park Road** opens to conventional vehicles and RVs around May 1. The **Moose–Wilson Road** opens to vehicles about the same time. Roads close to vehicles on November 1 and open for snowmobiles in mid-December, though they never close for nonmotorized use.

Montana's Average Monthly Temperatures (High/Low) °F

	Jan	Feb	Mar	Apr	May	June	July	Aug	Sept	Oct	Nov	Dec
Billings	36/12	44/17	52/24	63/33	72/42	81/50	89/55	88/53	76/43	66/34	49/23	38/14
Bozeman	33/13	38/18	44/23	55/31	64/39	74/46	82/52	81/51	70/42	59/33	43/23	34/15
Butte	29/5	34/10	40/17	50/26	60/34	70/42	80/46	78/44	66/35	56/26	39/16	29/6
Dillon	32/11	39/16	44/21	55/28	64/36	73/44	83/49	81/48	69/39	58/31	42/21	33/12
Glasgow	20/1	27/8	40/19	57/32	67/43	78/51	85/57	84/55	70/44	59/33	40/19	25/6
Great Falls	31/12	38/17	44/23	55/32	65/41	75/49	83/53	82/52	70/44	59/36	44/24	33/15
Havre	25/4	32/10	43/20	57/31	68/41	78/50	85/54	84/53	71/42	60/32	42/18	28/7
Helena	30/10	37/16	45/22	56/31	65/40	76/48	85/53	83/52	70/41	59/32	42/21	31/11
Kalispell	28/13	35/18	43/24	55/31	64/38	71/44	80/47	79/46	68/39	54/29	38/24	30/16
Lewistown	31/9	36/14	41/20	53/29	63/37	72/45	81/50	80/49	68/40	58/32	44/21	34/12
Libby	29/13	36/17	43/21	52/27	62/33	70/40	78/43	78/42	67/35	54/28	37/22	29/15
Miles City	26/6	33/13	44/22	58/34	69/45	80/54	89/61	87/59	73/47	60/36	42/22	29/9
Missoula	30/15	37/21	47/25	58/31	66/38	74/46	83/50	82/49	71/40	57/31	41/24	30/16
Sidney	24/2	32/8	44/19	60/30	72/42	80/51	86/55	85/53	73/42	61/33	41/19	28/6
W. Yellowstone	24/0	30/4	37/10	46/20	58/29	69/37	79/41	76/39	65/31	52/23	34/12	23/1

Wyoming's Average Monthly Temperatures (High/Low) °F

	Jan	Feb	Mar	Apr	May	June	July	Aug	Sept	Oct	Nov	Dec
Casper	33/12	37/16	45/22	56/30	67/38	79/47	88/54	86/52	74/42	61/32	44/22	34/14
Cheyenne	38/15	41/18	45/22	55/30	65/40	74/48	82/55	80/53	71/44	60/34	47/24	39/17
Cody	34/12	40/17	47/23	56/31	66/40	76/49	84/55	82/53	71/43	61/35	45/24	36/15
Devils Tower	34/4	39/10	48/18	60/28	70/38	80/47	88/53	87/50	76/39	64/28	46/17	35/7
Dubois	35/13	38/14	43/18	52/25	62/32	71/39	80/43	79/41	68/34	58/28	43/19	36/14
Gillette	30/10	36/15	44/21	55/30	64/39	76/49	85/55	84/53	71/43	60/33	43/21	33/12
Jackson	26/4	32/7	41/16	51/24	62/30	72/37	82/41	80/39	70/31	58/23	39/16	27/5
Kemmerer	28/5	32/6	39/13	50/22	62/32	72/39	82/45	79/43	69/34	56/25	40/15	30/6
Newcastle	33/11	38/15	47/23	59/33	69/43	80/52	88/59	86/56	74/46	61/35	45/23	35/13
Rawlins	30/11	33/14	40/20	52/28	63/36	75/45	83/52	80/50	69/41	56/31	41/21	31/13
Riverton	29/-2	37/6	48/18	59/28	69/38	80/46	89/51	87/48	75/38	62/27	43/13	30/0
Rock Springs	30/11	34/14	42/21	53/28	64/37	75/46	83/53	81/51	70/41	57/31	41/20	31/12
Sheridan	33/9	38/15	46/22	57/30	66/39	77/47	86/53	85/52	73/41	62/32	45/20	35/10
Thermopolis	35/6	42/13	51/22	61/31	71/39	82/47	90/54	88/51	76/41	65/31	47/19	36/8
Yellowstone	28/8	33/12	39/16	48/26	59/34	70/42	80/47	78/46	67/37	54/29	38/19	29/10

and you'll have the park more to yourself. Or, as we suggest over and over, abandon the pavement for the hiking trails.

Whenever you come, give these parks as much time as you can; you'll experience more at an unhurried pace.

3 Special Permits

BACKCOUNTRY PERMITS   If you want to sleep in the Yellowstone or Grand Teton backcountry, you have to get a permit, follow limits for length of stay and campfires, and stay in a designated area. The permit is free if you pick it up at the park earlier than 48 hours before you begin your trip or on the day of your trip. Or, you can reserve a site in advance by paying a $15 fee in either park. If you wish to reserve in advance, you must do so in writing, and you still need to pick up your permit in person upon your arrival in the park. Yellowstone reservations can be made after April 1 of the current year. In Grand Teton, you may reserve a permit from January 1 to May 15; thereafter all permits are first come, first served. If you're going during the parks' busy season, you'd be wise to reserve in advance.

In Yellowstone, permits can be obtained at any ranger station, most of which are open from 8am to 7pm. To make a reservation you must contact the park more than 48 hours in advance. You can request them by writing the **Backcountry Office,** P.O. Box 168, Yellowstone National Park, WY 82190, or by stopping in at a ranger station. Phone reservations are not accepted, but if you want information about the system, call ☎ **307/344-2160.**

In Grand Teton, permits are issued at the Moose and Colter Bay Visitor Centers and the Jenny Lake ranger station. Reservations may be made by writing the **Permits Office,** Grand Teton National Park, P.O. Box 170, Moose, WY 83012, or by sending a fax to 307/ 739-3438. Phone reservations are not accepted.

BOATING PERMITS   For motorized craft, the cost is $20 for annual permits and $10 for 7-day permits. Fees for nonmotorized boats are $10 for annual permits and $5 for 7-day permits. See the regulations section below for more information. Boating permits are required for all vessels. Motorized boating is restricted to designated areas. Boating is prohibited on all of Yellowstone's rivers and streams except for the Lewis River Channel, where hand-propelled vessels are permitted. The fees are the same in Grand Teton, where powerboaters are permitted on Jenny, Jackson and Phelps lakes, and nonmotorized boats are allowed on most park lakes and the Snake

River. Sailboats, windsurfers and jet skis are allowed only on Jackson Lake. U.S. Coast Guard–approved personal flotation devices are required for each person boating.

FISHING PERMITS   In **Yellowstone,** park permits are required for anglers 16 and over; the permit costs $10 for 10 days and $20 for the season. Youths 12 to 15 years of age must have a permit, but it's free. Children under 12 may fish without a permit. Permits are available at any ranger station, visitor center, Hamilton store, and most fishing shops in the gateways. The season usually begins on the Saturday of Memorial Day weekend and continues through the first Sunday in November. Exceptions to this rule are Yellowstone Lake, its tributaries, and sections of the Yellowstone River.

In **Grand Teton,** State of Wyoming fishing licenses are required for anyone over 14 years of age. An adult nonresident license costs $6 per day, $65 for the season. Youth fees (ages 14 to 18) are $10 for 10 days, $15 for the season. The river season generally opens April 1 and ends on October 31; Jackson Lake is closed October 1 to 31.

4 Getting There

If interstate highways and international airports are the measure of accessibility, then Yellowstone is as remote as Alaska's Denali National Park. But 3 million people make it here every year, on tour buses, in family vans, on bicycles and astride snowmobiles, even from the other side of the world.

Grand Teton's gateways are from the north, south and east. Drivers naturally enter from whichever side they approach the parks, but fliers have some choices to make.

THE NEAREST AIRPORTS

The closest airport to Yellowstone is in **West Yellowstone,** Montana, where the airport sits just 1 mile north of town (and the west entrance) on Highway 191. The airport has commercial air service seasonally, from June through September only, on Delta's commuter service, **Skywest** (☎ 800/453-9417 or 307/733-7920).

Visitors can land right in Grand Teton National Park when they fly to **Jackson,** Wyoming, and be only 56 miles of scenic driving from the southern entrance of Yellowstone. **American Airlines** (☎ 800/433-7300), **Delta** (☎ 800/221-1212), **Skywest** (see above), and **United Express** (☎ 800/241-6522) all have flights to and from **Jackson Airport.**

Driving Distances to Yellowstone National Park* (in miles)

Denver	563
Las Vegas	809
Salt Lake City	390
Portland	869
Seattle	827
Omaha	946
Washington, D.C.	2,081

*The difference in distance to Grand Teton is about 70 miles, depending on your route.

To the north, **Bozeman,** Montana, is 87 miles from the West Yellowstone entrance on U.S. 191. Or you can drive east from Bozeman to Livingston, a 20-mile journey on Interstate 90, and then south 53 miles on U.S. 89 to the northern entrance at Gardiner. Bozeman's airport, **Gallatin Field,** provides daily service via **Delta** (see above), **Northwest** (☎ 800/225-2525), and **United** (☎ 800/241-6522) as well as **Horizon** (☎ 800/547-9308) and **Skywest** (see above) commuter flights.

Also to the north, **Billings,** Montana, is 129 miles from the Cooke City entrance. Billings is home to the Montana's busiest airport, **Logan International,** 2 miles north of downtown. Daily intrastate service is provided by **Big Sky Airlines** (☎ 800/237-7788 or 406/245-2300), and regional daily service is provided by **Delta, Horizon, Northwest,** and **United** (see phone numbers above). From Billings, it's a 65-mile drive south on U.S. Highway 212 to Red Lodge, then 30 miles on the Beartooth Highway to the northeast entrance to the park.

From Cody, Wyoming, it's a gorgeous 53-mile drive west along U.S. Highway 16/14/20 to the east entrance of the park. **Cody's Yellowstone Regional Airport** (☎ 307/587-5096) serves the Bighorn Basin as well as the east and northeast entrances of Yellowstone National Park with year-round commercial flights via **SkyWest** and **United Express** (see phone numbers above).

Airfares to the small airports surrounding the parks can be pricey, so if you like to drive, consider flying in to Salt Lake City, Utah, and driving 280 miles to the park, a drive that has some nice scenic stretches. Even Denver, a much longer drive of over 400 miles, is

Driving Tips

The speed limit in Yellowstone and Grand Teton parks is 45 miles per hour (except on U.S. 191 through the east side of Grand Teton), but drivers go faster and sometimes much slower, often without any thought to the cars backed up behind them, the bicyclists trying to survive on the narrow shoulder, or the risks to their own passengers. In the winter, snowmobilers, too, must take it slow, or risk an accident or a ticket.

Wildlife such as bison often use the roads as well, especially during the winter—don't crowd them or try to pass. Drivers who gaze around at the sights risk running into a "bear jam" where people have pulled partway off the road, or simply slowed to a crawl. Use the pullouts and walk back to the view—it's safer, and you won't cause any "road rage."

Larger vehicles like RVs can also be a big irritation. They move slower than other traffic, and they block the view from smaller vehicles behind them. If you drive an RV, make a point of using the pullouts so folks behind you can have an unimpeded view.

an alternative for some, though it's a less beautiful drive than from Salt Lake.

RENTING A CAR   Most of the major auto-rental agencies have operations in the gateway cities. **Avis** (☎ 800/831-2847), **Budget** (☎ 800/527-0700), **Thrifty** (☎ 800/367-2277), **National** (☎ 800/227-7368), and **Hertz** (☎ 800/654-3131) all have operations in **Bozeman, Billings,** and **Jackson.** Cody is served by Thrifty, Avis, Hertz, and Budget. Alamo Auto Rental (☎ 800/327-9633) serves **Billings** and **Jackson.**

5   Tips for RVers

You love 'em or you hate 'em—the large, lumbering vehicles that serve some travelers as both transport and home. There are some retirees, self-named "full-timers," who sell their homes and their possessions and spend the rest of their lives chasing comfortable weather down the highway. Others may see it as a cost-saving way to vacation in the West, by renting a rolling room for the whole family at perhaps $1,000 per week plus gas. Is that a better deal than an economy car and less expensive motels? You do the math.

But you don't have to carry your bags, or even unpack them, and you'll sleep in campgrounds instead of motels, hear the sounds of the night outside, and have great flexibility in planning your itinerary. The trade-off will be making your own beds, doing without cable television, and making your own breakfast most of the time.

A few years back they tried to close the RV campground at Fishing Bridge, on the north end of Yellowstone Lake. The outcry was enormous, testimony to the immense popularity of RV travel, and so the Fishing Bridge facility remains open today. You can drive most of the major roads in both parks with an RV or trailer, but there will be some areas where large vehicles are prohibited, and most of the camping areas don't provide hookups—Colter Bay, Flagg Ranch, and Fishing Bridge are the exceptions.

For details on rentals, contact **America RV Rental,** a nationwide company with excellent references (☎ **541/926-7617;** www.limo.net/rv).

6 Learning Vacations & Special Programs

One of the best ways to turn a park vacation into an unforgettable experience is to join an educational program. There are no finals in these courses, they're just a relaxed, informative way to spend time outdoors.

The **Yellowstone Association Institute** (P.O. Box 117, Yellowstone National Park, WY 82190, ☎ **307/344-2294;** www.YellowstoneAssociation.org) operates at the old Buffalo Ranch, on the road through the Lamar Valley to the park's northeast entrance. The Institute offers more than 100 courses, winter and summer, covering everything from wildlife tracking in the snow to wilderness medicine. The courses, some of which are offered for college credit, run from 2 to 5 days, with forays into the field, and lectures and demonstrations at the Institute's cramped quarters. Participants share meals and stories in the common kitchen. Prices are reasonable, and some classes are specifically geared to families and youngsters.

For folks who want to make a genuine contribution to scientific research in the park, **Yellowstone Ecosystem Studies (YES)** (P.O. Box 6640, Bozeman, MT 59771, ☎ **406/587-7758;** www.yellowstone.org; e-mail: yes@yellowstone.org) Outdoor Field Studies program puts guests to work in the field following coyotes and wolves with telemetry equipment. You'll pay a hefty fee to participate, but you'll be contributing to crucial wildlife studies by biologist Bob Crabtree. (YES also rents cabins at its Science Center in Silver Gate, call ☎ **406/838-2222** for more information.)

Winter and summer, wildlife biologists lead enlightening tours of Grand Teton, Yellowstone and surrounding forest lands through the **Great Plains Wildlife Institute,** P.O. Box 7580, Jackson Hole, WY 83002 (☎ **307/773-2623;** www.wildlifesafari.com.com). By open-roofed van, raft, sleigh, and foot, these tours bring visitors closer to the wildlife than they're likely to get on their own, and guests sometimes participate in radio tracking and other research projects. The institute offers trips from a half-day sunset safari to week-long trips through the park, usually lodging in park hotels. Unlike the other schools described here, this is a for-profit operation, but the science is excellent.

The **Teton Science School,** P.O. Box 68, Kelly, WY 83011 (☎ **307/733-4765;** e-mail tss@wyoming.com), is a 30-year-old institution with a cabin campus in the park near the little town of Kelly that offers summer programs for students and adults. Classes cater to different ages, and the emphasis is on experiential, hands-on learning. College credit is available. Long and short classes review the ecology, geology, and wildlife of the park, with workshops in photography and tracking, too.

7 Clothing & Equipment

Nothing will ruin a trip to the parks faster than sore or wet feet. Take some time planning your travel wardrobe. Bring comfortable walking shoes, even if you plan to keep walking to a minimum. Bring shoes that are broken in, and if you plan to do some serious hiking, get sturdy boots that support your ankles and wick away water. Early in the season, trails may be wet or muddy; late in the fall, you can get snowed on. The more popular trails are sometimes also used by horses, which can make stream crossings a mucky mess.

Wear your clothing in layers, and bring a small back- or fanny pack so you can take those layers off and on as temperature, altitude and your physical exertion change. Gloves or mittens are useful before the park heats up, or in the evening when it cools down again, **even in summer.**

The atmosphere is thin at higher altitude, so protect your skin. Bring a strong sunblock, a hat with a brim, and sunglasses. We also recommend bringing insect repellent, water bottles, and a first-aid kit (our recommendations for its contents are discussed under "Protecting Your Health & Safety," below).

Take into account that elevations at the parks are between 5,000 and 11,000 feet, so in campgrounds and on hiking trails you'll want clothing appropriate to the temperatures—40° in the evening, 75° during the day.

8 Tips for Travelers with Disabilities

Both parks have in recent years become more user-friendly for travelers with disabilities.

YELLOWSTONE   **Accessible accommodations** are located in the Cascade Lodge at Canyon Village, in Grant Village, in the Old Faithful Inn, and in the Lake Yellowstone Hotel. For a free *Visitors Guide to Accessible Features in Yellowstone National Park,* write to the Park Accessibility Coordinator, P.O. Box 168, YNP, WY 82190, or pick up the guide at the gates or visitors centers. There are **accessible campsites** at Madison, Canyon, and Grant campgrounds, which may be reserved by calling ☎ **307/344-7311.**

Accessible rest rooms with sinks and flush toilets are located at all developed areas except West Thumb and Norris. Accessible vault toilets are found at West Thumb and Norris, as well as in most scenic areas and picnic areas.

Many of Yellowstone's **roadside attractions,** including the Grand Canyon of the Yellowstone's south rim, West Thumb Geyser Basin, much of the Norris and Upper Geyser Basins, and parts of the Mud Volcano and Fountain Paint Pot areas, are negotiable by wheelchair.

Visitor centers at Old Faithful, Grant Village, and Canyon are wheelchair-accessible, as are the Norris Museum and the Fishing Bridge Visitor Center.

Accessible parking is available at Old Faithful, Fishing Bridge, Canyon, Norris, and Grant Village, though you'll have to look for it; at some locations it is near a Hamilton store.

GRAND TETON   **Visitor centers** at Moose, Colter Bay, Jenny Lake, and Flagg Ranch provide interpretive programs, displays, and visitor information in several formats, including visual, audible, and tactile. Large-print scripts, Braille brochures, and narrative audiotapes are available at Moose and Colter Bay.

Accessible parking spaces are located close to all visitor center entrances; curb cuts are provided, as are **accessible rest room facilities.**

Campsites at Colter Bay, Jenny Lake, and Gros Ventre campgrounds are on relatively level terrain; Lizard Creek and Signal Mountain are hilly and less accessible. Picnic areas at String Lake and Cottonwood Creek are both accessible, though the toilet at Cottonwood is not.

Accessible dining facilities are located at Flagg Ranch, Leek's Marina, Jackson Lake Lodge, and Jenny Lake Lodge.

More information is available by contacting **Grand Teton National Park,** Drawer 170, Moose, WY 83012 (☎ **307/ 739-3600;** www.nps.gov/grte).

9 Tips for Travelers with Pets

Domestic animals and wild animals don't mix well, and park regulations reflect that. So as much as you may like traveling with Fido, don't bring him unless he likes the inside of a car and the end of a leash an awful lot. Pets must be leashed and are allowed only 25 feet away from roads and parking areas. They are prohibited on trails, in the backcountry, on boardwalks, and in thermal areas.

10 Tips for Travelers with Children

The best general advice we've discovered is in Lisa Evans's book *An Outdoor Family Guide to Yellowstone and Grand Teton National Parks* (The Mountaineers, 1996), which is easy to find in bookstores.

Older children will be entertained (distracted) and receive a nature lesson by enrolling in the **Yellowstone Junior Ranger Program** (no specific age restrictions) at any visitor center or ranger station. The $2 fee covers the cost of the activity paper for Junior Rangers, *Yellowstone's Nature,* which describes the requirements for attaining Junior Ranger status. Activities include attendance at a ranger-led program, hiking, and keeping a journal. When participants complete the program, it's announced to the public with great fanfare and a patch is awarded.

The **Young Naturalist** program at **Grand Teton** provides children with a similar opportunity to explore the natural world of the park, following an activity brochure. It costs $1 to participate, and when you complete the course, you're awarded a patch.

11 Protecting Your Health & Safety

Health hazards range from mild headaches to grizzly bear attacks, with their attendant high levels of pain and suffering.

Since most of us live at or near sea level, the most common health hazard is discomfort caused by **altitude sickness,** as we adjust to the parks' high elevations, a process that may take a day or more. Symptoms include headache, fatigue, nausea, loss of appetite, muscle pain, and lightheadedness. Doctors recommend that, until acclimated, travelers should avoid heavy exertion, consume light meals, and drink lots of liquids, avoiding those with caffeine or alcohol.

Two water-borne hazards are **giardia** and **campylobacter,** with symptoms that wreak havoc on the human digestive system. If you pick up these pesky bugs, they may accompany you on your trip home. Untreated water from the parks' lakes and streams should be boiled for 3 to 6 minutes before consumption, or pumped through a fine-mesh water filter specifically designed to remove giardia.

To be on the safe side, you may want to keep a **first-aid kit** in your car or luggage and have it handy when hiking. It should include, at the least, butterfly bandages, sterile gauze pads, adhesive tape, an antibiotic ointment, both children's and adult pain reliever, alcohol pads, a knife with scissors, and tweezers.

12 Planning a Backcountry Trip

While we've given the particulars for both Yellowstone and Grand Teton national parks in their respective chapters (see chapters 4 and 6), there are some general things to keep in mind when planning a backcountry trip.

REGULATIONS   The theme in the backcountry is "leave no trace," and that means packing out any garbage you take in, not taking pets, and avoiding leaving scars on the landscape by staying on designated trails and reusing existing, designated campsites. Fires are allowed only in established fire rings, and only dead and downed material may be used for firewood; fires are prohibited in some areas, but backpacking stoves are allowed throughout the parks. You must have a park permit for overnight stays in the backcountry. The complete lists of do's and don'ts is available in the ***Backcountry Trip Planner*** available at most visitor centers.

BACKPACKING FOR BEGINNERS   Be sure to wear comfortable, sturdy hiking shoes that will resist water if you're planning an early season hike; cotton socks are not a good idea, because the material holds moisture, whereas wool and synthetics like fleece "wick" it away from your body. Your sleeping bag should be rated for the low temperatures found at high elevations, and if you bring a down bag, keep it dry or suffer the consequences. Most campers are happy to have a sleeping pad. The argument rages about the merits of old-fashioned, external-frame packs and the newer, internal-frame models. Over the long run, the newer versions are

Bear Encounters

Most people have a healthy respect for bears, content to view them from a distance, but a close encounter can happen unexpectedly, and you need to know how to handle yourself. First, be aware that what matters most to a bear are food and cubs. If you get between a sow and her cubs, you could be in trouble. If a bear thinks the food in your backpack is his, you're in trouble.

Unless bears have been fed human food, though, they won't come looking for you. Make a lot of noise on the trail through bear habitat, and *Ursus horribilus* will give you a wide berth. Don't camp anywhere near the carcass of a dead animal; grizzlies sometimes partially bury carrion and return to it. Hang your food bag high in a tree and keep your cooking area distant from your campsite, and don't keep any food or utensils in your tent, or even the clothes worn while cooking. Soaps and other perfumed items can also be attractants.

Avoid hiking at night, or in meadowy mountain areas if visibility is poor. Bears have an extremely good sense of smell, but poor eyesight.

Should you encounter a bear, here are some things you should and should not do:

- **Do not run.** Anything that flees looks like prey to a bear, and it may attack. Bears can run at over 30 miles per hour. The bear may bluff charge, but you're best off holding your ground.
- **Avoid direct eye contact.**
- If the bear is unaware of you, stay downwind (so it can't catch your scent) and **detour away from it slowly.**
- If the bear is aware of you but has not acted aggressively, **slowly back away.**
- **Do not climb a tree.** Though black bears have more suitable claws for climbing, grizzly bears can climb trees too.
- If you're attacked, drop to the ground face down, clasp your hands over the back of your neck, tuck your knees to your chest, and **play dead.**
- If you carry **pepper spray,** be sure it's handy when you're in potential bear habitat, not buried in your backpack. If you use it, aim for the bear's face and eyes. After you use it, leave the area: Bears have been seen returning to sniff about an area where spray has been used.

more stable and comfortable, but a big frame pack can shoulder big-ger loads. Good padding, a lumbar support pad, and a wide hip belt are pluses. Be sure you've tried out the pack—wear it around the house!—before you take it on a long trip with heavy loads, so your body and the pack frame have a chance to adjust to each other.

PERSONAL SAFETY ISSUES   It's best not to hike alone, but if you must, be sure you have told both park rangers and friends where you'll be, and how long. Don't leave the parking lot without the following gear: a compass, topographical maps, first-aid kit, bug repellent, toilet paper and a trowel of some sort, a flashlight, matches, knife, a rope for hanging food supplies in a tree, and a bell or other noisemaker that will, we hope, alert any bears in the neigh-borhood to your presence, as well as tent, stove, and sleeping bag. At this altitude, sunscreen and sunglasses with UV protection are a wise addition. A recently developed bear repellent generically re-ferred to as "pepper spray," available in most sporting goods stores, has proven successful in countering bear attacks. You'll also need a good water filter, since that seemingly clear stream is filled with para-sites that are likely to cause intestinal disorders. If you don't have a filter, boil water for at least 5 minutes before you drink it.

3

Exploring Yellowstone

You can take the park in sections, or you can devote a summer to it.
One trip, however long, never seems to be enough. You can drive the
park, or you can hike. You can enjoy the old-style park hotels, or set
up your own tent. You can learn about the geology and flora and
fauna in visitor center exhibits, or venture forth with a naturalist.

There are 370 miles of paved roadway in Yellowstone, with a
figure-eight loop at the center that takes you to some key attractions:
You can cover that ground in one long day. But that's not the best
way to see Yellowstone, as I'm sure you know.

Give yourself a minimum of 3 days. Despite the crowds, you
should check the famous sites, because they're deserving of all the
attention: **Old Faithful,** the **Grand Canyon of the Yellowstone,
Fishing Bridge, Washburn Peak.** If you're seeking knowledge, take
a class at the Yellowstone Institute, or follow one of the rangers on
a nature hike. If you want solitude, go early in the morning up one
of the less used trails, like Mount Bunsen, or Mystic Falls.

You'll find more details in the chapters that follow on where to
hike, fish, sleep and enjoy yourself in the park.

1 Essentials

ACCESS/ENTRY POINTS   Yellowstone has five entrances. The
north entrance, near Mammoth Hot Springs, is located just south
of Gardiner, Montana, and U.S. Highway 89. In the winter, this is
the only access to Yellowstone by car.

The **west entrance,** just outside the town of West Yellowstone on
U.S. Highway 20, is the closest entry to Old Faithful. Inside the
park, you can turn south to Old Faithful or north to the Norris
Geyser Basin. This entrance is open to wheeled vehicles from April
to November and during the winter to snowmobiles and
snowcoaches.

The **south entrance,** on U.S. Highway 89/191/287, brings visitors into the park from neighboring Grand Teton National Park and
the Jackson area. Coming north from Jackson drivers get a
panoramic view of the Grand Tetons. Once in the park, the road

winds along the Lewis River to the south end of Yellowstone Lake, at West Thumb and Grant Village. It's open to cars from May to November and to snowmobiles and snowcoaches from December to March.

The **east entrance,** on U.S. Highway 14/16/20, is 52 miles west of Cody, Wyoming, and is open to cars from May to September and to snowmobiles and snowcoaches from December to March. The drive up the Wapiti Valley and over Sylvan Pass is especially beautiful, when not marred by road repair delays.

The **northeast entrance,** at Cooke City, Montana, is closest to the Tower-Roosevelt area, 29 miles to the west. This entrance is open to cars year-round, but beginning on October 15, when the Beartooth Highway closes, until around Memorial Day, the only route to Cooke City is through Mammoth Hot Springs. When it's open, the drive from Red Lodge to the park is a grand climb among the clouds.

Regardless of which entrance you choose, you'll be given a good map and up-to-date information on facilities, services, programs, fishing, camping, and more.

VISITOR CENTERS   There are five major visitor and information centers in the park, and each has something different to offer. Unless otherwise indicated, summer hours are 8am to 7pm.

The **Albright Visitor Center** (☎ 307/344-2263), at Mammoth Hot Springs, is the largest. It provides visitor information and publications about the park, exhibits depicting park history from prehistory through the creation of the National Park Service, and houses a wildlife display on the second floor.

The **Old Faithful Visitor Center** (☎ 307/545-2750) is another large facility. An excellent short film describing the geysers, *Yellowstone, A Living Sculpture,* is shown throughout the day in an air-conditioned auditorium. Rangers dispense various park publications and post projected geyser eruption times here. An informative seismographic exhibit is an added attraction.

The **Canyon Visitor Center** (☎ 307/242-2550), in Canyon Village, is the place to go for books and an informative display about bison in the park. It's staffed with friendly rangers used to dealing with crowds.

The **Fishing Bridge Visitor Center** (☎ 307/242-2450), near Fishing Bridge on the north shore of Yellowstone Lake, has an excellent wildlife display. You can get information and publications here as well.

The **Grant Village Visitor Center** (☎ **307/242-2650**) has information, publications, a slide program, and a fascinating exhibit that examines the effects of fire in Yellowstone.

Other sources of park information can be found at the Madison Information Station; the Museum of the National Park Ranger and the Norris Geyser Basin Museum, both at Norris; and the West Thumb Information Station.

ENTRANCE FEES   Park users are now asked to share more of the burden of park costs with taxpayers, but fees are still moderate: a 7-day pass costs $20 per automobile, and covers both Yellowstone and Grand Teton national parks. A snowmobile or motorcycle costs $15 for 7 days, and someone who comes in on bicycle, skis or foot pays $10. If you expect to visit the parks more than once in a year, buy an annual permit for $40. And if you visit parks and national monuments around the country, purchase a Golden Eagle Passport for $50: it's good for 365 days from the date of purchase at nearly all federal preserves. Senior citizens can get a Golden Age Passport for $10 annually, and blind or permanently disabled people can obtain a Golden Access Passport, which costs nothing.

Currently, about 80% of the fee increases made in 1996 are devoted to the park of origin, while the rest goes into a general pool for parks around the country. Stingy congressional appropriations make these funds crucial for park improvements.

CAMPING FEES   Fees for camping in **Yellowstone** range from $10 to $15 per night, depending on the number of amenities the campground offers. The RV Campground at Fishing Bridge charges $25 per night and has full hookups; while other campgrounds have sites suitable for RVs, this is the only one with hookups, and only RVs are allowed here. Flagg Ranch, just outside the south entrance, also has an RV camp with hookups.

For more information on camping, see the "Camping in Yellowstone" section in chapter 7. It is possible to make advance reservations at some campgrounds in both parks.

SPECIAL REGULATIONS & WARNINGS   More detailed information about these rules can be requested from the park rangers or at visitor centers throughout the parks or at www.nps.gov/yell/planvisit/rules.

- **Bicycles**   Bicycles are not allowed on the park's trails or boardwalks, but there are some designated off-pavement bicycling areas—contact the park for more information. Helmets and

Yellowstone National Park

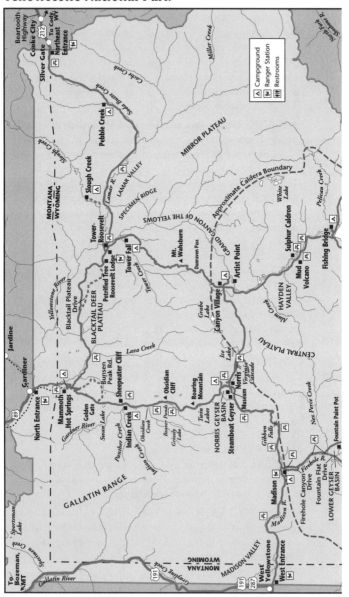

38

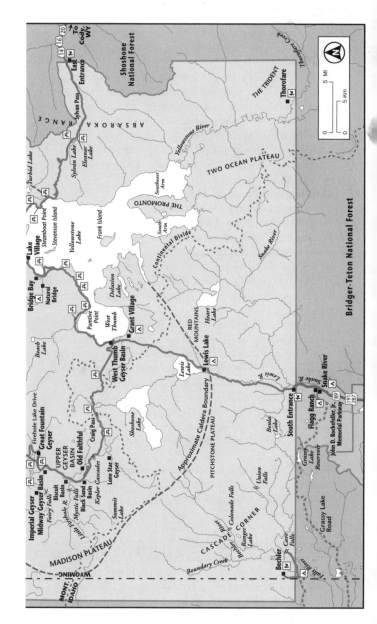

bright clothing are recommended because of the narrow, winding nature of park roads, and the large recreational vehicles with poor visibility.

- **Camping** In any given year, a person may camp for no more than 30 days in the park, and only 14 days during the summer season. Food, garbage or food utensils must be stored in a vehicle or container made of solid material and suspended at least 10 feet above the ground when not in use.

- **Climbing** Because of the loose, crumbly rock in Yellowstone, climbing is discouraged throughout the park, and prohibited in the Grand Canyon of the Yellowstone.

- **Defacing Park Features** Picking wildflowers, or collecting natural or archaeological objects, is illegal. Only dead-and-down wood can be collected for backcountry campfires.

- **Firearms** Firearms are not allowed in either park. However, unloaded firearms may be transported in a vehicle when cased, broken down, or rendered inoperable, and on certain trails for access to areas outside the park, with a special permit. Ammunition must be carried in a separate compartment of the vehicle.

- **Littering** Littering in the national parks is strictly prohibited—remember, if you take it in, you have to take it out. Throwing coins or other objects into thermal features is illegal.

- **Motorcycles** Motorcycles, motor scooters, and motor bikes are allowed only on park roads. No off-road or trail riding is allowed. Operator licenses and license plates are required.

- **Pets** Pets must be leashed and are prohibited in the backcountry, on trails, on boardwalks, and in thermal areas for obvious reasons. If you tie up a pet and leave it, you're breaking the law.

- **Smoking** No smoking in thermal areas, visitors centers or rangers stations, or any other posted public areas.

- **Snowmobiling** Snowmobilers must have valid drivers licenses and must stay on the designated unplowed roadways. Snowmobiles must obey posted speed limits.

- **Swimming** Swimming or wading is prohibited in thermal features or in streams whose waters flow from thermal features in Yellowstone. (An exception is the "Boiling River" near Mammoth, where visitors can take a warm soak between 5am and 6pm except during spring runoff). Swimming in Yellowstone Lake is discouraged because of the low water temperature and unpredictable weather.

• **Wildlife**   It is unlawful to approach within 100 yards of a bear or within 25 yards of other wildlife. Feeding any wildlife is illegal. Wildlife calls such as elk bugles or other artificial attractants are forbidden.

FAST FACTS: Yellowstone

ATMs   There are three ATMs in the park: at the Old Faithful Inn, Lake Yellowstone Hotel, and Canyon Lodge.

Audio Tours   Yellowstone National Park Lodges rents out self-guided audio tours you can take with you on your drive around Yellowstone. For further information, see "Self-Guided Driving Tours," below.

Car Trouble/Towing Services   If you have car trouble, you'll find car repair shops in Old Faithful, Canyon Village, Fishing Bridge, and Grant Village. Call the park's main information (☎ **307/344-7381**) 24 hours a day if you need to be towed.

Emergencies   Call ☎ **911** or the park's main information number (☎ **307/344-7381**), which is staffed 24 hours a day.

Gas Stations   You can purchase gasoline at Old Faithful, Canyon Village, Grant Village, Mammoth Hot Springs, Fishing Bridge, and Tower Junction.

Laundry   There are laundry facilities at Fishing Bridge RV Park, Canyon Village campground, and at the Grant Village Campground.

Medical Services   There are three **medical clinics** in the park: at Mammoth Hot Springs (☎ **307/344-7965**), Old Faithful (☎ **307/545-7325**), and the Yellowstone Lake Hotel (☎ **307/242-7241**), where there is a **pharmacy** and a small **hospital.** The Lake and Old Faithful clinics are open daily from May to October, while the Mammoth clinic is open weekdays year-round.

Permits   You can obtain fishing and backcountry permits at most visitor centers.

Post Offices   All the major visitor centers in Yellowstone have post offices (Mammoth, Old Faithful, Grant Village, Lake Village, and Canyon Village).

Supplies   Hamilton stores are located in all the park villages, with groceries, film and camera supplies, camping gear, and souvenirs.

Weather Updates   For weather updates and road conditions, call the park's main information number (☎ **307/344-7381**), which has recorded information.

2   The Highlights

This is a wonderland you can return to again and again, sampling a different pleasure each time. All the sites mentioned here are easily accessible along the loop roads of the park. But the further you get from the pavement, and the further from July and August you schedule your visit, the more private your experience will be.

THE UPPER LOOP

MAMMOTH HOT SPRINGS   Here, 5 miles south of the park's North Entrance at Gardiner, Montana, you'll find some of the park's spectacular thermal areas, including unique limestone terraces (the **Upper** and **Lower terraces,** which are described in "The Extended Tour," below). The Albright Visitor Center is here, with fine exhibits and books about Yellowstone for sale, as well as the Mammoth Hot Springs Hotel. Your best bet: Follow the Interpretive Trail through the terraces.

NORRIS GEYSER BASIN   South of Mammoth Hot Springs you'll find several impressive **geysers,** geothermal areas of different type and age, as well as two museums. Norris is conveniently close to the West Entrance of the park at West Yellowstone. You can follow boardwalks north and south (the south has more activity, but the north takes you across the dramatic Porcelain Basin. Best bet: Tour both of them.

CANYON VILLAGE AREA   East of Norris, the **Grand Canyon of the Yellowstone River** provides some of the park's best views. There are hikes of all lengths and for all abilities here. Canyon Village is one of the most developed sections of the park with lots of facilities, including comfortable new lodges. The canyon may not be as big as the Grand Canyon in Arizona, but it's got its own dynamic beauty.

TOWER-ROOSEVELT AREA   The closest of the major park areas to the Northeast Entrance (which is near Cooke City,

Traveler's Tip

If you are considering making your trip to the parks before mid-June, think about beginning your exploration in Grand Teton and working north to Yellowstone. Elevations in Grand Teton are slightly less and snow melts earlier, so accumulations on trails are reduced, and temperatures are more moderate.

Montana), this is also one of the most uncrowded and easygoing areas of the park, and a short drive from the beautiful **Lamar Valley.** The Roosevelt Lodge Cabins are a good budget lodging if you want to rough it, and **Tower Falls** provides a dramatic backdrop for photos. Your best bet: Try the buckboard ride from Roosevelt Lodge to the **evening barbecue.**

THE LOWER LOOP

OLD FAITHFUL AREA   **Old Faithful** remains an enduring symbol of Yellowstone, even as it slows down with age, and you'll find the benches filled for each eruption. The historic **Old Faithful Inn** (with its fine restaurant) is located here, and the new **Old Faithful Snow Lodge** is a great addition. This area is most conveniently accessed from West Yellowstone and the park's West Entrance. And don't miss the **Riverside Geyser.**

LAKE VILLAGE AREA   On the north shore of Yellowstone Lake you'll find many fishing and boating opportunities, as well as fine dining and lodging choices. The Lake Yellowstone Hotel is one of the two best choices in the park. This area is the closest to Yellowstone's East Entrance, which is about 50 miles from Cody, Wyoming. The Hayden Valley is nearby. You can rent a boat at Bay Bridge to get out and try to catch one of those lake trout.

GRANT VILLAGE/WEST THUMB AREAS   Grant Village is the southernmost of the park's developments, an uninspired collection of modern buildings on the south end of Lake Yellowstone. Nearby is **West Thumb Geyser Basin** and the Grant Village Visitor Center. The geyser basin has a boardwalk that allows views of geysers that are beneath the surface of Yellowstone Lake.

3 If You Have Only 1 or 2 Days (the Short Tour)

If you are so pinched for time that you have only 1 or 2 days to tour Yellowstone, here's an itinerary that highlights the best of the best. If you'll be spending the night, reserve a room at either Old Faithful Inn or the Lake Hotel—if those are booked full, try the new Yellowstone Snow Lodge, or get a campsite at Norris or Indian Creek.

The quickest route to the inner road loops of the park is by the west entrance road, so come in that way, stopping perhaps for a stroll along the banks of the **Madison River,** where you can see the forest recovering from the 1988 fires. You'll also spot wildlife: ducks and trumpeter swans on the river, grazing elk and bison. Turn north at Madison Junction to **Norris Geyser Basin,** where there are two boardwalk tours, and take the southern one if you're in a hurry, because there you can wait for the **Echinus Geyster** pool to fill and erupt.

You're now driving the **upper loop,** which goes north to **Mammoth Hot Springs,** east to **Tower-Roosevelt,** south to **Canyon Village,** and west again to Norris, finally returning to Madison Junction, a circuit of about 85 miles. If you go south rather than west at Canyon Village you'll be on the southern loop, which will take you to **Fishing Bridge** and **Lake Village,** then by **West Thumb,** west over Craig Pass to **Old Faithful,** and back to the Madison Junction. The entire lower loop covers 96 miles.

Altogether, this 2-day circuit is called the "Grand Loop," taking you through all the major areas of the park except the road between Norris and Canyon Village. You could do it in a day—it's only 120 miles long—but you'd scare a lot of other travelers as you sped by.

THE UPPER LOOP   If you're pressed for time, the Norris Geyser basin is a major concentration of **thermal attractions,** including Porcelain Basin, and has a nice **museum.** Mammoth has one of the park's major attractions, the ever-growing **terraces** of Mammoth Hot Springs. In addition to the natural attraction, the **Albright Visitor Center** provides excellent historical background for everything you'll see in the park. There is a fine old hotel at Mammoth, and lodging just outside the park in Gardiner, too, but we recommend you continue further around the loop on your first day.

From Mammoth, the route winds through forested areas that lead to the edge of the **Lamar Valley,** a deep, rounded path for the Lamar River that is a major wildlife repository. You could stop for the night at nearby Roosevelt Lodge, or continue south to Yellowstone's **Grand Canyon,** one of the most dramatic sights in park.

✪ **THE LOWER LOOP**   This is a better way to go in our opinion if you have only 1 day. You'll also see the two largest geyser areas in Yellowstone—**Norris** to the north and the park's signature attraction, **Old Faithful,** to the south. On the eastern side of this route, you'll find the **Grand Canyon of the Yellowstone** and **Hayden Valley,** where you'll find resident herds of buffalo. Farther south, the **Yellowstone Lake** area is a haven for water-lovers: There's fishing, boating, and places for picnicking on the shore of the lake.

4 Yellowstone: The Extended Tour

Stretching your visit to 4 or 5 days has several advantages. You'll have more time to visit the most popular areas of the park, you can walk a few of the trails, and you'll have time to learn from the exhibits at the visitor centers instead of blasting by them.

The **visitors centers** are a good source of information about the ecosystem, the flora and fauna, and the history of the park, and they're staffed by knowledgeable rangers who can answer your questions. There are eight altogether, but some may be closed if you visit the parks during the off seasons. The **Albright Visitor Center** is open year-round, and the **Old Faithful Visitor Center** is open during summer months and December to March. The others usually open concurrently with the lodging facilities in their area of the park. Ask the rangers about programs in their area, and check whether any geothermal features have undergone a change in their activity recently—geysers have been known to revive suddenly after years of quiescence.

The roads in Yellowstone are organized into a series of interconnecting loops, which you can come into from any of the park's five entrances. To simplify things, we will discuss attractions and activities going clockwise along each section of the **Grand Loop Road,** beginning at the **Madison Junction.** But you can enter the loop at any point and pick up our tour as long as you are traveling clockwise. We haven't suggested an optimum amount of time to spend on each leg of the loop since that will depend on your particular interests. If you want to get away from the crowds, take your time and try to get off the pavement and out into the park away from the main roads.

WEST YELLOWSTONE TO NORRIS

Closest Entrance: West Yellowstone (West Entrance).

Distances: 14 miles from West Yellowstone to Madison; 14 miles from Madison to Norris.

Since the largest percentage of visitors to Yellowstone enter at the **West Yellowstone Entrance,** we'll use that as a jumping-off point to begin an extended tour of the park. As you travel the 14 miles from the gate to **Madison Junction,** you will find the **Two Ribbons Trail,** which offers an opportunity to walk through and inspect the effects of the 1988 fire. The trailhead is 3 miles east of the West Yellowstone entrance at a well-marked turnout. Along this 0.75-mile loop trail, you'll see a mosaic of blackened, singed, and unburned trees—charred snags and green trees side by side among boulders shattered by the heat. The scraggly, deformed branches and piles of rock are surrounded by bushes and fresh, bright green tree shoots that are only now emerging from the soil.

Park maps don't identify all the observation points and side roads in the area, so now is the time to begin forming the habit of driving off the beaten path, even when you may not know where you're going. Keep a sharp eye peeled for the poorly marked **Riverside turnout** on the Madison River side of the road; it's a paved road on the north side of the highway about 6 miles from the entrance. This back road takes you along a river, removed from most traffic, with a number of turnouts perfectly situated to look for resident swans, enjoy a picnic, or test your fly-fishing ability.

As you continue toward Madison Junction, you'll see vivid evidence of the 1988 fire and, odds are, a herd of bison that frequents the area during summer months. As frightening as the fire was, it had its good points: There is evidence that the 1988 fire burned hotter here because the old lodgepole pines had been infected by beetles, which decimated the trees. The good news is that the fire killed the beetles and remineralized the soil. When temperatures exceeded 500°F, pine seeds were released from fire-adapted pine cones, which has quickened the rebirth cycle. The hundreds of tiny trees poking through the soil are evidence that the forest is recovering quickly.

The 0.5-mile round-trip **Harlequin Lake Trail,** located 1.5 miles west of the Madison campground on the West Entrance Road, offers an excellent, easy opportunity to explore the area. It winds through the burned forest to a small lake that is populated by various types of waterfowl. But don't get your hopes up; sightings of the rare harlequin ducks are rare.

An alternative hike, one of the best in the area, is up the **Purple Mountain Trail,** which begins 0.25 mile north of the Madison Junction on the Norris Road. This hike requires more physical exertion, as it winds 6 miles (round-trip) through a burned forest to the top of what many consider only a tall hill, with an elevation gain of 1,400 feet.

Madison Junction is a focal point of the most widely known Yellowstone myth, namely that in September 1870, Cornelius Hedges and a group of explorers agreed that the land should be protected from those who would exploit its resources and began making plans to promote the creation of a national park. In reality, this conversation never happened. Madison Junction is also the confluence of the Gibbon and Firehole rivers, two famous trout streams, which meet to form the Madison River, one of three which join to form the Missouri.

The **Madison Campground,** one of the largest and most popular in the park, is situated at the junction, with hiking trails and sites in view of the river. If you're planning a stay here, it's wise to arrive by 8am or you may be disappointed.

This is where you'll enter the northern loop toward Norris Junction, along a windy 14-mile section of road that parallels the **Gibbon River.** The river was named for Gen. John Gibbon, who explored here in 1872 but whose main, dubious, claims to fame were as the cavalry leader who buried Custer's army, and who chased Chief Joseph and the Nez Perce Indians from the park as they attempted to escape to Canada.

At 84-foot **Gibbon Falls,** you'll see water bursting out of the edge of a caldera in a rocky canyon, the walls of which were hidden from view for several hundred years until being exposed by the fire of 1988. There's a delightful **picnic area** just below the falls on an open plateau overlooking the Gibbon River.

Before arriving at Norris Junction, you'll discover the **Artist Paint Pot Trail** in Gibbon Meadows, 4.5 miles south of the Norris Junction, an interesting, worthwhile, and easy 0.5-mile stroll that winds through a lodgepole-pine forest to a mud pot at the top of a hill. This thermal area contains some small geysers, hot pools, and steam vents.

Across the road from the trailhead is **Elk Park,** where you can expect to see a large resident herd of—yes—elk.

NORRIS GEYSER BASIN

Closest Entrances & Distances: 28 miles from West Yellowstone (West) Entrance; 26 miles from Gardiner (North) Entrance.

Perhaps more than any other area in Yellowstone, this basin is living testimony to the park's unique thermal activity. It is never the same, changing from year to year as thermal activity and the ravages of wind, rain, and snow create new and different ponds and landscapes. Trees fall, slides occur, and geysers erupt. The ✪ **Norris Geyser Basin** was named for the second superintendent of the park, an outgoing sort whose name graces many park roads and attractions. It is also the location of one of the park's highest concentration of thermal features, including the most active geysers, with underground water temperatures that reach 459°F.

There are two loop trails here, both mostly level with wheelchair access, to the Porcelain Basin and the Back Basin. If you take in both of them, you'll see most of the area's interesting thermal features. If you're pressed for time, take the shorter, **Porcelain Basin Trail,** a boardwalk that takes only 45 minutes. To me, this area is especially spectacular on summer days when thermal activity takes place on the ground and thunder and lightning storms boom overhead.

The **Porcelain Basin Trail** is a 0.75-mile round-trip that can be completed in 45 minutes; on it are Black Growler Steam Vent, Ledge Geyser, and descriptively named Whale's Mouth.

The 1.5-mile **Back Basin Loop** is easily negotiable in 1 hour and passes by **Steamboat Geyser,** which has been known to produce the world's highest and most memorable eruptions. However, these 400-foot waterspouts occur infrequently, so it will take some luck to see one. Conversely, **Echinus Geyser** erupts several times a day.

Warning: In thermal areas, the ground may be only a thin crust above boiling hot springs, and there's no way to guess where a safe path is. New hazards can bubble up overnight, and pools are acidic enough to burn through boots, so you must stay in designated walking areas.

Among the many highlights of the area is the **Norris Geyser Basin Museum,** a beautiful, single-story stone-and-log building, the stone archway of which leads to an overlook of the Porcelain Basin. The museum houses several excellent exhibits that explain the nature of the area; with luck you'll arrive in time for a ranger-led tour. In the past, ranger programs have been scheduled four times a day; ask at a visitor center for current schedules.

Also nearby is the **Museum of the National Park Ranger,** which is little more than a room full of artifacts in a small building near the campground (see below).

Both museums open in mid- to late May, weather permitting, and are open until September; hours vary by season, but you can expect the museums to be open from 8am to 6pm during the busiest times (roughly Memorial Day to Labor Day, but again weather is a factor here).

The **Norris Campground,** which is just slightly north of the Norris Junction, is another very popular campground, so plan an early arrival or be prepared to look for an alternative site, which isn't easy during the peak season. Part of the appeal of the campground is its proximity to the Gibbon River and to an old cavalry building from the 1880s, which houses the Museum of the National Park Ranger.

NORRIS TO MAMMOTH HOT SPRINGS

Closest Entrances: Norris is 28 miles from the West Yellowstone (West) Entrance; Mammoth Hot Springs is 5 miles from the Gardiner (North) Entrance.

Distance: 21 miles from Norris to Mammoth Hot Springs.

From Norris Geyser Basin, it's a 21-mile drive north to Mammoth Hot Springs, past the **Twin Lakes,** beautiful, watery jewels surrounded by trees. During the early months of the park year, the water is milky green because of the runoff of ice and snow. This is an excellent place to do some bird watching.

This stretch of road, between Norris Junction and Mammoth Hot Springs, presents yet another excellent opportunity to see the effects of the 1988 fire. Try to use one of the turnouts to avoid blocking the roads. The large **meadow** on the west side of the highway that begins 3 miles from Norris is popular with moose, thanks to water from bogs, marshes, and a creek. As you travel alongside **Obsidian Creek,** you'll notice the smell of sulfur in the air, evidence of thermal vents.

On the east side of the road 4 miles from Norris is **Roaring Mountain,** a patch of ground totally devoid of brush and plant life, covered with trees and stumps from the fire. Its bareness is attributed to the fact that, as steam vents developed here, the ground became hot and acidic, which bleached and crumbled the rock, taking the undergrowth with it. Historians say that the noise from the Roaring Mountain was once so loud that it could be heard as far as 4 miles away; these days it is very quiet.

Just up the road 2 miles is the **Beaver Lake Picnic Area,** an excellent little spot for a snack. Keep an eye out for moose.

As you wend your way a 0.5 mile to Obsidian Cliff, across the road from the picnic area the terrain changes quickly, and you'll find yourself driving through a narrow valley bisected by a beautiful green stream. **Obsidian Cliff** is where ancient peoples of North America gathered to collect obsidian, a hard, black rock that was used to make weapons and tools.

If you didn't stop at Beaver Lake, consider taking time for a short (3-min.) detour on the road to **Sheepeater Cliffs** (unless you're driving an RV or pulling a trailer), which, like most park attractions, is in a well-marked area just off the pavement. Though close to the main road, this quiet, secluded spot sits on the banks of the Gardner River beside a cliff comprised of columnar basalt rock that was formed by cooling lava following a volcanic eruption. This area, once inhabited by the Sheepeater Indians, is today home to yellow-bellied marmots that live in the rocks, safe from flying predators and coyotes.

As you travel the final few miles to Mammoth Hot Springs, you'll be in an area whose geologic diversity is especially interesting. You'll see evidence of the fire, large springs and ponds, and enormous glaciated rock terraces and cliffs.

Exiting the valley, head north onto a high plateau, where you'll find **Swan Lake,** flanked by Little Quadrant Mountain and Antler Peak to the west, and Bunsen Peak to the north.

At the northernmost edge of the Yellowstone Plateau, you'll begin a descent through **Golden Gate.** This steep, narrow stretch of road was once a stagecoach route constructed of wooden planks anchored to the mountain by a massive rock called the **Pillar of Hercules,** the largest rock in an unmarked pile that sits next to the road.

Beyond Hercules are **The Hoodoos,** an ominous looking jumble of travertine boulders on the north side of the road that have tumbled off Terrace Mountain to create a pile of unusual formations.

From the 45th parallel parking area on the North Entrance road north of Mammoth Hot Springs, a short hike leads to the **Boiling River.** Here you can take a dip during daylight hours, where a hot spring empties into the Gardner River. There are no facilities, though, so you're on your own.

MAMMOTH HOT SPRINGS

Closest Entrance: 5 miles from the Gardiner (North) Entrance.

The large **Albright Visitor Center** (☎ **307/344-2263**), near park headquarters, has more visitor information and publications than other centers, and significant exhibits telling the story of the park from prehistory through the creation of the National Park Service. It's open from 8am to 8pm during peak season. Enclosed in floor-to-ceiling glass cases are uniforms, furniture, sidearms, and memorabilia that reflect the park's varied history. There are excellent photography exhibits, much of it by the first park photographer, William Henry Jackson. A second level is filled with displays of the wildlife that inhabits the park, including wolves, mountain lions, waterfowl, and other birds. *The Challenge of Yellowstone,* a film addressing the concept of the national park, is shown throughout the day.

This area may offer the best argument for getting off the roads, out of your car, and into the environment. Though it's possible to see most of the wildlife and the major thermal areas from behind car windows, your experience of the park will be multiplied tenfold

Mammoth Hot Springs

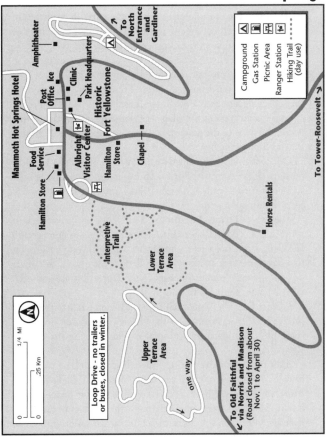

through the expenditure of a small amount of energy. Most people in average shape are capable of negotiating the trails here, a significant percentage of which are level or only moderately inclined boardwalks. Even the more challenging trails frequently have rest areas where you can catch your breath or, more important, stop and absorb the magnificent views.

One of Yellowstone's most unique, beautiful, and fascinating areas is the **Upper** and **Lower terraces.** Strolling among them, you can observe Mother Nature going about the business of mixing and matching heat, water, limestone, and rock fractures to sculpt the area. With the exception of the Grand Canyon of the Yellowstone

River, this is the most colorful area of the park; its tapestries of orange, pink, yellow, green, and brown, formed by masses of bacteria and algae, seem to change colors before your eyes.

The mineral-rich hot waters that flow to the surface here do so at an unusually constant rate, roughly 750,000 gallons per day, which results in the deposit of almost 2 tons of limestone on these ever-changing terraces. Contours are constantly changing in the hot springs, as formations are shaped by large quantities of flowing water, the slope of the ground, and trees and rocks that determine the direction of the flow.

On the flip side of the equation, nature has a way of playing tricks on some of her creatures: **Poison Spring** is a sinkhole on the trail, so named because carbon dioxide collects there, often killing creatures that stop for a drink.

The **Lower Terrace Interpretive Trail** is one of the best ways to see this area. The trail starts at 6,280 feet and climbs another 300 feet along rather steep grades, through a bare, rocky, thermal region to a flat alpine area and observation deck at the top. A park guide says the 1.5-mile round-trip walk to the Upper Terrace and back takes 2 hours, but it can be done in less.

Liberty Cap is a 37-foot tall dome at the entrance to the interpretive trail. It was named by the Hayden Expedition because it resembles hats worn by Colonial patriots during the French Revolution.

After passing **Palette Spring,** where bacteria create a collage of browns, greens, and oranges, you're on your way to **Cleopatra** and **Minerva terraces.** Minerva is a favorite of visitors because of its bright colors and travertine formations, the product of limestone deposits. In nature's way, these attractions have occasionally become so undisciplined as to spray deposits of water and mineral deposits large enough to bury the boardwalk.

The hike up the last 150 feet to the Upper Terrace Loop Drive is slightly steeper, though there are benches at frequent intervals. From here you can see all the terraces and several springs—**Canary Spring** and **New Blue Spring** being the most distinctive—and the red-roofed buildings of **Fort Yellowstone,** which is now the park headquarters.

If you wish, you can continue walking along **Upper Terrace Loop Drive,** which is also accessible by car. The Upper Terrace has its own unique attractions, including **New Highland Terrace,** which is a forest of tree skeletons engulfed by travertine, and **Angel Terrace,** known for its pure white formations.

Just steps from the lower terrace is the trailhead for the **Beaver Ponds Loop Trail,** a 5-mile jaunt through shaded woods along a trail that follows **Clematis Creek.** The ponds, which have been dammed by beavers, are some 2.5 easy miles from the trailhead. You may be forced to adjust your body clock to catch a glimpse of these toothy engineers, since they're most active early in the morning and in the evening. The area is also a hangout for elk, pronghorn, and bears, so it may be closed early in the year. If you get tired, there are several shady areas along the creek to stop and soak your feet.

MAMMOTH HOT SPRINGS TO TOWER JUNCTION

Closest Entrance: Mammoth is 5 miles from the Gardiner (North) Entrance.
Distance: 18 miles from Mammoth to Tower.

Heading east from Mammoth on the Tower road, a 6-mile drive will bring you to the **All Person's Fire Trail,** so named because this flat, easy stroll along a boardwalk offers an excellent opportunity to educate yourself about the effects of the fire on the environment.

Two miles later is **Blacktail Plateau Drive,** a 7-mile, one-way dirt road that offers great wildlife-viewing opportunities and a bit more solitude. You'll be more or less following the route of the Bannock Trail, made by the long-vanished Indian inhabitants of the area. For centuries, the trail was used by Bannock Indians as they trekked from Idaho to buffalo hunting grounds in eastern Montana; scars in the land made by their travois—twin poles tied to a horse that were used as a luggage rack—are still evident along the trail. You'll emerge back onto the Mammoth–Tower road, about a mile west of the turnoff to the Petrified Tree.

Turn right onto this 0.5-mile long road that dead ends at the **Petrified Tree,** a redwood that, while standing, was burned by volcanic ash more than 50 million years ago. If you have the time and energy, park your car at the base of the road after you turn off the Mammoth–Tower road and hike up, since the parking area is often congested. After your stop, continue on to Tower Junction.

TOWER-ROOSEVELT

Closest Entrances & Distances: 23 miles from the Gardiner (North) Entrance; 29 miles from the Cooke City (Northeast) Entrance.

Just beyond the Petrified Tree, you'll come to **Tower-Roosevelt,** the most relaxed of the park's villages and a great place to take a break from the more crowded attractions. Even if you aren't going to stay, you might want to make a quick stop at the **Tower Soldier Station,** now the ranger residence at Tower Junction, one of three surviving outposts from the era of U.S. Cavalry management of the park. Also here is **Roosevelt Lodge,** a rustic building that commemorates Pres. Theodore Roosevelt's camping excursion to this area of the park in 1903. It now serves as a dining hall, bar, and registration area for visitors staying at nearby frontier cabins. You can get into the cowboy spirit by taking a guided trail ride, a stagecoach ride, or a wagon ride. A more adventurous alternative to the rather rustic dining-room atmosphere at Roosevelt Lodge is an Old West cook-out to which you will arrive by either horseback or wagon for a hearty meal. There's a range of other services in this spot, including a Hamilton store if you need to buy provisions, and a gas station.

At **Specimen Ridge,** 2.5 miles east of the Tower Junction on the Northeast Entrance road, you'll find a ridge that entombs one of the world's most extensive fossil forests. Between 45 million and 50 million years ago, the mature forest that stood here was engulfed by deep volcanic ash some 27 times; subsequent erosion has exposed more than 100 different fossilized species in an area that spans 40 square miles.

A DETOUR: THE CHIEF JOSEPH HIGHWAY
Closest Entrance & Distance: 29 miles to the Cooke City (East) Entrance.

Because all the major attractions in Yellowstone are located on the loop roads, some of the park's most beautiful and secluded areas go unnoticed by travelers. If you have an additional day or two, I suggest you head for the eastern entrances on another loop tour. From Tower Junction, go east to Cooke City, and then continue to Cody; or, from Fishing Bridge, head across Sylvan Pass to Cody. If you hurry, you can complete the trip in a day, though you'll miss the Cody rodeo.

From **Tower Junction,** you'll traverse the ✪ **Lamar Valley,** one of the prettiest and lesser-traveled areas of the park. This valley was covered with a thick crust of ice during the last ice age, which began 25,000 years ago and ended 10,000 years later, leaving a valley shaped by melting glaciers that is dotted by glacial ponds and strewn with boulders dropped by moving ice. Fifty million years ago, the mature forest that stood here was engulfed by deep volcanic ash. If you stop to look at the Specimen Ridge wayside, you'll be able to see the results. In addition to the region's natural beauty, it's also the new home of packs of transplanted wolves and offers excellent fishing in the Lamar River.

Cooke City could best be described as an outpost that provides essential services including restaurants, motels, gas stations, and grocery stores, but it's a long way from being as nice or well turned out as its sister gateway cities.

Fourteen miles outside of Cooke City, take the **Chief Joseph Scenic Highway** (WY 296), which connects to WY 120 into Cody. This highway, also called the Sunlight Basin Road, offers great opportunities for viewing deer, coyotes, and other wildlife.

Cody is the quintessential Western town. Folks are friendly, accommodations are well turned out and moderately priced, and there are enough tourist attractions—the nightly rodeo and a rebuilt historical town are most famous—to make it worth the detour.

From Cody, return to Yellowstone's East Entrance on U.S. 12/ 16/20. After you reenter the park, you'll cross 8,541-foot **Sylvan Pass** and travel through the Absaroka mountain range, estimated to be 50 million years old. Driving along the shores of Yellowstone Lake, you'll pass **Mary Bay,** yet another crater created by a volcanic explosion. You'll return to the main area of the park at **Fishing Bridge Junction,** where you can rejoin the Grand Loop Road and continue your tour.

FROM TOWER JUNCTION TO THE GRAND CANYON OF THE YELLOWSTONE

Closest Entrances: 23 miles from the Gardiner (North) Entrance; 29 miles from the Cooke City (Northeast) Entrance.

Distance: 19 miles from Tower Junction to Canyon Village.

A few minutes' drive from the Tower area is the **Calcite Springs Overlook.** A short loop along a boardwalk leads to the overlook at the rim of **The Narrows,** the narrowest part of the canyon. You can hear the river raging through the canyon some 500 feet below, and look across at the canyon walls comprised of rock spires and bands of columnar basalt. Just downstream is the most prominent feature in the canyon, **Bumpus Butte.**

The trail to the 132-foot **Tower Fall** begins within footsteps of the Hamilton Store and leads to an overlook that is typically crowded with sightseers. You'll have a more interesting and photogenic view if you continue on the path to the base of the falls where Tower Creek flows into the Yellowstone River.

Continuing south, you'll travel through the **Washburn Range,** an area in which the 1988 fire ran especially hot and fast. The terrain changes dramatically as the road climbs along some major hills toward **Mount Washburn.** The twistiest section of this road is the aptly named **Mae West Curve.** One stretch of this highway, just before the curve is a favorite summer haunt of the grizzly bear, which overlooks stands of aspen trees. Other sections are covered with sagebrush. During the fire, the sagebrush was incinerated, but roots were uninjured, so it now grows vigorously in soil that is fertilized by ash leached into the earth by snowmelt, another example of nature's artful ways.

There are trailheads for the **Mount Washburn Trail,** one of our favorites, on each side of the summit. One is at the end of Old Chittenden Road (the turnoff to this road from the Tower–Canyon Road is well marked); the other begins at Dunraven Pass, about a mile further down the highway. Both hikes take the same time, but Old Chittenden has the larger parking lot, so it may be more crowded; it's also more scenic (though steeper).

As you approach **Dunraven Pass** (8,859 ft.), keep your eyes peeled for the shy bighorn sheep, since this is one of their prime habitats.

One mile further south is the **Washburn Hot Springs Overlook,** which offers sweeping views of the canyon. On a clear day, you can see 50 to 100 miles south, beyond Yellowstone Lake. Get out of the car and take a look. As you wander the immediate area on foot, you will often see fox and marmots amid the flower-covered alpine meadows.

CANYON VILLAGE

Closest Entrances & Distances: 40 miles from West Yellowstone (West) Entrance; 38 miles from Gardiner (North) Entrance; 48 miles from the Cooke City (Northeast) Entrance; 43 miles the from East Entrance.

You're in for yet another eyeful when you reach the **Grand Canyon** of Yellowstone National Park, which offers a vivid example of nature unleashing its destructive power to create what is now a dramatic piece of real estate.

The canyon has its geologic origins in the same volcanic eruptions that created Yellowstone Lake. As lava flows created lakes that overflowed their banks, rhyolite, a hard, granitelike rock, carved the canyon, which was subsequently blocked by glaciers. Eventually, when the ice melted, floods recarved each end of the canyon, deepening it and removing sand and gravel.

The result: a 20-mile ditch that at some points is 1,200 feet deep and 4,000 feet wide, and two waterfalls, one of which is twice as high as Niagara Falls. Even the most reluctant hiker will be rewarded

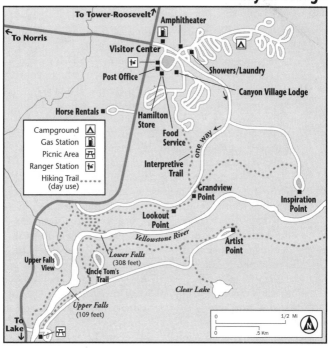

To Tower-Roosevelt

To Norris

Amphitheater

Visitor Center

Post Office

Showers/Laundry

Canyon Village Lodge

Horse Rentals

Hamilton Store

Food Service

Campground
Gas Station
Picnic Area
Ranger Station
Hiking Trail
(day use)

Interpretive Trail

one way

Grandview Point

Inspiration Point

Lookout Point

Yellowstone River

Artist Point

Upper Falls View

Lower Falls (308 feet)

Uncle Tom's Trail

Clear Lake

Upper Falls (109 feet)

To Lake

0   1/2 Mi
0   .5 Km

with sites as colorful as those seen in "the other canyon." Compared to the Grand Canyon of Arizona, Yellowstone's Grand Canyon is relatively narrow; however, it's equally impressive because of the steepness of the cliffs, which descend hundreds of feet to the bottom of a gorge where the Yellowstone River flows. It's also equally colorful with displays of oranges, reds, yellows, and golds. You won't find thermal vents in Arizona, but you will find them here, a constant reminder of ongoing underground activity.

You should plan on encountering crowds when you reach **Canyon Village.** And though it is overdeveloped, you'll find many necessary services here, including a post office and two stores stocked with fresh and preserved foodstuffs, camping gear, and souvenirs. Meals are served in a cafeteria, restaurant, and an old-fashioned snack shop to visitors perched on bright red stools. Accommodations are in cabins, and a large campground. Concessionaires offer horseback trail rides, from a nearby stable, and guided tours.

The **Canyon Visitor Center** (☎ **307/242-2550**) is the place to go for books and a new exhibit on bison. It's also staffed with friendly rangers used to dealing with the crowds here.

An auto tour of the canyon follows **North Rim Drive,** a two-lane, one-way road that begins in Canyon Village, to your first stop, **Inspiration Point.** On the way, you'll pass a **glacial boulder** estimated to weigh 500 tons that was deposited by melting ice more than 10,000 years ago. Geologists estimate that this chunk of rock was carried 40 miles to its present location.

At **Inspiration Point,** a moderately strenuous descent down 57 steps takes you to an overlook with views of the Lower Falls and canyon. (At 8,000 feet, the hike will cause your pulse rate and blood pressure to rise, so it is wise to pause for a few extra minutes before making the return.) Evidence of current earthquake activity is beneath the soles of your shoes. The viewing platform once extended 100 feet farther over the canyon; on June 30, 1975, it was shattered by an earthquake, and tumbled into the canyon. There are several other viewpoints you can stop at along North Rim Drive before you reconnect with the main Canyon Village–Yellowstone Lake Road, which will take you down to South Rim Drive.

Along the way, you can also stop at **Grandview Point,** where the river flows some 750 feet below the observation platform. During summer months, Grandview is an excellent spot from which to view ospreys, which normally nest in this area and can be seen riding the thermals. **Lookout Point** provides a better view of the Lower Falls; however, the observation deck is at the end of a steep, 150-foot trail. Going down is the easy part; the return trip is not recommended for those with heart or lung problems.

For the adventurous, an alternative to driving from one overlook to another is to negotiate the **North Rim Trail,** which is slightly more than 2.25 miles long, beginning at Inspiration Point. This trail ends at the Upper Falls parking area, where the Upper Falls Trail begins; it's another 0.75 mile to the South Rim Drive bridge. Unfortunately, the North Rim Trail is not a loop, so if you take the hike, you'll have to backtrack to get your car at Inspiration Point. The footpath brings you closer to what you want to see, and you won't be fighting for elbow room, as you will at the overlooks that are only accessible to cars.

Whether you drive or walk, you should go down to the **Upper Falls View,** where a 0.25-mile trail leads down from the parking lot to the brink of the **Upper Falls,** an overlook within splashing distance of the rushing river, and the waterfall. At this point you won't just hear, you'll feel the power of the river as it begins its course down the canyon.

The **South Rim Drive** leads to several overlooks and better views of the Lower Falls. The most impressive vantage point is from the bottom of **Uncle Tom's Trail,** a steep, 500-foot route to the river's edge that begins at the first South Rim parking lot. The trail is named after Tom Richardson, an adventuresome early day guide who led travelers to the base of the falls with ropes and ladders; these days, the trip is down 328 steps and paved inclines. The trail is rather steep, but it can be negotiated in about an hour, though it will be challenging for the neophyte hiker (an experienced hiker might be able to negotiate this distance in somewhat less time).

South Rim Road continues to a second, lower parking lot and a trail that leads to **Artist Point.** The view here is astounding, one of our favorites in the park and is best in the early morning. It was at this point that Thomas Moran was inspired to create his famous painting of the falls, reproductions of which are seen in galleries and print shops throughout the world. Watching shutterbugs can be fun too, as they go through various contortions, trying to record the perfect Kodak moment.

The **South Rim Trail** is an alternative to viewing the Lower Falls and the canyon from wooden observation decks. From the first South Rim parking lot, which is just beyond the South Rim Drive Bridge, follow trail markers to the partially paved trail, then 1.75 miles to Artist Point. (The trail follows the canyon for 3.25 miles beyond Artist Point to **Point Sublime,** where you must double back along the same route.) You'll have several different views of the falls, and you can always hop off to access Uncle Tom's Trail, Artist Point, and **Lily Pad Lake.** Neither Point Sublime nor Lily Pad Lake is accessible to those in cars.

A DETOUR: CANYON VILLAGE TO NORRIS

Distance: 12 miles from Canyon Village to Norris.

Before proceeding to the Yellowstone Lake area, consider backtracking 12 miles on the road from Canyon Village to Norris Geyser Basin. About three-quarters of the way to Norris, you'll find a turn-off for **Virginia Cascades Drive,** a 3-mile road that winds along the Gibbon River as it flows off the Solfatara Plateau to create the 60-foot high Virginia Cascade. The road is open only to hikers and bikers, and the cascades are beautiful, so it's an excellent hideaway from the crowds and a great spot to call a timeout from your tour. Virginia Cascades Drive winds back in the direction of Canyon Village.

CANYON VILLAGE TO FISHING BRIDGE

Closest Entrances: 27 miles to the East Entrance; 43 miles to the South Entrance.

Distance: 16 miles from Canyon Village to Fishing Bridge.

The road winds through the **Hayden Valley,** which is a vast expanse of beautiful green meadows accented by brown cuts where the soil is eroded along the banks of the Yellowstone River. Imagine this: 10,000 years before Ferdinand V. Hayden led the survey expedition of 1871, the entire Hayden Valley, except for the tallest peaks that surround it, was covered with a 4,000-foot-thick layer of ice. Today, wooded banks define what was once a shoreline. The valley is now a wide, sprawling area where bison play and where trumpeter swans, white pelicans, and Canada geese float along the river. This is also a prime habitat for the grizzly, so during early spring months pay close attention to binoculars-toting visitors grouped beside the road.

Nature is at her acidic best at the **Sulphur Caldron** and **Mud Volcano** areas, 12 miles south of the Canyon Junction, which were described by the frontier minister Edwin Stanley as "unsightly, unsavory, and villainous." We think he was right on the money, so you'll certainly not want to miss this area. There's nothing quite like the sound of burping mud pots.

By 1984, the vapors from Sulphur Caldron (on the east side of the road) had rotted the foundations on which the overlook was constructed, and it collapsed. The pH of the caldron is twice that of battery acid. The pools are so acidic that if you stepped in one, your shoes would be reduced to ashes.

At **Dragon's Mouth Spring,** turbid water from an underground cavern is propelled by escaping steam and sulfurous gases to an earth-side exit where it colors the earth with shades of orange and green. The belching of steam from the cavern and the attendant sound, which is due to the splash of 180°F water against the wall in a subterranean cavern, creates a medieval quality; hence, the name of the spring.

Nearby **Mud Volcano** is an unappetizing mud spring, the product of vigorous activity caused by escaping sulfurous gases and steam.

Photo Tip

The Hayden Valley offers excellent opportunities to photograph bison. They are less harassed by tourists here and less confined.

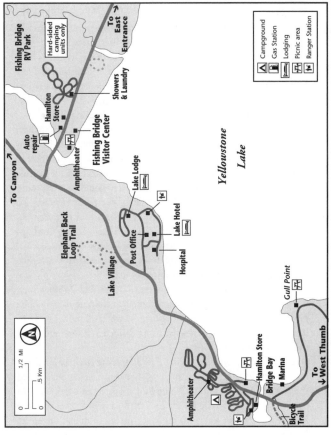

The youngest feature in the area is **Black Dragon's Caldron,** which is often referred to as the demon of the backwoods and rightly so. The caldron emerged from its subterranean birthplace for the first time in 1948 when it announced its presence by blowing a hole in the landscape, scattering mature trees hundreds of feet in all directions. Since then, continual seismic activity and intermittent earthquakes in the area have caused it to move 200 feet south of its original position.

Le Hardy Rapids, a shaded area 2 miles farther south, is an ideal spot for a stroll along a shaded section of the river. This is a prime route for cutthroat trout in the early summer on their way to spawn.

It is also popular with the shy harlequin ducks. The scary side of the equation is that this innocent-looking stretch of water flows across a fault in the earth. Some geologists believe that this will be the spot where the next major eruption will occur, and that it will be as large as, or larger than, the eruption that created the Yellowstone Caldera 600,000 years ago. Their guess: The explosion could occur anytime in the next 100,000 years; tomorrow, for instance.

The road across the Yellowstone River at **Fishing Bridge** was once the only eastern exit in the park, the route leading over Sylvan Pass to Cody, Wyoming. The bridge, which was built in 1937, spans the Yellowstone River as it exits Yellowstone Lake and is another prime spawning area for native trout. As a consequence, it became so popular that as many as 50,000 fishermen would beat the water into a froth every year in their search for the perfect entree. To protect the trout, fishing was banned in the '60s, but it remains an excellent vantage point from which to watch them as they head upstream. The bridge is also an excellent spot for observing waterfowl, especially the large, white pelicans and Canada geese that inhabit the area, seemingly oblivious to the crowds.

The **Fishing Bridge Visitor Center** (☎ 307/242-2450), which is open from 8am to 6pm, has an excellent wildlife display. The nearby Hamilton store sells provisions, as well as liquor. The Fishing Bridge **RV Park** is restricted to hard-sided vehicles only, since this is a prime grizzly habitat.

You'll find an excellent hiking trail, **Elephant Back Loop Trail,** leading off the short strip of highway between Fishing Village and the Lake Village area. The 2-mile loop leads to an overlook with panoramic views of Yellowstone Lake and its islands, the Absaroka Range, and Pelican Valley to the east. Instead of taking the entire loop around to the overlook, you can shorten the hike a 0.5 mile by taking the left fork approximately 1 mile from the trailhead and doubling back after you get to the overlook.

YELLOWSTONE LAKE AREA

Closest Entrances: Approximately 31 miles from Fishing Bridge to the East Entrance; approximately 39 miles from Fishing Bridge to the South Entrance.

Distances: The lakefront from Fishing Bridge to the West Thumb Geyser Basin is 21 miles.

As if the park didn't have enough record-setting attractions, at 7,773 feet **Yellowstone Lake** is North America's largest high-altitude lake. It is also 20 miles long, 14 miles wide, contains 110 miles of shoreline, has depths ranging to 390 feet, and is *very* cold. Because the

Photo Tip

If the weather looks promising, be certain to schedule an early morning wake-up call, then head for a scenic vantage point near the edge of the lake just before sunrise. If conditions are right, the surface of the lake will be flat and enshrouded in fog. As you watch, the sun heats the surface and the fog rises to reveal an island (Stevenson) that seems to have magically appeared from the sky.

surface freezes by December and remains crusted until late May, the temperature at the bottom remains at 39°F year-round, and the surface temperature isn't a lot warmer. Considering its size relative to the entire volcanic caldera, the lake is considered by many to be just a puddle. At one point in its history, the entire area was filled with ice, most of which has since melted, so the lake relies on 124 tributaries, including the Yellowstone River, to maintain its present level.

The lake exhibits its multifaceted personalities every day, which range on the emotional scale from a placid, mirrorlike surface to a cauldron whipped by southerly winds that create 3- to 4-foot waves. Boaters are warned to be especially cautious because of the number of boat-related fatalities related to hypothermia. Compelling evidence of the ongoing changes occurring in the park as a consequence of subsurface thermal activity is the fact that the lake bottom is rising and tilting about 1 inch per year, a veritable sprinter's pace in geologic time. Trees on the south end of the lake are drowning while new beaches are coming into being on the north end, and existing beaches are expanding.

Because the lake has the largest population of native cutthroat trout in North America, it makes an ideal fishing spot in summer. (See chapters 2 and 4 for information on fishing regulations.) The lake is also an ornithologist's paradise; the skies are filled with osprey, bald eagles, white pelicans, and cormorants. Shoreside, moose and grizzly bear are especially prevalent during the trout runs in spring.

Lake Village, on the northwest shore of the lake, offers a wide range of amenities, the most prominent of which is the majestic 100-year-old **Yellowstone Lake Hotel,** perhaps the most beautiful structure in the park. You'll find excellent food in the restaurant, as well as a postage-stamp-sized deli. Hamburgers and the like are available at the Hamilton Store. Lodging is in the hotel, its annex and cabins, and at Lake Lodge, which offers sleeping accommodations in modestly priced, rustic, frontier-style cabins.

Just south of Lake Village is the **Bridge Bay Marina,** the center of the park's water activities. Here you can arrange for guided fishing trips or small boat rentals, or learn more about the lake during an informative and entertaining 1-hour narrated boat tour. The views are magnificent, and the skipper shares fascinating facts about the area's history. The marina is usually open from mid-June to mid-September.

Campers will discover a large **campground** here with sites for RVs and tent campers. Though the campground area is surrounded by trees, the area itself is very large and has been cleared, so it offers very little privacy.

Though the **Natural Bridge,** near Bridge Bay, is well marked on park maps, it's one of the park's best-kept secrets, and you may end up enjoying it by yourself. The mile-long path down to the bridge, a geologic masterpiece consisting of a massive rock arch 51 feet overhead, spanning Bridge Creek, is an excellent bike route.

Looking for a picnic area? Keep a sharp eye out for an inconspicuous paved road on the lake side of the highway 13 miles west of Fishing Bridge that leads down to a secluded spot near **Pumice Point.**

The **West Thumb** area along the western shoreline is the deepest part of Yellowstone Lake. Because of its suspiciously craterlike contours, many scientists speculate that this 4-mile wide, 6-mile long, water-filled crater was created during volcanic eruptions approximately 125,000 years ago.

The **West Thumb Geyser Basin** is notable for a unique series of geysers. Some are situated right on the shores, some overlook the lake, and some can be seen *beneath* the lake surface. Three of the shoreline geysers, the most famous of which is **Fishing Cone,** are occasionally marooned offshore when the lake level rises. Fortunately, the area is surrounded by a half mile of boardwalks, so it's easy to negotiate.

Near the center of an area that is totally surrounded by healthy growing trees is a **tree graveyard.** These pale, limbless trees were killed when thermal activity caused hot water to move toward them. When their roots absorbed the hot water, the trees were cooked from the inside out.

Details about the area, and maps, are available in the **West Thumb Information Station,** which is housed in a log structure that functioned as the original West Thumb Ranger Station. The center is open daily from May through September from 9am to 5pm.

As you depart the West Thumb area, you are presented with two choices: Either to head south toward Grand Teton National Park or to head west across the **Continental Divide** at Craig Pass, en route to Old Faithful.

GRANT VILLAGE TO THE SOUTH ENTRANCE

Distance: 22 miles from Grant Village to the South Entrance.

Located on the southern shore of Yellowstone Lake, Grant Village offers dramatic views of summer squalls and one of Yellowstone's most inspiring sunrises. Perhaps the primary appeal of the village, the southernmost outpost in the park, is its location as a jumping-off place for travelers leaving for Grand Teton National Park, or a place for them to spend their first night in Yellowstone. Named for Pres. Ulysses S. Grant, the village was completed in 1984. It's the newest of Yellowstone's villages and home to the park's most modern facilities.

The **Grant Village Visitor Center** (☎ **307/242-2650**) has information, publications, a slide program, and a fascinating exhibit examining the effects of fire in Yellowstone. *The Unfinished Song,* a film about the fires of 1988, is shown daily. A Kodak-sponsored slide presentation of the park is also worth the investment of half an hour.

The **Grant Village Restaurant** has an excellent dining room with views of the lake. Reservations are recommended. Nearby is **Lake House,** which serves primarily steak and chicken dinners in a dining room closer to the shoreline. Guest accommodations are in a motel-style building. Other services include a general store that serves light meals and fast food, a modest gift shop, and a service station. Given a choice, I'd head north to a different destination, or continue south to Grand Teton.

In contrast to this forgettable village is the beautiful 22-mile drive to **Grand Teton** along high mountain passes and **Lewis Lake.** The lake, which is 108 feet deep, is the third largest in the park, and is connected to Shoshone Lake by a narrow channel that, rumor has it, is populated by German Brown trout. After the lake loses its winter coat of ice, it is a popular spot for early season anglers who are unable to fish streams that are clouded by the spring runoff.

Beyond the lake, the road follows the Lewis River through an alpine area and along the **Pitchstone Plateau,** a pile of lava more than 2,000 feet high and 20 miles wide that was created some 500,000 years ago. A high gorge overlooking the river provides views that are different from, but equally spectacular to, those in

West Thumb & Grant Village

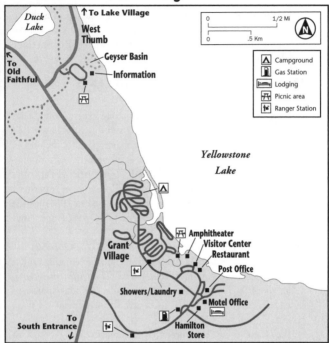

other sections of the park. At its highest point, the road winds across a high plateau that is accented with forests of dead, limbless lodgepoles—remnants of the 1988 fire.

WEST THUMB TO OLD FAITHFUL

Distance: 17 miles from West Thumb Geyser Basin to Old Faithful area.

Craig Pass is an important geologic landmark since it is here, at the Continental Divide in the Yellowstone-Teton area, that the headwaters of two major rivers are formed, one emptying into the Pacific Ocean, the other into the Gulf of Mexico. The Snake River winds from Grand Teton through Idaho to meet the Columbia River in Oregon and then drains into the Pacific Ocean at Astoria, Oregon. The Yellowstone River, which begins south of Yellowstone Park, drains into the Missouri River, which drains into the Mississippi, which empties into the Gulf of Mexico.

The most interesting phenomenon on the Old Faithful route is **Isa Lake** at Craig Pass. Unlike most lakes and streams in the parks, it has both eastern and western drainages and ends up in both the Pacific Ocean and the Gulf of Mexico. Amazingly, as a consequence of a gyroscopic maneuver, the outlet on the *east* curves *west* and drains to the Pacific, and the outlet on the *west* curves *east* and drains to the Gulf.

Before you reach the Old Faithful geyser area, two additional detours are recommended. Two and a half miles south of Old Faithful is an overlook at the spectacular **Kepler Cascades,** a 150-foot stair-step waterfall on the Firehole River that is steps from the parking lot.

Near that parking lot is the trailhead for the second detour, a 5-mile round-trip to the **Lone Star Geyser** (on the eponymous trail), which erupts every 3 hours, sending steaming water 30 to 50 feet from its 12-foot cone. The hike, which winds along a gentle trail bordering the Firehole River through pastoral meadows and a forest, is a must-do. Even when others are on the trail, the area exudes a solitary air because it is possible to abandon the trail, follow the meandering stream, and find flat, open places to relax or picnic.

OLD FAITHFUL GEYSER AREA

Closest Entrance & Distances: 16 miles from Old Faithful geyser to Madison Junction, then another 14 miles to West Yellowstone (West) Entrance.

Despite the overwhelming sight of the geysers and steam vents that populate the Old Faithful area, we suggest you resist the temptation to explore until you've stopped at the **Old Faithful Visitor Center** (☎ **307/545-2751**). It has a larger staff and more facilities than most of the other park visitor centers. An excellent film describing the geysers, *Yellowstone, A Living Sculpture,* is shown throughout the day in an air-conditioned auditorium that provides relief from hot July afternoons. Various park publications and an informative seismographic exhibit are added attractions. You will also want to check the information board for estimated times of geyser eruptions, and plan your time accordingly.

The Yellowstone Association's guides for **Old Faithful** and the **Fountain Paint Pots** include complete maps and explanations of the 150 geysers and many hot springs in the area, which happen to be a quarter of the world's total. Priced at 25¢ they're the best bargain in the park.

The number and variety of accommodations here is greater than at any other park center. The **Old Faithful Inn** is said to be the largest log structure in the world. Depending upon which brochure you're reading, the ceiling is either 79 or 84 feet high. The Inn was

Old Faithful Area

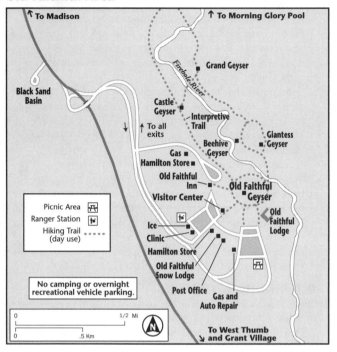

finished in 1904 and is a National Historic Landmark. There are two other accommodations in this bustling center of activity: **Old Faithful Lodge,** which has rustic frontier cabins for rent, and **Old Faithful Snow Lodge,** which offers rooms in a motel-like structure that once was a dormitory for the hired help.

Several **dining** choices are available, the nicest of which is the dining room in the Inn, where three meals are served daily; the requisite deli is situated off the lobby. A coffee shop–style restaurant is situated in Snow Lodge; a cafeteria with food to satisfy various ethnic palates and an ice cream stand are in the Lodge, as is a large gift shop. Nearby are a Hamilton store with various provisions and souvenirs, a gasoline station, an auto repair shop, a post office, and a medical clinic.

The Old Faithful area is generally divided into four sections: **Upper Geyser Basin,** which includes Geyser Hill, **Black Sand Basin, Biscuit Basin,** and **Midway Geyser Basin.** All of these areas are

connected to the Old Faithful area by paved tra
allows, hike the area; it's fairly level, and distanc
Between the Old Faithful area and Madison
find the justifiably famous **Lower Geyser Basin,** including Fountain Paint Pot and the trails surrounding it. You can see some of
these geysers on Firehole Lake Drive.

Though ✪ **Old Faithful** is not the largest geyser in the park, and
seems less inclined these days to be faithfully "regular," its image has
been seen on everything from postage stamps to whiskey bottles. It
acquired its name when the Washburn Expedition of 1870 observed
its predictable pattern of eruptions. Seismic activity has wrought
changes in the geyser's habits, but it's still pretty regular, erupting
with an average interval of 88 minutes, though it may vary 20 minutes in either direction. A typical eruption lasts 1.5 to 5 minutes,
during which 3,700 to 8,400 gallons of water are thrust upward to
heights of 180 feet. For the best views, and photo ops, of the eruption in the boardwalk area, plan on arriving at least 15 minutes
before the scheduled show so as to assure a first-row view.

An alternative to a seat on the crowded boardwalk is a stroll from
the Old Faithful Geyser up the **Observation Point Trail** to an
observation area that provides better views of the entire geyser
basin. The path up to the observation point is approximately
0.5 mile, and the elevation gain is only 200 feet, so it's an easy
15-minute hike. The view of the eruption of the geyser is more
spectacular from here and the crowds less obtrusive.

From the vantage point of the Observation Point Trail, you'll
have a different perspective of the entire **Upper Geyser Basin;** it's
possible to see most of the major geysers as well as inaccessible steam
vents in the middle of wooded areas. On clear, sunny days, sun-
beams highlight the colors of the ponds and geysers in the valleys
below.

Warning: The shaded trail area is a popular spot with resident
bison, so don't be surprised to find yourself sharing the trail with
them; be sure to yield the right of way.

Interested in continuing your hike? From the top of the boardwalk continue to the **Solitary Geyser** on a loop that leads back to
the Inn, adding only 1.1 miles to the trip on a mostly downhill trail.

Accessible by walkways from Old Faithful Village, the **Upper
Geyser Basin Loop** is referred to as Geyser Hill on some maps. The
1.3-mile loop trail winds among several thermal attractions.
Anemone Geyser may offer the best display of the various stages of

pical eruption as the pool fills and overflows, after which bubbles
rising to the surface begin throwing water in 10-foot eruptions, a
cycle that is repeated every 7 to 10 minutes.

The **Lion Group** consists of four geysers that are interconnected
beneath the surface. The eruptions of the **Lion Geyser,** the largest
of the quartet, are usually preceded by gushes of steam and a deep
roaring sound, from which it derives its name. **Doublet Pool** is
especially popular with photographers who are attracted by a complex series of ledges and deep blue waters. Further along the trail is
Giantess Geyser, known for its violent eruptions, which cause the
surrounding area to shake and quake as underground steam explodes
before reaching the surface, where it may burst at heights of 200 feet.
It erupts infrequently, at unscheduled intervals, so you should check
with rangers to see if it's active. The colors of **Emerald Pool** algae—
blues, greens, yellows, and oranges—offer an excellent example of
the effects of water temperature and sunlight on what are, after all,
living organisms.

Two other stars of the show in the Upper Geyser Basin are **Castle
Geyser** and **Grand Geyser.** Castle Geyser, which has the largest
cone of any geyser in the park, currently erupts for 20 minutes
every 10 to 12 hours, after which a noisy steam phase may continue
for half an hour. Grand Geyser, the tallest predictable geyser in the
world, usually erupts every 7 to 15 hours with powerful bursts that
produce streams of water that may reach 200 feet in height.

The **Riverside Geyser** is situated on the bank of the Firehole
River, near **Morning Glory Pool.** One of the most picturesque geysers in the park, its 75-foot column of water creates an arch over the
river. **Morning Glory Pool** was named for its likeness to its name-
sake flower in the 1880s but has since lost its bloom. Vandals have
tossed so much debris into its core over the years that it now suffers
from poor circulation and reduced temperatures, which are causing
unsightly brown and green bacteria to grow on its surface.

The **Black Sand Basin** is a cluster of especially colorful hot
springs and geysers located 1 mile north of Old Faithful. It is interesting primarily because of its black sand, a derivative of obsidian.
Biscuit Basin, located 2 miles further up the road, was named for
biscuitlike deposits that surrounded colorful **Sapphire Pool** until a
1959 earthquake caused the pool to erupt, sending them skyward.
Both the Black Sand Basin and the Biscuit Basin can be viewed from
flat, interpretive boardwalks.

The **Midway Geyser Basin** extends for about 1 mile along the Firehole River. The major attractions here are the **Excelsior Geyser,** the third-largest geyser in the world and once the park's most powerful geyser, and the well-known **Grand Prismatic Spring,** the largest hot spring in Yellowstone, and the second largest in the world. A boardwalk leads to Excelsior, which in the 1880s erupted to 300 feet, creating a 300-foot wide crater in the process. Just beyond is Grand Prismatic Spring. Those colorful bands of yellow, red, and green are thermal algae.

OLD FAITHFUL TO MADISON JUNCTION

Closest Entrance: 30 miles from Old Faithful area to the West Yellowstone (West) Entrance; 39 miles to the South Entrance.

Distance: 16 miles from Old Faithful area to Madison.

Believe it or not, there are other superb geysers and hot springs on **Firehole Lake Drive,** all viewable without leaving your vehicle, along a 3-mile, one-way road that passes several of them. The turnoff for Firehole Lake Drive is about 8 miles north of Old Faithful area. There are three geysers of particular interest on this road. The largest is **Great Fountain Geyser,** which erupts every 8 to 12 hours, typically spouting water some 100 feet high for periods of 45 to 60 minutes. However, lucky visitors may see the occasional "superburst" that reaches heights of 200 feet or more.

Estimates are that **White Dome Geyser** has been erupting for hundreds of years. Unfortunately, the age and height of this massive cone are not matched by spectacular eruptions. The vent on top of the cone has been nearly sealed with deposits of "geyserite," so eruptions now reach only 30 feet. However, the cone itself is worth a trip down this road.

Further on, **Pink Cone Geyser** couldn't be closer to the road, since road builders cut into the geyser's mound during construction.

About 0.25-mile north of where Firehole Lake Drive rejoins the Grand Loop Road is the **Fountain Paint Pots** area. This is a very popular spot, so you may be forced to wait for a parking place. Though it's not large or spectacular, it's one of the most interesting areas in the park. All the various types of thermal activity are on display here, so as you stroll along the easy, 0.5-mile boardwalk, you'll be in an area that may have six geysers popping their lids at the same time. Though less impressive than other basins, these ponds, pots, and vents are among the most active in the park.

The first part of this natural exhibit, **Bacteria,** offers an excellent example of how algae and bacteria are at work in these thermal areas. The centerpiece, literally, of this region is **Fountain Paint Pot,** which changes character as summer temperatures increase, causing once thin, watery mud to become very thick. The mud is composed of clay and particles of silica that are trapped in the paint pots. (If you see a bubble forming on the surface, be prepared for a burst that may throw mud over the guard rail.) **Leather Pool** has undergone a transformation since the 1959 Hebgen Lake earthquake. It was once a warm, 143°F pool lined with leatherlike algae, but its temperature increased so dramatically after the quake that the algae were killed. **Red Spouter** changes its temperament with the seasons as its water table changes. During summer months, when the water table is low, it is a fumarole; from late fall through the winter it spouts red water and mud. The Fountain Pots themselves are very colorful with orange, yellow, blue, and green pots surrounded by bleached mud, gurgling like experiments in high school chemistry labs. All in all, it takes roughly 20 minutes to do the whole tour. Before departing, take a look across the large grassy area called **Fountain Flat.**

As you continue toward the Madison Junction, consider a detour along **Fountain Flat Drive,** a left turn about 2 miles beyond Fountain Paint Pot. This scenic paved road ends 0.25 mile north of Ojo Caliente, after which it is open only to hikers and bikers. One mile south of the Firehole River bridge, where you'll find the **Imperial Meadows Trailhead** (for a description, see chapter 4). Park the car and head up the 3-mile trail to the 200-foot **Fairy Falls.** This trail gets less traffic than the popular Lonestar and Dunraven trails.

Though a detour along **Firehole Canyon Drive** will require backtracking when you're approaching Madison from the south, the trip is worth the time you'll spend. There are great views of the canyon and **Firehole Falls.** The 2-mile, one-way road, which is a left

Know Your Bacteria

Even the most casual visitor can do some scientific sleuthing here, learning to identify water temperature by observing the colors in the pots. The colors result from different types of bacteria that survive at specific water temperatures. Some turn yellow until temperatures reach 161°F, above which bacteria cannot live. As temperatures approach boiling—199°F at this elevation—pinks begin to appear.

turn off the Grand Loop Road just before you get to the Madison Junction, skirts 800-foot lava cliffs as it meanders along the canyon of the Firehole River in the shadow of National Park Mountain before rejoining the Grand Loop Road. Like much of the park, this area was burned by the 1988 fire, so it offers excellent opportunities to see how quickly new growth is reconstituting the forest.

There are excellent views of the beautiful Firehole River as it rages through this narrow canyon, highlighted by a close-up of Firehole Falls. Be sure and bring a camera. Near the end of this 2-mile road is a popular swimming hole (though you'll need to change into your swimwear before arriving). There are several places to soak weary feet during the hot days of July and August.

5 Self-Guided Driving Tours

Depending on your driving skills and your tolerance for large numbers of cars, recreational vehicles, and auto-towed trailers, there is no substitute for a self-driven tour of the park. Though roads are narrow, there are hundreds of turnouts that afford opportunities to take in the views. On the downside, the roads can be windy and change elevation frequently, so there's no hope for setting a land speed record.

Self-guided car audio tours are a great way to get the most out of a drive through the park in your own vehicle. Just rent an audioplayer that plugs into your vehicle's cigarette lighter and plays through your FM radio, sit back, and listen as prerecorded messages describe park routes and attractions and provide historical and environmental information; there's even a section that addresses the interests of younger travelers. The system, which rents for $25 for a full day or $16 for a half day, is available from **Yellowstone National Park Lodges** at all hotel activity desks and is highly recommended.

6 Organized Tours

A number of companies offer bus tours of the park originating in gateway communities: **Powder River Coach USA** (☎ 800/ 527-6316) out of Cody has day-long trips; **Gray Line of Yellowstone** (☎ 800/523-3102) takes travelers around the park from West Yellowstone, as does **Buffalo Bus Lines** (☎ 800/ 426-7669). If you are looking for specialized guided trips—such as photo safaris or snowmobile tours—contact the chambers of commerce in the gateway community where you want to begin.

Photo Tip

Shutterbugs who want to increase the odds of taking the perfect photo can receive hands-on instruction from a professional photographer, compliments of Kodak. Beginning in mid-June, talks and photo walks are scheduled in the park's most photogenic areas. These no-fee programs generally last 2 hours and are conveniently scheduled throughout the day. For information, check in the Yellowstone news-letter (handed out at the entry gates) or at the Fishing Bridge Visitors Center.

Within the park, the hotel concessionaire, **Yellowstone National Park Lodges** (☎ **307/344-7311;** ynp-lodges.com), has a variety of general and specialized tours. Three different motor-coach tours are available from all of Yellowstone's villages. For about $27 ($14 for children) you can explore the Upper Loop (Norris Geyser Basin, the Grand Canyon of the Yellowstone and Mammoth Hot Springs), or for $29 (children $15) the Lower Basin (Old Faithful, Yellowstone Lake, the Hayden Valley). For about $33 (children $17), you can do the whole thing, the Grand Loop. These are full-day tours, with stops at all the sights and informative talks by the guides. Specialty trips include photo safaris, wildlife trips up the Lamar Valley (try it in winter), and special group charters of the historic yellow tour buses from the 1930s.

At Bridge Bay Marina, 1-hour **scenicruiser tours** depart through-out the day from June to the end of September for a trip around the northern end of giant Yellowstone Lake. You view the Lake Hotel from the water, and visit Stevenson Island, while a guide fills you in on the history, geology and biology of the area. Fares are $9 for adults, $5 for children 2 to 12. Guided fishing trips on 22-foot and 34-foot cabin cruisers are also available from Yellowstone National Park Lodges at Bridge Bay, and you can rent smaller outboard and rowboats.

Buses are replaced in the winter by **snowcoach tours.** The snowcoach can pick you up at the south or west entrances, or at Mammoth, and take you all over the park. You can spend a night at Old Faithful and then snowcoach up to Mammoth the next night, or do round trip tours from the gates or wherever you're lodged in the park. One-way trips range from $40 to $44, while round-trips cost $79 to $88. No special prices for children. For more on snowcoaches, see "Winter Sports & Activities" in chapter 4.

One- and 2-hour **guided horseback trail rides** are available at Mammoth Hot Springs, Roosevelt Lodge, and Canyon Village Corrals. Children must be 8 years old and at least 48 inches tall. Tour prices are $20 for a 1-hour ride and $32 for a 2-hour ride. No children's prices. Check any activity desk for times and dates. Reservations are recommended and may be made at **Yellowstone National Park Lodges** activity centers in the hotels, though not before you leave home.

7 Ranger Programs

Yellowstone and Grand Teton national parks continue to offer free **ranger-led educational programs** that will significantly enhance a visitor's understanding of the history, culture, and wildlife in the area in which they are traveling. Most programs run through late September. For a schedule, check the park newsletter you receive when you enter the park.

On a more informal basis, you'll run into ranger-naturalists roaming the geyser basins, along the rim of the Grand Canyon in Yellowstone, and in areas where wildlife gather in both parks. They are available to answer questions as well.

Evening campfire programs are presented nightly in the summer at campgrounds at Mammoth Hot Springs, Norris, Madison, Old Faithful, Grant, Bridge Bay and Canyon, and three times weekly at Lewis Lake campground and the Tower Falls Amphitheater. Many of these activities are accessible to the disabled. It's a good idea to bring a flashlight, warm clothing, and rain gear. Rangers also conduct walking, talking, and hiking programs throughout the park.

As one would expect, there are more tours and evening programs in the **Old Faithful** area than anywhere else in the park. The topics of the guided walks, which can run as long as 1.5 hours, usually focus on the geysers, their fragile plumbing, and their role in the Yellowstone ecosystem. It's not necessary to have the dexterity of a mountain goat to manage the majority of the terrain around Old Faithful. Beginning in June, daily hikes in the **Canyon** area head out to the Hayden Valley and the rim of the Grand Canyon; a ranger talk on the art inspired by the falls is held several times a day at the lower platform of Artist's Point. An explanation of the origins of the hot pools and mud pots is conducted daily beginning in June at the **Grant** area as part of a walk of the Lakeshore area of the West Thumb Geyser Basin. The **Lake/Fishing Bridge** agenda includes walking tours of the Mud Volcano area, and along the shores of

Yellowstone Lake and Indian Pond. There is an afternoon talk at the Fishing Bridge Visitor Center about managing wildlife like grizzlies and wolves, and a discussion of fisheries management that is held on the west end of the Fishing Bridge. Once a week, a park ranger dressed in mountain man regalia demonstrates the skills of the early mountain men at the Elephant Back Trailhead. Fire ecology, wildlife biology, and aquatic resources are discussed during daily strolls that originate at the Two Ribbons trailhead of the **Madison** area. Bring mosquito repellant.

Two of the more interesting ranger talks are held at **Mammoth Hot Springs,** one is a talk about Yellowstone's diverse wildlife, the second is a historical tour of the original site of Fort Yellowstone, established more than 125 years ago. There is also a guided tour of the hot springs terraces. The hottest, most dynamic, and oldest geyser basin in the park is at **Norris,** where a popular 1.5-hour tour begins at the Norris museum four times daily.

4

Hikes & Other Outdoor Pursuits in Yellowstone National Park

*T*hose who complain that Yellowstone's 3 million visitors have compromised the park's wilderness just need to take a walk, because there's plenty of virtually undisturbed, wild country here. If you want a wilderness experience with privacy, abundant wildlife, hot springs, trout streams, and thrilling scenery, Yellowstone is in fact a wonderful choice.

There are short hikes where you never lose sight of the road or a visitors center, moderate hikes where you might spend an afternoon penetrating the forest to visit a spot of secluded beauty, and overnight trips where you can hike and camp for days without running into another visitor.

In fact, there's so much to see and do in Yellowstone you could easily get overwhelmed. We've tried to make it easier for you by describing our favorite day hikes, as well as our favorite backcountry experiences and other park activities.

For a more extensive and more detailed list of trails than what follows here, pick up Mark C. Marschall's excellent *Yellowstone Trails* (Yellowstone Association, $9.95), or the maps provided by the park.

1 Day Hikes

Here is a small selection of good hikes, long and short. The **Continental Divide Trail (CDT)** links many of these individual hikes together as part of a continuous trail from Mexico to Canada, roughly following the spine of the continent. The Yellowstone Backcountry Office maintains a guide to CDT trails. The **Howard Eaton Trail** system once went all through the park, but was largely supplanted by the Grand Loop Road. Sections of the old trail are still maintained and will be found in trail guides, though some of them closely parallel park roads.

Wherever you go, if you're planning to hike for more than 30 minutes, be sure to carry a supply of water.

WEST YELLOWSTONE TO MADISON

Artist Paint Pot Trail. 0.5 mile. Easy. Access: Trailhead is 4.5 miles south of Norris Junction in Gibbon Meadow.

This interesting and easy 0.5-mile stroll along a relatively level path winds through a lodgepole-pine forest in Gibbon Meadows to a mud pot at the top of a hill. This thermal area contains some small geysers, hot pools, and steam vents.

Harlequin Lake Trail. 0.5 mile RT. Easy. Access: Trailhead is 1.5 miles west of the Madison Campground on the West Entrance road.

This trail offers an excellent, easy opportunity to explore the area by following a 0.5-mile trail that winds through the burned forest to a small lake that is populated by various types of waterfowl.

Purple Mountain Trail. 6 miles RT. Easy. Access: Trailhead is 0.25 mile north of the Madison Junction on the Madison-Norris Road.

This hike requires more physical exertion as it winds 3 miles through a burned forest to the top of what many consider only a tall hill with an elevation gain of 1,400 feet.

Two Ribbons Trail. 0.75 mile RT. Easy. Access: Trailhead is 3 miles east of the West Entrance at a turnout on the north side of the road.

This trail offers an opportunity to inspect the effects of the 1988 fire. Along this 0.75-mile loop trail, you'll see a mosaic of blackened, singed, and unburned trees—charred snags and green trees side by side among boulders shattered by the heat. The scraggly, deformed branches and piles of rock are surrounded by bushes and fresh, bright green tree shoots that are only now emerging from the soil.

NORRIS GEYSER BASIN

Back Basin Loop. 1.5 miles RT. Easy. Access: Trailhead is located at Norris Geyser Basin.

This level boardwalk is easily negotiable in an hour and passes by **Steamboat Geyser,** which has been known to produce the world's highest and most memorable eruptions. How often? Almost never. Wait instead by **Echinus Geyser,** as its colorful pool fills and then erupts several times a day.

Porcelain Basin Trail. 0.75 mile RT. Easy. Access: Trailhead is located at Norris Geyser Basin.

You'll share this boardwalk with other folks, but it takes you across a broad flat basin where steaming water makes colorful trails. You can complete the walk in less than an hour, but you'll probably stop to look closely at some of these geothermal features, a few of which periodically spit and rumble in small eruptions.

MAMMOTH HOT SPRINGS AREA

All Person's Fire Trail. 0.5 mile RT. Easy. Access: The trailhead is on Tower Road, 8 miles east of Mammoth Hot Springs.

This flat, easy stroll along a boardwalk presents an excellent opportunity to learn about the effects of the fire on the environment.

Beaver Ponds Loop Trail. 5 miles RT. Easy. Access: Trailhead is located at Mammoth Hot Springs Terrace.

Start at Clematis Gulch and make your way to a series of beaver ponds, your best chances of seeing the big-tailed beasts is early morning or afternoon. There are some good views, coming and going, including Mount Everts.

Bunsen Peak Trail. 4.2 miles RT. Moderate. Access: Trailhead across the road from the Glen Creek Trailhead, 5 miles south of Mammoth on the Mammoth–Norris Road.

This trail leads takes you up 1,300 feet in 2 miles to the 8,564-foot summit. Make the hike early and you can watch the morning sun strike Electric Mountain. You can take an alternative route back down to the Osprey Falls Trail (see below).

Osprey Falls Trail. 10 miles RT. Moderate. Access: Trailhead is at Bunsen Peak Trailhead 5 miles south of Mammoth Hot Spring on Mammoth–Norris Road.

The first 3 miles of this hike lead along an old road bed at the base of Bunsen Peak. From the Osprey Falls Trail turnoff, it's another 2 miles through a series of switchbacks in Sheepeater Canyon to a waterfall on the Gardner River.

Glen Creek Trail. 6 miles RT. Easy to moderate. Access: Trailhead is 5 miles south of Mammoth on the Mammoth–Norris Road.

The Glen Creek Trailhead presents hikers with several alternative paths through the Sepulcher Mountain area. During the early summer, this plateau is a beautiful, wide-open area that follows the base of Terrace Mountain. Huge expanses of sagebrush and pines are interspersed with the brilliant yellows and blues of wildflowers, reaching to the horizon. This is an excellent place to escape the crowds. You will also get a feel for the real park in this wilderness area without making much of a physical commitment. Since the trail is in the Gallatin Bear Management Area, you'll want to make noise, or tie a bell to a shoe, while hiking here. You will notice very quickly

Mammoth Area Trails

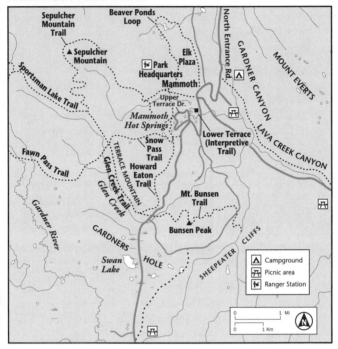

that elk and other wildlife aren't nearly as tame as those that wander around the parking lots at the tourist centers; you'll see them, but they are likely to vanish quickly. Be sure to include a pair of binoculars in your backpack.

Three miles from the trailhead, you'll arrive at a fork in the trail. Now you have to make your choice: Continue another 2 miles up the steeper **Sepulcher Mountain Trail** to the mountain's summit; continue on to the east on the Terrace Mountain loop of the **Snow Pass Trail;** or retrace your steps to the trailhead. If you're continuing, we recommend the Sepulcher Mountain Trail. It's a moderate hike that climbs 2,300 feet as the trail winds through a diverse selection of wildlife and scenery.

Lower Terrace Interpretive Trail. 1.5 miles RT. Easy. Access: Trailhead is south of the village on the road to Norris.

This interpretive trail is one of the best ways to see this area. The trail starts at 6,280 feet and climbs another 300 feet along marginally steep grades, through a bare, rocky, thermal region to a flat alpine area and observation deck at the top, but it's not a difficult climb. A park guide says the 1.5-mile round-trip walk to the Upper Terrace and back takes 2 hours, but it can be done in less.

GRAND CANYON OF THE YELLOWSTONE RIVER AREA

Clear Lake and Ribbon Lake Loop Trail. 6 miles RT. Moderate. Access: Trailhead is across the street from the South Rim parking lot.

The hike to Clear Lake is 1.5 miles, a gradual climb across a high plateau, and Ribbon Lake lies less than 2 miles beyond. Views of the plateau improve with each footstep until you find yourself surrounded by a panoramic view of the mountains surrounding the Canyon area. Clear Lake itself is intimately small, and gives you the opportunity to see subsurface activity of the thermal areas below the lake. On a circumnavigation of the lake along a trail, you will see and smell venting activity making its way to the surface; in some spots the lake looks like a small, boiling pot. There is bear activity in this area early in the year, so check with rangers for current conditions before heading out.

Howard Eaton Trail. 14 miles one-way. Moderate to difficult. Access: Trailhead across the street from the South Rim parking lot.

Either the Clear Lake or Ribbon Lake trails gives access to the Howard Eaton Trail. This is an arduous 14-mile trail to Fishing Bridge and Yellowstone Lake. There is bear activity in this area early in the year; check with rangers for current conditions before heading out.

✪ **Mount Washburn Trail.** 6 miles RT. Moderate. Access: Trailheads at the end of Old Chittenden Road and at Dunraven Pass.

This is a short hike to panoramic views, with wildflowers decorating the way and nonchalant bighorn sheep often browsing nearby. Trailheads are located at the summit at Dunraven Pass (elevation 8,895 ft.), and on Old Chittenden Road, where there's more parking available. Either hike is 6 miles round-trip with an increase in elevation of 1,400 feet, however, the climbs are fairly gradual and interspersed with long level stretches. From the summit, the park will lie before you like a map on a table: You'll see the Absaroka Mountains to the east, Yellowstone Lake to the south, and the Gallatin Mountains to the west and north. In addition to the sheep, you may see marmots and red fox; for a few years, two grizzly bears were regulars rooting in a meadow across from the Dunraven Pass trailhead. You'll be climbing a summit over 10,000 feet, so pace

Canyon Area Trails

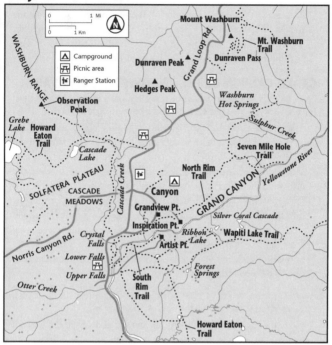

yourself, and bring a wind shell and warm clothing to fend off the wind that often buffets the top. The hike to the summit is an easy 90-minute walk at a steady pace. There's a warming hut in the base of the ranger lookout, with viewing telescopes and rest rooms.

North Rim Trail. 2 miles one-way. Easy. Access: Trailhead at Inspiration Point.

This trail, which is described more fully in the Grand Canyon section of chapter 3, offers better views of the falls and the river than you'll get from the parking areas. It's a nice way to see a longer stretch of the canyon.

South Rim Trail. 3.2 miles one-way. Easy. Access: Trailhead at the parking lot just beyond South Rim Drive bridge.

Like the North Rim Trail, there are more and better views of the canyon and river than you can see from a vehicle. It's easy, not long, and yet you'll have it mostly to yourself because most folks are in and out of the bus at the parking lots.

7-Mile Hole Trail. 5.5 miles one-way. Moderate to difficult. Access: Trailhead off North Rim Trail.

You'll see the Silver Cord Cascade from the rim, and then drop down to the river after a couple of miles in an area where the canyon widens enough for trees. There are some active hot springs along this hike. This is quite a drop (1,400 ft.), and out-of-shape hikers should remember that whatever goes down must come up.

Uncle Tom's Trail. 500 feet. Moderate. Access: Trailhead is located at the South Rim parking lot.

The short trip is down 328 stairs and paved inclines that lead to the river. The trail is rather steep but can be negotiated in an hour, though it will be challenging for the neophyte hiker. Watch for ice on cold mornings.

YELLOWSTONE LAKE AREA

Elephant Back Loop Trail. 2 miles RT. Easy. Access: From the east, the trailhead is on the right side of the road, just before the turnoff for the Lake Yellowstone Hotel.

Here's an opportunity to look down on (literally!) the island-dotted expanse of Yellowstone Lake, the Absaroka Mountains, and the Pelican Valley. A photo opportunity, and a fairly easy 2-mile loop.

Storm Point Trail. 2 miles RT. Easy. Access: Trailhead is 3.5 miles east of Fishing Bridge, directly across from the Pelican Valley Trailhead (on the lake side of the road).

The Storm Point Trail follows a level path that terminates at a point jutting into the lake with panoramic views. It begins near Indian Pond. During spring months, this is a popular spot with grizzlies, so the trail may be closed; however, even when it's open, check with rangers regarding bear activity.

Pelican Valley Trail. 7–16 miles RT. Moderate. Access: Trailhead is across from Lake Yellowstone north shore.

This loop explores an area north of the lake loaded with elk, bison, sandhill cranes, trout, eagles, grizzly, and the new kids on the block, wolves. You can take hikes of different length, up to a 16-mile loop, but a lot of folks, having had their fill of wildflowers and beasts, go no farther than Pelican Creek Bridge, about 3.5 miles in. If you continue on, you'll pass through forest and "bear meadows," where you should be watchful and respectful of wildlife—I once had to make a huge detour around a bison, which kept moving up the trail where I wanted to go. This is a daytime-only hiking area, and it's closed in the early summer until July 4 because of bear activity.

OLD FAITHFUL AREA

Fairy Falls Trail. 12 miles RT. Moderate. Access: Trailhead located at Imperial Meadows in Biscuit Basin.

Though longer than the Mystic Falls Trail, the Fairy Falls Trail is popular because it leads to a taller waterfall, which drops 200 feet. The easy 6-mile hike begins at the Imperial Meadows Trailhead, 1 mile south of the Firehole River bridge on Fountain Flat Drive. It winds through an area populated by elk along Fairy Creek, then past the Imperial Geyser. From here, it joins Fairy Creek Trail and travels east to the base of the falls. The total gain in elevation is only 100 feet.

Fountain Paint Pot Trail. 0.5 mile RT. Easy. Access: Trailhead begins at Fountain Paint Pot parking lot.

This is a very accessible, popular area, so you may be forced to wait for a parking place. All types of thermal activity are on display, so as you stroll along the boardwalk you'll be distracted at every turn by another bubbling pool or colorful mud pot.

Geyser Hill Loop. 1.3 miles RT. Easy. Access: Trailhead at Old Faithful Boardwalk.

One of the most interesting, and easiest, loops in the area, this trail winds among several thermal attractions. Anemone Geyser puts on a good display of the various stages of a typical eruption as the pool fills and overflows; the Lion Group consists of four geysers interconnected beneath the surface; Doublet Pool is popular with photographers who are attracted by a complex series of ledges and deep blue waters; and Giantess Geyser is known for its violent eruptions.

✪ **Lonestar Geyser Trail.** 5 miles RT. Easy. Access: Trailhead at the parking lot opposite Kepler Cascades.

The popularity of this trail takes away from the pleasure of walking a fairly level, forested trail along the Firehole River, interrupted now and then by broad riverbank meadows. The geyser itself sits in a meadow pocked by steam vents and thermal features. About every 3 hours it spouts about 50 feet in the air, from a vanilla-chocolate colored cone. The path is partially paved and open to bicycles as far as the geyser (hikers can go further, over Grants Pass). In the winter, skiers come this way.

Mystic Falls Trail. 1.1 miles one-way. Easy. Access: Trailhead located at Imperial Meadows in Biscuit Basin.

This trail leads to a waterfall on the Little Firehole River that drops more than 100 feet, one of the steepest in the park. The trail starts

Old Faithful Area Trails

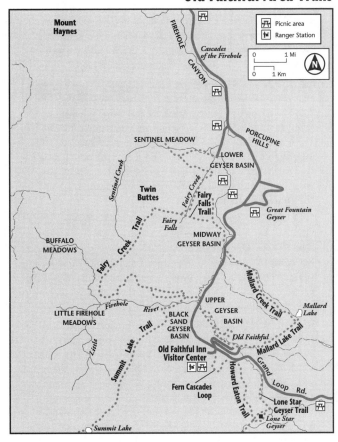

at Biscuit Basin, crosses the river, then disappears into the forest. The total distance to the base of the falls is only 1.1 miles; there's a trail to take you to the top, and if you want to take a different way home, connect with the **Little Firehole Meadows Trail,** with long-distance views of Old Faithful, back to Biscuit Basin.

Observation Point Trail—Solitary Geyser. 2.1 miles RT. Easy. Access: Trailhead at Old Faithful boardwalk.

For a spectacular view of Old Faithful and the geyser basin from above, take this 2-mile loop. The path up to the observation point is just half a mile, the elevation gain only 200 feet, an easy 15-minute hike. From the top you can see most of the major geysers, as well as inaccessible steam vents located in the middle of wooded areas. From the top of the boardwalk continue to the Solitary Geyser on a downhill slope that leads past the geyser, through the basin, and back to the Old Faithful Inn, which completes the loop.

2 Exploring the Backcountry

The backcountry of Yellowstone is the real thing: a domain of free-roaming wildlife, untracked by humans, and largely unpatrolled. The National Park Service, through its system of permits, designated camping areas, and rules (for more on these, see below), has managed to preserve a true wilderness. Yellowstone has more than 1,200 miles of trails (most of which are in the backcountry) and 300 backcountry campsites.

For **general information** on backpacking and safety, see chapter 2.

INFORMATION BEFORE YOU GO   Contact the **Yellowstone Backcountry Office** (P.O. Box 168, Yellowstone National Park, WY 82190) and they'll send you a useful *Backcountry Trip Planner* with a detailed map showing where the campsites are, how to make reservations, and how to prepare.

BACKCOUNTRY PERMITS   Backcountry permits are free, but you have to have one for any overnight trip, on foot, horseback or by boat. Camping is allowed only in designated campsites, many of which are equipped with food storage poles to keep wildlife out of your stores. These sites are primitive and well situated, and you won't feel like you're in a campground.

Pick up your permit in the park within 48 hours of your departure, at one of the following visitor ranger stations any day of the week during the summer: Bechler, Canyon, Mammoth, Old

Planning Ahead

You can pick up a permit the day before beginning a trip, but if you'll be traveling during peak season, try to make a reservation in advance. If you don't, and someone else has reserved the campsites in the area you want to go, you're out of luck. It costs $20 to hold a site, and you can begin making reservations for the upcoming year on April 1.

Caution: The reservation is just that, a reservation; upon your arrival at the park, you'll need to secure the permit, which is valid only on the dates for which it is issued.

Faithful, Tower, West Entrance, Grant Village, Lake, South Entrance, and Bridge Bay.

WHEN TO GO   Many of the trails into the park backcountry remain covered with snow, or muddy in the first weeks of melt, well into June. At the higher elevations, over 9,000 feet, summer doesn't really start until July. Trail maintenance in the backcountry is much less thorough than on the more public trails near the roads: Creeks and streams described as "intermittent" during summer months may be filled with melting snowpack that converts them to impassable, swiftly running rivers, some of the water running down the trails themselves. Look in the Backcountry Trip Planner for approximate dates when specific campsites will be habitable.

MAPS   Park rangers suggest using the "Yellowstone Series" of maps produced by **Trails Illustrated.** Each of the four maps in the collection covers about nine of those produced by the U. S. Geologic Survey and is printed on durable plastic; the maps also show backcountry campsite locations. For more information, contact **Trails Illustrated,** Box 3610, Evergreen, CO 82438 (☎ **800/ 962-1643**), or the **Yellowstone Association Institute,** P.O. Box 117, Yellowstone National Park, WY 82190 (☎ **307/344-2294;** www.YellowstoneAssociation.org).

OUTFITTERS   An alternative to going on your own is to go with an outfitter. Outfitters provide most equipment, which can offset the cost of their services, which may include setting up tents and making meals.

In Gardiner, at the North Entrance to the park, **Wilderness Connection Inc.** (☎ **406/848-7287;** fax 406/848-2131), offers horseback trips in the park for groups of 2 to 10; rates begin at $200 per person, per day. **Yellowstone Guidelines** (☎ **800/314-4506**) offers customized, guided hikes and horseback trips with meals and lodging in tents or nearby hostelries. Plan on spending $250 per day or more, depending upon where you bed down. **Yellowstone Llamas** (☎ **406/586-6872**) offers an excellent compromise: Beasts of burden that carry the heavy gear, leaving you free to wander the trails. The trips typically cover 5 to 8 miles per day in the park and gourmet meals are served at the end of the day. Cost is $160 per day, per person.

Also, many Jackson, Wyoming-based outfitters conduct trips into Yellowstone. Don't forget to check out chapter 6, "Hikes & Other Outdoor Pursuits in Grand Teton National Park," for more outfitters.

THE YELLOWSTONE BACKCOUNTRY   If you just can't get your fill of geysers, or if you've had your fill of people, several trails lead to more isolated backcountry. The **Shoshone Geyser Basin** and **Heart Lake Geyser Basin** contain active geysers, as do **Ponuntpa Springs** and the **Mudkettles** in the Pelican Valley Area, **Imperial Geyser** in the Firehole area, and the **Highland Hot Springs** on the Mary Mountain Trail. If you head in these directions, be careful about walking on unstable surfaces: A young man died in 1988 when he fell into a superheated pool.

SHOSHONE LAKE   Shoshone Lake is the park's largest backcountry lake and a popular spot for backcountry hikers. The shortest route to the lake is via the **Delacy Creek Trail,** which begins 8 miles east of Old Faithful on the Old Faithful–West Thumb road. From here, the trail winds 3 miles along Delacy creek through moose country and the edge of the forest at the lake. At this point, it's a toss-up: You can head around the lake in either direction. Assuming you take a clockwise track around the lake— a distance of 18 miles—you'll take the **East Shore Trail** to its intersection with **Dogshead Trail,** then head west on the **South Shore Trail** until it intersects with the North Shore Trail and returns to your starting point.

A detour: At the western end of the lake you'll arrive at the 1-mile-long **Shoshone Geyser Basin Trail,** which loops through a number of geysers, hot springs, and meadows that during spring months are ankle-deep in water and mud. Union Geyser, which erupts sporadically, is impressive, since eruptions occur from three vents simultaneously. Because the crust of the earth is so thin here, your footsteps may sound like thumping on a hollow gourd.

As you travel the lake's loop trail along the **East Shore Trail,** you'll have views of the lake at the top of a 100-foot rise. Then, on the **South Shore Trail,** you'll cross the Lewis Channel, which may have thigh-high water as late as July. Beyond that, the trail is a series of rises that are easily negotiable by the average hiker, passing across shallow Moose Creek and through meadows where you may spot deer or moose early in the morning or evening.

The 7-mile **North Shore Trail** is a mostly level path (there is one 200-foot-tall ridge) that winds through a lodgepole-pine forest. The best views of the lake are from cliffs on this trail. The loop trail is especially popular with overnighters, since there are 26 campsites on the loop, the largest of which has space for eight campers.

THE BECHLER REGION   This area in the park's southwest section is often referred to as the Cascade Corner because it contains a majority of the park's waterfalls. It was not scarred by the fires of 1988 and offers great opportunities to view thermal features. Many backpacking routes cut through this region, including one that leads to Old Faithful on the **Bechler River Trail.**

To begin your hike, drive into the park from Ashton, Idaho, and check in at the Bechler Ranger Station. To reach the ranger station, drive east 17 miles from Ashton on the Cave Falls Road; 3 miles before reaching Cave Falls, you'll find the ranger station turnoff. The ranger station is 1.5 miles down the gravel road.

The **Bechler Meadows Trail** takes you into this southwest corner, rich in waterfalls, cascades, and thermal areas that rarely have human visitors. About 6 miles into the journey, the trail fords the river several times as it enters Bechler Canyon, where it passes Collonade and Iris Falls. There are places on this trail where you can view the Grand Tetons in the distance, and hot springs that provide warm bathing in creeks. You can cover a good 30 miles, depending on what turns you take. It's a camping trip best made late in the summer to avoid high water during creek crossings. For a shorter trip, hike 3.5 miles along the **Bechler River Trail** to the **Boundary Creek Trail,** then return to the station via the **Bechler Meadows Trails,** a round-trip of 7 miles.

The most adventurous, and scenic, route takes you 30 miles from the ranger station to the end of the trail at the **Lonestar Trailhead** near Old Faithful. Beyond Iris Falls, and then Ragged Falls, you'll reach a patrol cabin at Three Rivers Junction at the 13-mile mark, a popular camping area with room for 12 people. There are a total of ten campsites between the ranger station and Three Rivers. If you continue towards Old Faithful, you'll intersect the **Shoshone Lake Trail** at the 23.5-mile mark and exit 6.5 miles later.

THOROFARE AREA   When you enter this country in the park's southeast corner, you're venturing into the most remote roadless area in the Lower 48. You can make a round-trip of around 70 miles deep into the wilderness, or shorter hikes, such as a trip from the park's east entrance road to the Yellowstone River inlet on Yellowstone Lake's southeast arm. The remoteness of this country discourages many hikers, so you'll have it mostly to yourself. Along the way teepee rings and lean-tos are reminders that Indians once used this trail as the main route between Jackson Hole and points north.

The **Thorofare Trail** follows the eastern shore of Yellowstone Lake and then trails the Yellowstone River up into some of the most remote and beautiful backcountry in the Rockies. It's a lot of miles and climbing, but you'll be rewarded with views of the Upper Yellowstone Valley, Two Oceans Plateau and abundant wildlife. You'll reach the Park Service's Thorofare Ranger Station at 32 miles, and a few miles further you'll come to Bridger Lake, outside the park, and a gorgeous alpine valley with a ranger station known as Hawk's Rest. Fishers love this area—so do grizzly bears, especially during the cutthroat trout spawning season in early summer. You'll be a good 35 miles from the trailhead at the lake, and even the most capable hikers should consider riding with an outfitter. You can cut the journey shorter by getting a boat "shuttle" to the mouth of the lake's southwest arm; call **Yellowstone National Park Lodges** (☎ **307/344-7901**). Only nonmotorized boats are allowed into the arm to the Yellowstone River outlet. You can canoe in, a wonderful trip in good weather, or you can come into Thorofare through Bridger-Teton National Forest up the North Fork of the Buffalo Fork to the south (check with the forest's Blackrock Ranger Station).

Other than bears, the major obstacle to early season trips in the Thorofare is water; you'll encounter knee-deep water at **Beaverdam Creek** and at **Trapper Creek,** as late as July.

THE SPORTSMAN LAKE TRAIL   This trail begins near Mammoth Hot Springs and extends west toward U.S. 191 to Sportsman Lake: a moderate, 14-mile trail which displays a diverse combination of flora and fauna. From the Glen Creek Trailhead 5 miles south of Mammoth Hot Springs, you'll spend 2 miles on the Glen Creek Trail as you traverse a mostly level, wide-open plateau, covered with sagebrush, that is the home of herds of elk and a bear management area. At the **Sepulcher Mountain Trail** at the 3-mile mark, the terrain becomes steeper as you continue northwest on the **Sportsman Lake Trail**—the elevation gain is approximately 2,300 feet to the Sepulcher summit (though you don't go to it on this route). The trail eventually enters the forest and descends to a log that is used to cross Gardner River. Then, it's uphill for another 4 miles to **Electric Divide,** another 2,000-foot gain in elevation. From there, the trail descends 2,100 feet in 3 miles to Sportsman Lake, which is located in an area burned by the 1988 conflagration. The lake, which sits in a meadow populated by moose and elk, is teeming with cutthroat trout. Two campsites provide overnight spaces for a total of 30 visitors.

THE SLOUGH CREEK TRAIL   Beginning in the Lamar Valley of the park's northeast corner, this trail takes hikers through some of the best wildlife habitat in the park. You can see elk, bison, trumpeter swans, sometimes grizzly bears, and now wolves that have quite happily taken up residence among abundant prey. The presence of wolves has made this area more popular, and the trail is also used by horse-packers. The trail starts from the road to Slough Creek campground, following the creek's valley north, then crossing a ridge to a second valley. You can hike a few miles, or take your camping gear and head for the park boundary, 11 miles to the north.

3 Other Activities

BIKING   Considering the vast expanse of real estate the parks cover, the challenging terrain, and the miles of paved roads and trails, a cyclist might conclude that the parks are prime areas for biking, on or off the roads.

It looks good on paper, but the reality is more harrowing. The roads are narrow and twisty; there are no bike lanes, so bikers continually fight for elbow room with wide-bodied RVs and trailers, some of which have side-view mirrors designed to decapitate bicyclists. Off-road opportunities are limited because of the small number of trails on which bikes are allowed.

Nevertheless, plenty of bicyclists take the challenge. The following trails are available, but you'll be sharing the roads with hikers. The **Mt. Washburn trail,** leaving from the Old Chittenden Road, is a strenuous trail that climbs 1,400 feet. The **Lone Star Geyser trail,** accessed at Kepler Cascade near Old Faithful, is an easy 1-hour ride on a user-friendly, partly paved road. Near Mammoth Hot Springs, **Bunsen Peak Road** and **Osprey Falls trails** present a combination ride/hike: The first 6 miles travel around Bunsen Peak; getting to the top requires a hike. A hike down to Osprey Falls adds 3 miles to the journey.

Bike rentals are available in the gateway towns of West Yellowstone (**Yellowstone Bicycles** (☎ **406/646-7815**) and Jackson **Hoback Sports,** (☎ **307/733-5335**) or **The Edge Sports,** 490 W. Broadway (☎ **307/734-3916**). Rental fees for traditional bikes are about $20 to $25 a day; for a full suspension mountain bike $25 to $35 a day.

BOATING   The best place to enjoy boating in Yellowstone is on **Yellowstone Lake,** which has easy access and beautiful, panoramic views. The lake is also one of the few areas where power boats are

---

ii Especially for Kids

You may find that several of the ranger programs will appeal to kids. And don't forget the **All Person's Fire Trail,** an interpretive trail leading through a burned-out area of the park with signs to teach the young ones about forest fires. It's located on Tower Road, just east of Mammoth Hot Springs (described in more detail in "Day Hikes," above in the Mammoth section).

Like many national parks, Yellowstone has a **Junior Ranger Program** for kids ages 5 to 12. For $2, you get a special activity paper, *Yellowstone's Nature.* (Sign up at any visitor center.) Kids get a Junior Ranger badge for completing certain activities.

There's also a unique education residential program for kids in 4th, 5th, and 6th grades at Yellowstone called *Expedition: Yellowstone!* This is a residential program where kids learn about the park, combining classroom work with a trip to Yellowstone. For more information, write: **Expedition Yellowstone Coordinator,** P.O. Box 168, Yellowstone National Park, WY 82190-0168.

---

allowed. Rowboats and outboard motorboats can be rented at **Bridge Bay Marina** (☎ **307/344-7381**). Costs for rowboats are about $28 per day or $6 per hour; an outboard with room for six rents for $29 per hour. Sea kayakers and canoeists should stay close to the shore on Yellowstone Lake because of high winds that can easily capsize a small, nonmotorized craft. Motorboats, canoes, and kayaks can be used on Lewis Lake as well.

FISHING   Seven varieties of game fish live in the parks: native cutthroat, rainbow, brown, brook and lake trout, grayling, and mountain whitefish. Of the trout, only the cutthroat are native, and they are being pressured in the big lake by the larger lake trout. As a result, you can't keep any pink-meat cutthroat caught in Yellowstone Lake, and you *must* keep any lake trout. These limits seem to have diminished the number of fishing boats on Yellowstone Lake in recent years, but they're necessary. The Yellowstone season typically opens on the Saturday of Memorial Day weekend and ends on the first Sunday in November. Yellowstone Lake has a slightly shorter season, and the lake's tributaries are closed until July 15 to avoid conflicts between humans and grizzly bears, both of which are attracted to spawning trout.

Many fine anglers come to Yellowstone, and they are well informed about which seasons are best on which stretches of river. In June, try the **Yellowstone River** downstream of Yellowstone Lake, where the cutthroat trout spawn. In July, fish the **Madison River** near the west entrance, and again in late fall for rainbow and some brown trout. In late summer, you can try to hook the cutthroats that thin out by September on the **Lamar River** in the park's beautiful northeast corner.

Fishing on **Yellowstone Lake** has been popular until recent years, when regulations designed to bring back the waning population of cutthroat trout have sent some of the trolling powerboats elsewhere. The problem is the introduced lake trout, which compete with and eat the cutthroat. If you catch a lake trout, you *must* kill it, and if you catch a large cutthroat, you *must* throw it back. Certain areas of the lake, like the southeast arm, are closed to motorized boats—this makes the Yellowstone River inlet a wonderful area to canoe and camp and fish.

You can fish the **Yellowstone River** below the Grand Canyon by hiking down into **Seven Mile Hole,** a great place to cast (not much vegetation to snag on) for cutthroat trout from July to September, you'll have the best luck around Sulphur Creek.

Other good fishing stretches include the **Gibbon** and **Firehole** Rivers, which merge to form the Madison River on the park's west side, and the 3-mile **Lewis River Channel** between Shoshone and Lewis lakes during the fall spawning run of brown trout.

There is an access for handicapped anglers to the Madison River, 3.5 miles west of Madison Junction at the Haynes Overlook, where you'll find a wheelchair-accessible fishing platform overhanging the river's edge along 70 feet of the bank.

Suggested Reading   Two reference guides present excellent information about park fishing opportunities and requirements: *Fishing Yellowstone National Park,* by Richard Parks (Falcon Press), and *The Yellowstone Fly-Fishing Guide,* by Craig Mathews and Clayton Molinero (published by Lyons and Burford). Both can be purchased from the Yellowstone Association.

Permits   The required Yellowstone fishing permit is available at any ranger station, visitor center, or Hamilton Store in the park. Anyone older than 15 needs a fishing permit, which costs $10 for 10 days or $20 for the season. Kids ages 12 to 15 also need a permit, but it's free. Anyone under 12 must be supervised by an adult. Season permits can be obtained by mail (**Visitors Services,** P.O. Box

168, Yellowstone National Park, WY 82190); 10-day licenses must be purchased at the park visitors centers, ranger stations, or Hamilton Stores.

Supplies & Fishing Guides   If you need supplies, in Gardiner, stop at **Parks' Fly Shop,** Highway 89 (☎ **406/848-7314**). In West Yellowstone, check at **Bud Lilly's,** 39 Madison Ave. (☎ **406/ 646-7801**), or **Blue Ribbon Flies,** 315 Canyon St. (☎ **406/ 646-7642**).

In **West Yellowstone,** the following tackle shops offer the full gamut of guided fishing trips and schools—1-day trips and weeklong excursions: **Arrick's Fishing Flies,** 128 Madison Ave. (☎ **406/646-7290**); **Bud Lilly's Trout Shop,** 39 Madison Ave. (☎ **406/646-7801**); **Eagle's Tackle Shop,** 3 Canyon St. (☎ **406/646-7521**); **Jacklin's,** 105 Yellowstone Ave. (☎ **406/646-7336**); and **Madison River Outfitters,** 117 Canyon St. (☎ **406/646-9644**).

Also, several Jackson, Wyoming-based fishing guides lead trips into Yellowstone. See the fishing section in chapter 6.

HORSEBACK RIDING   People who want to pack their gear on a horse, llama, or mule must get permits to enter the Yellowstone backcountry, or hire an outfitter with a permit (see below). Other visitors who want to get in the saddle but not disappear in the wilderness can put themselves in the hands of the concessionaire, **Yellowstone National Park Lodges.** Stables are located at Canyon Village, Roosevelt Lodge, and Mammoth Hot Springs. Roosevelt Lodge also offers **evening rides** from June into September. Choices are 1- and 2-hour guided trail rides daily aboard well-broken, tame animals. Wranglers refer to these as "nose-and-tail" tours, and an experienced rider is likely to find them awfully tame.

If you're looking for a longer, overnight horsepacking experience, contact the park and request a list of approved concessionaires that lead backcountry expeditions. Most offer customized, guided trips, with meals, horses, and camping and riding gear provided. Costs will run from $200 to $400 per day per person, depending on the length of trip and number of people. In Gardiner, at the north entrance to the park, **Wilderness Connection Inc.** (☎ **406/848-7287**) offers horseback trips in the park for groups of 2 to 10; rates begin at $200 per day for customized, guided hikes and horseback trips, with meals and lodging in tents or nearby hostelries. On the south side of the park, try **Press Stephens, Outfitter** (☎ **307/455-2250**). While not a horsepacking excursion per se, you might also try **Yellowstone Llamas** (☎ **406/586-6872**). They offer an excellent compromise:

Llamas carry the heavy gear, leaving you free to wander the trails. They typically cover 5 to 8 miles per day in the park, and serve gourmet meals at the end of the day. Cost is $160 per day, per person.

4 Winter Sports & Activities

The average snowfall in a Yellowstone winter is nearly 50 inches, creating a beautiful setting for sightseers, and a wonderful resource for outdoor winter recreation. The steaming hot pools and geysers generate little islands of warmth and clear ground, attracting not just tourists but wildlife as well. Nearby trees are transformed into "snow ghosts" by frozen thermal vapors. Bison become frosted, shaggy beasts, easily spotted as they take advantage of the more accessible vegetation on the thawed ground. Yellowstone Lake's surface freezes to an average thickness of 3 feet, creating a vast ice sheet that sings and moans as the huge plates of ice shift. But the ice is thinner where hot springs come up on the lake bottom, and you'll see otters surfacing at the breaks in the ice. Waterfalls become astounding pieces of frozen sculpture. Snow-white trumpeter swans glide through geyser-fed streams under clear-blue skies of clean, crisp mountain air.

Only two of the park's hostelries, **Mammoth Hot Springs** and the **Old Faithful Snow Lodge,** provide accommodations from December through March, as does **Flagg Ranch,** just outside the park's south entrance (see chapter 7 for more information). The only road that's open for cars is the **Mammoth Hot Springs–Cooke City Road.** Most visitors these days come into Yellowstone in winter from the west or south by snowcoach or snowmobile.

For additional information on all of the following winter activities and accommodations, as well as snowcoach reservations, contact **Yellowstone National Park Lodges,** (☎ 307/344-7311). There are also many activities, outfitters, and rental shops in the park's gateway towns.

The **Yellowstone Association** (☎ 307/344-2294) offers winter courses based out of its headquarters at the old Buffalo Ranch in Lamar Valley. Past offerings have included 3-day classes devoted to "Backcountry by Ski," "Yellowstone's Winter World," and "Tracking Yellowstone's Wolves" (it's a howl watching instructor Jim Halfpenny get down on all-fours to demonstrate wolf gaits and "marking").

CROSS-COUNTRY SKIING   There are 40 miles of **cross-country trails** in the Old Faithful area, including the popular **Lone Star Geyser Trail,** an 8-mile trail in a remote setting that starts at the Old Faithful Snow Lodge; and the **Fern Cascades trail,** which winds for 3 miles through a rolling woodland landscape on a short loop close to the Old Faithful area. In the Mammoth area, try the **Upper Geyser Basin and Biscuit Basin trail** (about 6 miles), which some say is the best in Yellowstone, though it may take an entire day to negotiate.

Equipment rentals (about $12 per day), ski instruction, ski shuttles to various locations, and guided ski tours are all available at the **Old Faithful Snow Lodge** and the **Mammoth Hot Springs Hotel,** the park's two winter lodging options. Discounts are available for multiday rentals of skis or snowshoes. Ski instruction costs $17 per person for a 2-hour group lesson. A half-day guided excursion (two-person minimum) is around $32 per person; a full day is $69 per person. For groups of three or more, the cost is considerably lower: $21 per person for a half day, $48 per person for a full day.

ICE-SKATING   **The Mammoth Skating Rink** is located behind the Mammoth Hot Springs Recreation Center. On a crisp winter's night you can rent a pair of skates ($1 per hour, $4 per day) and glide across the ice while seasonal melodies are broadcast over the PA system. It's cold out there, but there's a warming fire at the rink's edge.

SNOWMOBILING   Roads that are jammed with cars during the summer fill up with bison and snowmobiles during the winter. In deference to the shaggier road warriors, moderate speed limits are strictly enforced, but this is still an excellent way to sightsee at your own pace. A driver's license is required for rental ($120 for a single rider, $135 per day for two at **Mammoth Hot Springs Hotel** or **Old Faithful Snow Lodge**) and a quick lesson will put even a first-timer at ease. A helmet is included with the snowmobile, and you can rent a clothing package for protection against the bitter cold. **Warming huts** are located at Mammoth, Indian Creek, Canyon, Madison, West Thumb, and Fishing Bridge. They offer snacks, a hot cup of coffee or chocolate, and an excellent opportunity to recover from a chill. *A precaution:* Keep an eye on snow conditions. While it's true that snowmobile trails are groomed for travel, when snow cover is scanty, a normally smooth trip can become something akin to riding on a jackhammer. Also, if engine noise is what you came to Yellowstone to escape, this is probably not for you.

Snowmobile rentals are also available in the **gateway communities** of Gardiner and West Yellowstone, Montana, and at Flagg

Winter Road Conditions

Due to the high elevation and the abundance of snow, most of the roads in Yellowstone are closed to all wheeled vehicles during winter. The only major park area that is accessible by car is Mammoth Hot Springs; cars are allowed to drive in the village at Mammoth Hot Springs. Signs will alert you as to how far south into the park you can actually go from here (usually to Tower Junction, 18 miles away). From Tower Junction, it's another 29 miles to the Northeast Entrance. This entrance is open but not accessible from Red Lodge, Montana, and points east (since the Beartooth Highway is closed in winter). You can only go as far as Cooke City, Montana, and the roads are kept open specifically so that the folks in Cooke City aren't totally stranded during the long winters. Snowcoaches, snowmobiles, and cross-country skiers, however, use park roads regularly throughout the winter season. For up-to-the-minute information on weather and road conditions, call the **Visitor Information Center** at ☎ **307/344-7381.**

Ranch (see section 2 of this chapter for recommended outfitters). Most rental shops accept reservations weeks in advance, so reserving at least a day or 2 weeks ahead of time is a good idea. Plan on making reservations for the week between Christmas and New Year's at least 6 months in advance.

Basing Yourself in West Yellowstone   From the West Yellowstone entrance, you're only 14 miles to the Madison Junction, which presents opportunities to head south to Old Faithful or north to the Grand Canyon and Mammoth Hot Springs. Since this is the most popular way to access the park, plan on making reservations early.

In West Yellowstone, contact **Alpine West,** 601 U.S. 20 (☎ **800/858-9224** or 406/646-7633); **Hi Country Snowmobile Rental,** 530 Gibbon (☎ **406/646-7541**); and **Old Faithful Snowmobile Rentals,** 215 Canyon (☎ **406/646-9695**), to arrange reservations. Expect to pay $100 to $125 per day per machine; however, unless you own winter gear that's adequate for temperatures in the teens and a helmet, plan on spending another $25 for clothing.

Basing Yourself at Flagg Ranch   Accessing the Old Faithful area of Yellowstone from the south requires a greater commitment of time, money, and physical exertion.

After flying into Jackson, you can find lodging there, or head north 51 miles on U.S. 89 to **Flagg Ranch,** where you'll find lodging, a restaurant, bar, and snowmobile and snowcoach rentals. Depending upon road conditions, the trip can take 2 hours by auto. For information about accommodations or snowmobile rentals, contact Flagg Ranch (☎ **800/443-2311**).

Flagg Ranch is within minutes—even by snowmobile—of the park's South Entrance. From there it's a 22-mile trip to the West Thumb Junction and 17 miles to the Old Faithful geyser basin and Old Faithful Snow Lodge. Depending upon weather and road conditions, the trip may be arduous, especially if winds are blowing snow across the roads and creating bone-chilling temperatures.

Tip: Since there's so much traffic on park roads and snowmobiles and snowcoaches make deep ruts in the snow, traveling two to a snowmobile can be especially uncomfortable for the person on the back, especially when you're covering long distances.

It's cold, too.

SNOWCOACH TOURS   It is possible to enjoy the sights and sounds of Yellowstone without raising a finger, except to write a check or sign a credit card voucher, by taking one of the scenic snowcoach tours that are available at various locations in the park for about $12.

If you've never seen a snowcoach, you're in for a treat. Don't be fooled into thinking that this distinctively Yellowstone mode of transportation is merely a fancy name for a bus that provides tours during winter. Imagine instead an Econoline van with tank treads for tires and water skis extending from its front, and you won't be surprised when you see this unusual-looking vehicle. The interiors are toasty-warm with seating for a large group, and they usually allow each passenger two bags. They aren't the fastest, smoothest, or most comfortable form of transportation, but they do allow large groups to travel together, and they're cheaper and warmer than snowmobiles. They're also available for hire by groups at many snowmobile locations. Guides provide interesting and entertaining facts and stories of the areas as you cruise the park trails, and they give you opportunities to photograph scenery and wildlife.

In West Yellowstone, contact **Three Bear Lodge** (☎ 800/221-1551); **Yellowstone Arctic** (☎ 800/646-7365 or 800/221-1151); or **Yellowstone Alpen Guides** (☎ 406/646-7242).

For Flagg Ranch or Jackson snowcoach information, contact **Flagg Ranch** (☎ 800/443-2311) or **Yellowstone National Park Lodges** (☎ 307/344-7311).

5

Exploring Grand Teton National Park

*T*hough Grand Teton National Park is much smaller than Yellowstone, there is much more to it than just its peaks, seven of which climb to elevations greater than 12,000 feet. Because it's only 54 miles the long way, from north to south, you can catch some of its highlights in a day. But you'd be missing a great deal—the beautiful views from its trails, an exciting float of the Snake River, the fun you can have out on Jackson Lake.

Whether you spend half a day or 2 weeks in the park, it has the distinct advantage of its proximity to the town of Jackson. You can come off a climb of the Grand Teton and be living it up at the Cowboy Bar that evening, or dining in a fine restaurant—then, the next day, you can return to the peace of the park.

1 Essentials

ACCESS/ENTRY POINTS   Grand Teton National Park is a strip of real estate running along a north-south axis. Teton Park Road, the primary thoroughfare, skirts along the lakes that pool at the mountains' base. From the **north,** you can enter the park from Yellowstone National Park, which is linked to Grand Teton by the **John D. Rockefeller, Jr., Memorial Parkway** (U.S. Highways 89/191/287), an 8-mile stretch of highway where you may see wildlife through the trees, some of which are bare and blackened from the 1988 fires. When you come this way, you will already have paid your entrance to both parks, but you can stop at a park information center at Flagg Ranch, just outside Yellowstone, and get Grand Teton information. From December to March, Yellowstone's south entrance is open only to snowmobiles and snowcoaches, and there are connecting snowmobile trails to Grand Teton.

You can also approach the park from the **east,** via U.S. Highways 26/287. This route comes from Dubois, 55 miles east on the other side of the Absaroka and Wind River Mountains, and crosses

Togwotee Pass, where you'll get your first and one of the best views of the Tetons from above the valley. Travelers who come this way can continue south on U.S. 26/89/191 to Jackson without paying an entrance fee, though they are within the park boundaries, and enjoy spectacular mountain and Snake River views.

Finally, you can enter Grand Teton from Jackson in the **south,** driving about 12 miles north on U.S. Highways 26/89/191 to the Moose turnoff and the park's south entrance. Here you'll find the park headquarters and Moose Visitor Center, and a small community that includes dining and shops.

VISITOR CENTERS & INFORMATION   There are three visitor centers in Grand Teton National Park. The **Moose Visitor Center** (☎ 307/739-3399), mentioned above, is a half mile west of Moose Junction at the southern end of the park; it's open 8am to 7pm daily from June through Labor day, and 8am to 5pm the rest of the year. The **Colter Bay Visitor Center** (☎ 307/739-3594), the northernmost of the park's visitor centers, is open 8am to 8pm from early June through Labor Day, and from 8am to 5pm from Labor Day through early October. There is also **Jenny Lake Visitor Center,** open 8am to 7pm daily from early June through Labor Day and 8am to 5pm from Labor Day through early October. Maps and ranger assistance are available at all three, and there are bookstores and exhibits at Moose and Colter Bay. Finally, there is an information station at the **Flagg Ranch** complex (no phone), which is located approximately 5 miles north of the park's northern boundary.

To receive park maps before your arrival, contact **Grand Teton National Park,** P.O. Drawer 170, Moose, WY 83012 (☎ 307/739-3600; www.nps.gov/grte).

FEES   There are no park gates on US Highway 26/89/191, so you get a free ride through the park on that route, but if you want to get off the highway and explore, you'll pay $20 per automobile for a 7-day pass. If you expect to visit Yellowstone and Grand Teton (admission is good for both) more than once a year, buy a $40 annual permit. Better yet, if you visit parks elsewhere in the country, buy a $50 **Golden Eagle passport,** good for all parks and national monuments for a year from the month of purchase.

Senior citizens can get a **Golden Age Passport** for $10 annually, and blind or permanently disabled people can obtain a **Golden Access Passport,** which costs nothing. Most of the money from entrance fees goes back into the park where it was collected, so consider it a contribution worth making: In Grand Teton, this revenue has been spent on rehabbing the Jenny Lake Overlook, trail maintenance and restoring the lakeshore at Jenny Lake, among other things.

Fees for **camping** in Grand Teton are $12 per night at all the park campgrounds. For recorded information on campgrounds, call ☎ **307/739-3603.** For more information on camping, see the "Camping in Grand Teton" section in chapter 7. It is not possible to make advance reservations at campgrounds in Grand Teton.

SPECIAL REGULATIONS & WARNINGS   See chapter 3 "Exploring Yellowstone" for a summary of the major park regulations, which are generally similar in both parks.

FAST FACTS: Grand Teton

ATMs   There is an ATM at the Jackson Lake Lodge; another is located at the Dornan's Store in Moose.

Car Trouble/Towing Services   There are no towing services inside the park; if you are not a member of an automobile club, try one of the services in nearby Jackson, Wyoming. The park's main information number is ☎ **307/739-3600.**

Emergencies   Dial ☎ **911,** or 307/739-3300 and ask for park dispatch.

Gas Stations   Gasoline is available at Flagg Ranch, Colter Bay Village, the Jackson Lake Lodge, the Signal Mountain Resort Lodge, and Dornan's in Moose.

Laundry   There are laundry facilities at the Colter Bay Village.

Medical Services   There is a medical clinic at Jackson Lake Lodge and a hospital in Jackson, WY.

Permits   Boating permits and backcountry permits can be obtained at the Colter Bay and Moose visitor centers and at the Jenny Lake Ranger Station. For recorded information on climbing, call ☎ **307/739-3604.**

Post Offices   There are post offices in Moose (☎ **307/733-3336**) and Moran (☎ **307/543-2527**).

Supplies   You'll find a well-stocked general store in the Dornan's complex at Moose Village; there are convenience stores at Flagg Ranch, Colter Bay Village, the Signal Mountain Resort Lodge, and South Jenny Lake.

Weather Updates   Call ☎ **307/739-3611** for weather information.

Grand Teton National Park

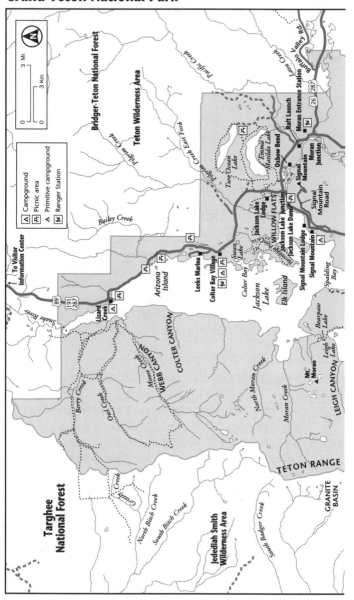

102

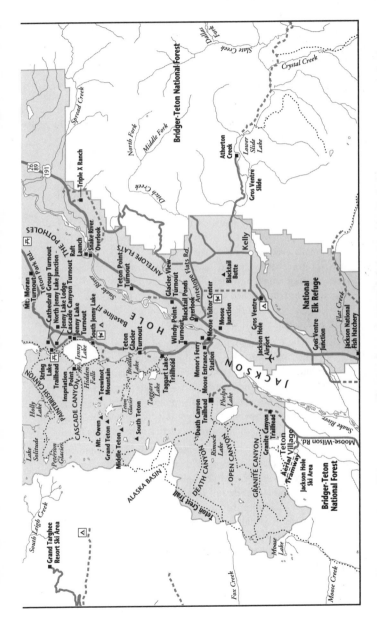

2 The Highlights

No matter what you do in Grand Teton, you are nearly always in view of the big granite peaks dominating the western skyline. Let's give them top billing in our highlights section, then.

THE PEAKS The ✪ Cathedral Group is comprised of **Grand Teton** (elevation 13,770 ft.), **Middle Teton** (elevation 12,804 ft.), and **Mt. Owen** (elevation 12,928 feet). Nearby, almost as impressive, are **South Teton** (elevation 12,514 ft.) and **Teewinot** (elevation 12,325 ft.). To the north, **Mt. Moran**, at 12,605 feet, is the fourth largest of the Tetons (on a clear day, though, you can take a great photograph of this peak all the way from Colter Bay to North Jenny Lake Junction). If you come from the east, you will pass no toll booths on your way south on U.S. Highway 191/26/89, but there are frequent pullouts on the west side of the road that give you a panoramic overview of the Snake River and the Tetons. For that matter, you get a more distant, but equally grand, view of the mountains coming over **Togwotee Pass** on U.S. Highway 26-287. **Signal Mountain,** reached off Teton Park Road by Jackson Lake, is less a peak to look at than to look off—you can drive or hike to the top for a grand view.

COLTER BAY At the north end of the park, alongside Jackson Lake, Colter Bay offers a busy mix of information, services, activities on and off the water, and shopping. The **Visitors Center** (☎ **307/739-3594**) provides wildlife videos, slide programs, natural history hikes and evening amphitheater programs. Most remarkable is the **Indian Arts Museum,** which houses a collection of American Indian crafts, clothing, and beadwork, covering rooms on two floors.

JACKSON LAKE This biggest of park lakes was dammed to provide more water for potato farmers in Idaho, but that also makes it a good place to sail, fish and ride around on powerboats. Several lodges dot its shores, but the one that bears its name, **Jackson Lake Lodge,** is set back from the lake by some flats and marshlands—good places to spot wildlife. You can't beat the views, either, and some good hikes begin here.

SIGNAL MOUNTAIN AREA The **Signal Mountain campground** is a favorite of park visitors, conveniently on the lakeshore for folks with watercraft, and the **Signal Mountain Lodge** is a fine place to stop for a meal with a view or perhaps a night with a roof overhead. Across the road, you can climb the mountain, by foot or

car, and get a panoramic view of the valley and mountains—the best way to study the skid marks and other remnants left by glaciers.

JENNY LAKE   A loop off Teton Park Road takes you close to String and Jenny lakes, and the exclusive **Jenny Lake Lodge** (which has the park's finest restaurant). Day visitors can go to the south end of the lake, the point of origin of both boat rides and great hiking trails, like the one to **Inspiration Point and Hidden Falls,** on the west side of the lake. There's also a small store. If you've got your wide-angle lens handy, stop at the **Cathedral Group Turnout,** a terrific spot for photographers.

MOOSE   Except for lodging, you'll find plenty of services and shops here—even a fine wine store—and the park **headquarters** and **visitors center.** It's been a service area since the days of Bill Menor, who ran a river ferry and a country store here a century ago. Half a mile from the park offices, the store and ferry have been recreated at the **Menor/Noble Historic District.** The nearby **Chapel of the Transfiguration** is a log church built in 1925. The altar window frames a view of the Grand Teton.

SNAKE RIVER   From below the Jackson Lake Dam, the Snake River winds its way east and south, eventually turning west toward Idaho in Snake River Canyon. There are beautiful stretches of river in the park like the Oxbow, where trumpeter swans and moose appear, and a good paddle down to Moose. To the east and up on the flats, U.S. Highway 191/89/26 follows the river from Moran Junction to Jackson, with several pullouts and overlooks.

3 If You Have Only 1 Day

A 1-day trip around this park is not unreasonable, given its size, and you can do a loop where you see many major attractions without having to retrace your steps. For more complete information on what you'll see along the way, read the next section on touring the park. Although this 1-day itinerary assumes you are entering Grand Teton from the north, after visiting Yellowstone, you could just as easily begin your itinerary in Jackson, which is 8 miles south of the Moose Entrance Station.

Begin at the south entrance of Yellowstone National Park, driving the **John D. Rockefeller, Jr., Memorial Parkway** (U.S. 89/181/287) south past the **Flagg Ranch Information Station** and to the park. As you drive south, you'll find yourself skirting the

northern shore of Jackson Lake, with a view of **Mt. Moran** to the west, and, further south, the towering **Cathedral Group.**

Colter Bay Village on the northeast shore is one of the park's busiest spots. You can rent boats, take scenic cruises, go on guided fishing trips, buy fishing licenses and supplies, rent a cabin, or camp. Several popular hiking trails start here, and there's also a visitor center. If you turn right at Colter Bay Junction and go another 0.5 mile, you'll be at the **Colter Bay Visitor Center;** stop here only if you wish to take in the **Indian Arts Museum.**

The **Lakeshore Trail** begins at the marina entrance and runs along the harbor for an easy 2-mile round-trip. It's level, paved, shady, and wheelchair-accessible, the best opportunity for a hike in this area if you don't have much time. Nearby, on the shore of the lake, is an amphitheater where ranger-naturalists conduct evening programs. The Douglas firs and pine trees here are greener and healthier than the lodgepole pines you see at higher elevations in Yellowstone.

A few minutes' drive south of Colter Bay you'll pass Jackson Lake Lodge (you might want to look in the lobby and out the big picture window), and then **Jackson Lake Junction,** where a right turn puts you on **Teton Park Road,** the beginning of a 43-mile loop tour. You'll be driving parallel to the mountain range, with Grand Teton the 13,770-foot centerpiece. You'll see lakes created by glaciers thousands of years ago, bordering a sagebrush valley inhabited by pronghorn and elk.

Just 5 miles down the road along Jackson Lake, a left hand (east) turn will take you up **Signal Mountain,** where you'll have a 360° view of the valley. You might want to grab a quick lunch at **Signal Mountain Lodge,** a friendly place with a beautiful view. Then continue down Teton Park Road to **South Jenny Lake,** where there is a huge parking area (and a store) for the many people who stop to either hike around the lake or take a boat ride across. If you have time, get to the other side (it's a 2-mile hike) and make the short climb to **Hidden Falls.** Otherwise, the best day hike in this area is the **Moose Ponds Trail** (see chapter 6.)

When you leave South Jenny Lake, you'll drive a flat, sagebrush stretch to Moose, the southernmost of the park's service centers. A half mile before Moose Junction is the **Moose Visitor Center,** which features exhibits of the Greater Yellowstone area's rare and endangered species, a video room, and an extensive bookstore. While you're in Moose, you might wish to visit the **Menor/Noble Historic District** and the **Chapel of the Transfiguration.**

Traveler's Tip

If you see an ungated road leading off any main highway, give it a try. You may be surprised to find quiet overlooks that don't appear on park maps.

Coming out of Moose, take a left (north) on **U.S. 26/89/191,** which crosses the open flats above the Snake River to Moran Junction. The best views along this road are the **Glacier View Turnout** and the **Snake River Overlook,** both of which are right off the road and well marked. At Moran Junction, turn left for a final 5-mile drive back to Jackson Lake Junction, past **Oxbow Bend,** a great spot for wildlife-viewing.

Worn out? Catch the dramatic sundown behind the Tetons, then head for your campsite (if you're tenting, stake out a spot early), or a room at one of the park's three resort hotels, or 13 miles south of the Moose entrance in Jackson, Wyoming.

4 Touring Grand Teton

A 1-day whirlwind tour of Grand Teton is not for everyone. A better idea is to allow at least 2 days. That leaves time for some relaxed hikes, picnics, touring the visitor centers, and getting a real feel for the park and the history and culture of the area. A day at the Jenny Lake area, for instance, will provide some of the best views of the peaks and a chance to walk the trails around the lake, to Inspiration Point or beyond up Cascade Canyon. You could also easily spend a day in the ✪ **Jackson Lake Lodge** area where there are several wildlife viewing spots and places for a secluded picnic.

As with the short tour in the previous section, we begin at the northern end of the park. But you could just as easily start exploring from the southern end near Jackson. From Jackson, it's 13 miles to the Moose Entrance Station, another 8 miles to the Jenny Lake Visitor Center, another 12 miles to the Jackson Lake Junction, and 5 more miles to Colter Bay.

JACKSON LAKE & THE NORTH END OF THE PARK

A great many people enter Grand Teton National Park from the north end, emerging from Yellowstone's south entrance with a 7-day park pass that gets them into Grand Teton as well. Yellowstone is connected to Grand Teton by a wilderness corridor through which the **John D. Rockefeller, Jr., Memorial Parkway** runs for 56 miles, past meadows sometimes dotted with elk, over the Snake River above Jackson Lake, and through forests that in some places still show the mosaic burns of the 1988 fires.

Along the parkway, not far from Yellowstone, you'll come to the recently modernized **Flagg Ranch** (see chapter 7), with gas, restaurants, lodging and other services. In the winter this is a busy staging area for the snowcoach and snowmobiling crowd.

Giant **Jackson Lake,** a huge expanse of water filling a deep gouge left 10,000 years ago by retreating glaciers, dominates the north end of the park. Though it empties east into the Snake River, curving around in the languid **Oxbow Bend**—a favorite wildlife-viewing float for canoeists—the water from Jackson Lake eventually turns south and then west through Snake River Canyon and into Idaho. Stream flow from the dam is regulated both for potato farmers downstream in Idaho and for rafters in the canyon, and, for better or ill, we have an irrigation dam in a national park. Elsewhere on the lake, things look quite natural, except when water gets low in the fall.

As the road follows the east shore of the lake from the north, the first development travelers encounter is **Leeks Marina,** where boats can launch, gas up and moor from mid-May to mid-September. There is a casual restaurant serving light fare and pizza during the summer. There are also numerous scenic pullouts along the lake, some good for picnics.

Just south of Leeks is **Colter Bay,** a busy outpost of park services where you can get groceries, postcards and stamps, T-shirts, and advice. At the **Colter Bay Visitors Center** you can view park and wildlife videotapes and attend a park orientation slide program throughout the day. Ranger-led activities include museum tours, park orientation talks, natural history hikes, and evening amphitheater programs. Colter Bay has lots of overnight options, from its cabins to its old-fashioned tent camps to its trailer park and campground. There is also a general store, a laundry, two restaurants, a boat launch and boat rentals, and tours. You can take pleasant short hikes in this area, including a walk around the bay or out to **Hermitage Point** (see chapter 6).

The **Indian Arts Museum** (☎ **307/543-2467**) at the Colter Bay Visitors Center is worth a visit, though it is not strictly about the Native American cultures of this area. The artifacts are mostly from Plains Indian tribes, but there are also some Navajo items from the Southwest. The collection was assembled by David T. Vernon, and

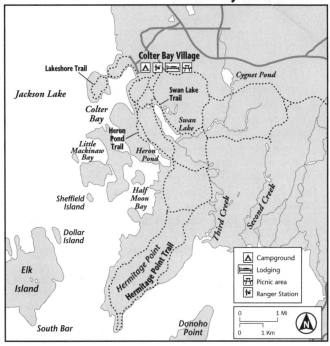

Colter Bay Village

Lakeshore Trail

Cygnet Pond

Jackson Lake

Colter Bay

Swan Lake Trail

Swan Lake

Heron Pond Trail

Little Mackinaw Bay

Heron Pond

Sheffield Island

Half Moon Bay

Dollar Island

Elk Island

Hermitage Point

Hermitage Point Trail

Third Creek

Second Creek

△ Campground
🛏 Lodging
🛆 Picnic area
🛉 Ranger Station

0   1 Mi
0   1 Km

South Bar

Donoho Point

N

includes pipes, shields, dolls, and war clubs sometimes called "skull crackers." There are large historic photos in the exhibit area.

From Colter Bay, the road swerves east and then south again past **Jackson Lake Lodge** (see chapter 7), a well-heeled 1950s-style resort with a great view of the Tetons and brushy flats in the foreground where moose often roam. Numerous trails emanate from here, both to the lakeshore and east to **Emma Matilda Lake** (see chapter 6). The road then comes to **Jackson Lake Junction,** where you can either continue west along the lakeshore or go east to the park's Moran Entrance Station. Here the park's odd entrance configuration comes into play. If you go out through the Moran entrance you are still in the park, and may turn south on U.S. Highway 26/89/191 and drive along the Snake River to Jackson, making most of your journey within the park's borders.

But if you're here to enjoy the park, you should turn right (west) on **Teton Park Road** at Jackson Lake Junction. After only 5 miles, you will arrive at **Signal Mountain.** Like its counterpart at Colter

Bay, this developed recreation area, on Jackson Lake's southeast shore, offers camping sites, accommodations in cabins and multiplex units, two restaurants, and a lounge with one of the few live televisions in the park. If you need to stock up with gas or food, do so at the small convenience store here. Boat rentals and scenic cruises of the lake are also available.

If you turn east instead of west off Teton Park Road at Signal Mountain, you can drive up a narrow, twisty road to the **top of the mountain,** 1,000 feet above the valley, where you'll have a fine view of the ring of mountains—Absarokas, Gros Ventres, Tetons, and Yellowstone Plateau—that create the Jackson "Hole." Note also the potholes created in the valley's hilly moraines left by retreating glaciers. Below the summit, about 3 miles from the base of the hill, is **Jackson Point Overlook,** a paved path 100 yards long leading to the spot where the Hayden Expedition's photographer William Henry Jackson shot his famous wet plate photographs of Jackson Lake and the Tetons more than a century ago—proof to the world that such spectacular places really existed.

Looking for a hideaway? On the right (west) side of the road between Signal Mountain and North Jenny Lake Junction, approximately 2 miles south of the Mt. Moran Turnout, is an unmarked, unpaved road leading to **Spalding Bay.** It's a sheltered little campsite and boat launch area with a primitive rest room. There isn't much space if others have beaten you there, but it's a great place to be alone with great views of the lake and mountains. If you decide to camp, be sure and get a park permit. An automobile or SUV will have no problem with this road, taking it slowly. You'll pass through brush and forest and might spot a moose.

JENNY LAKE & THE SOUTH END OF THE PARK

Continuing south along Teton Park Road, you move into the park's southern half, where the tallest peaks rise abruptly above a string of smaller lakes strung together in the foothills—**Leigh Lake,** the appropriately named **String Lake,** and **Jenny Lake,** many visitors' favorite. At North Jenny Lake Junction, you can take a turnoff west to **Jenny Lake Lodge** (see chapter 7). The road then continues as a one-way scenic loop along the lakeshore before rejoining Teton Park Road about 4 miles later.

Beautiful **Jenny Lake** gets a lot of traffic throughout the summer, both from hikers who circumnavigate the lake on a 6-mile trail and from more sedentary folks who pay for a boat ride across the lake

Signal Mountain to Jackson Lodge & Trails

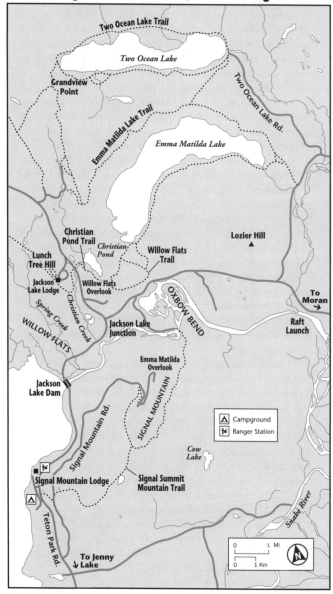

to Hidden Falls and the short steep climb to Inspiration Point (see "Hiking," below). The parking lot at **South Jenny Lake** is often jammed, and there can be a long wait for the boat ride, so you might want to get there early in the day. Or you can save your money by taking the 2-mile hike around the lake—it's level and easy. There is also a tents-only campground, a visitor center, and a general store stocked with a modest supply of prepackaged foods, and even less fresh produce and vegetables. You'll have to buy a ticket and wait in line for the trip across the lake in a powerboat that holds about 30 people. Contact **Teton Boating Company** (☎ **307/733-2703**).

South of the lake, Teton Park Road crosses open sagebrush plains with never-ending views of the mountains. You'll pass the **Climbers' Ranch**—an inexpensive dorm lodging alternative for climbers, run by the American Alpine Association—and some trailheads for enjoyable hikes to **Taggart Lake** and elsewhere. Look closely in the sagebrush for the shy pronghorn, more commonly called antelope. This handsome animal, with tan cheeks and black accent stripes, can spring up to 60 miles an hour. If you wander in the sagebrush here, you may encounter a badger, a shy but mean-spirited creature that sometimes comes out of its hole in the morning or at twilight.

The **Teton Glacier Turnout** presents a view of a glacier that grew for several hundred years until, pressured by the hotter summer temperatures in the past century, it reversed direction, and began retreating.

The road arrives at the park's south entrance—again, actually well within the park's boundaries—and the sprawling **Moose Visitor Center,** which is also park headquarters. If you are approaching the park from the south, rather than the north, this is where you'll get maps, advice, and some interpretive displays.

Just behind the visitor's center is **Menor's Ferry.** Bill Menor had a country store and operated a ferry across the Snake River at Moose back in the late 1800s. The ferry and store have been reconstructed, and you can buy items like those once sold here. Nearly is a cabin where a bunch of conservationist conspirators met in 1923 to plot the protection of the natural and scenic quality of the area, an idea that eventually led to the creation of the national park.

Also in this area is the **Chapel of the Transfiguration.** In 1925 this chapel was built in Moose so that settlers wouldn't have to make the long buckboard ride into Jackson. It's still in use for Episcopal services from spring to fall, and it's a popular place to get hitched, with a view of the Tetons through a window behind the altar.

Jenny Lake Area & Trails

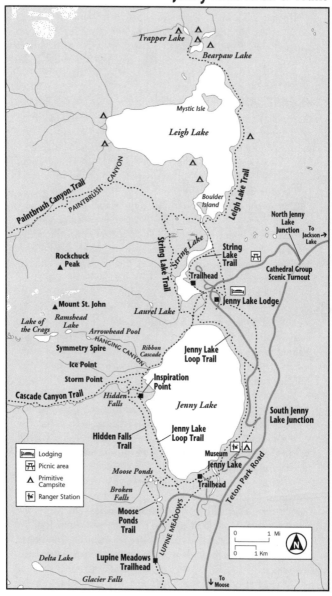

Trapper Lake

Bearpaw Lake

Mystic Isle

Leigh Lake

Boulder Island

Paintbrush Canyon Trail

PAINTBRUSH CANYON

String Lake Trail

String Lake

Leigh Lake Trail

North Jenny Lake Junction

To Jackson → Lake

String Lake Trail

Picnic area

Cathedral Group Scenic Turnout

Rockchuck Peak

Trailhead

Jenny Lake Lodge

Mount St. John

Laurel Lake

Lake of the Crags

Ramshead Lake

Arrowhead Pool

HANGING CANYON

Symmetry Spire

Ribbon Cascade

Jenny Lake Loop Trail

Ice Point

Storm Point

Inspiration Point

Cascade Canyon Trail

Hidden Falls

Jenny Lake

South Jenny Lake Junction

Hidden Falls Trail

Jenny Lake Loop Trail

Museum

Jenny Lake

Moose Ponds

Trailhead

Broken Falls

LUPINE MEADOWS

Teton Park Road

Moose Ponds Trail

Delta Lake

Lupine Meadows Trailhead

Glacier Falls

↓ To Moose

Lodging
Picnic area
Primitive Campsite
Ranger Station

0   1 Mi
0   1 Km

N

113

Dornan's is a small village area just south of the visitors center on a private holding of land owned by one of the area's earliest homesteading families. There are a few shops and a semigourmet grocery store, a post office, a bar with occasional live music, and a first-rate wine shop, of all things.

THE EAST SIDE OF THE PARK

At Moose Junction, just east of the visitors center, drivers can rejoin the highway and either turn south to Jackson and the Gros Ventre turn, or cruise north up U.S. Highway 89/26/191 to Moran Junction. This 18-mile trip is the fastest route through Grand Teton National Park, and, being further from the mountains, offers views of a broader mountain tableau.

The junction of U.S. 89 with **Antelope Flats Road** is 1.2 miles north of the Moose Junction. The 20-mile route beginning here is an acceptable biking route. It's all on level terrain, passing by the town of Kelly and the Gros Ventre campground before looping back to U.S. 26/89/191 at the Gros Ventre Junction to the south. (If you're interested in the area, you might also look at the end of the "Day Hikes" section in the next chapter, where there's a short description of Kelly and the Gros Ventre Slide area, which can be viewed just beyond the park boundaries to the east.) If you continue straight on Antelope Flats Road, you'll reach the **Teton Science School** at the road's end, about a 5-mile trip. The school offers interesting learning vacation programs, which are described more fully in chapter 2.

Less than a mile further along U.S. 26/89/191, on the left, **Blacktail Ponds Overlook** offers an opportunity to see how beavers build dams and the effect these hard-working creatures have on the flow of the streams. The area is marshy early in summer, but it's still worth the 0.25-mile hike down to the streams where the beaver activity can be viewed more closely.

Two miles further along U.S. 89 brings you to the **Glacier View Turnout,** which offers views of an area that 140,000 to 160,000 years ago was filled with a 4,000-foot-thick glacier. The view of the gulch between the peaks offers vivid testimony of the power of the glaciers that carved this landscape. Lower **Schwabacher Landing** is at the end of a 1-mile, fairly well maintained dirt road that leads down to the Snake River; you'll see the turnoff 4.5 miles north of the Moose Junction. The road winds through an area filled with glacial moraine (the rocks, sand, gravel, and so forth that were left behind as glaciers passed through the area), the leftovers of the Ice

Age. At the end of the road is a popular launch site for float trips and for fly-fishing. It's also an ideal place to retreat from the crowds. Don't be surprised to see bald eagles, osprey, moose, river otter, and beaver, which regularly patrol the area.

The **Snake River Overlook,** approximately 4 miles down the road beyond the Glacier View Turnout, is the most famous view of the Teton Range and the Snake River, immortalized by Ansel Adams. From this overlook, you'll also see at least three separate, distinctive, 200-foot-high plateaus that roll from the riverbed to the valley floor, leaving a vivid example of the power of the glaciers and ice floes as they sculpted this area. In the early 1800s, this was a prime hunting ground for John Jacob Astor's Pacific Fur Company and a certain David E. Jackson, for whom the lake and valley are named. But by 1840 the popularity of the silk hat had put an end to fur trapping, and the hunters disappeared. Good thing; by the time they departed, the beaver population was almost decimated.

A half mile north of the Snake River Overlook, signs warn that the road to **Deadman's Bar Overlook,** which leads to a clearing on the river bank, should only be negotiated by four-wheel drive vehicles. Though the 1-mile road is unpaved and bumpy, it is maintained well enough to be handled by most cars if there's no snow on the road and if it has not been raining.

Cunningham Cabin, 1.75 miles north of Deadman's Bar Overlook, is a nondescript historic site at which the first homesteaders, Pierce and Margaret Cunningham, built their ranch in 1890. By 1928, they had been defeated by the elements and sold out to Rockefeller's Snake River Land Co. You can visit it at any time.

If you head down the highway in the other direction (south) from Moose Junction, on U.S. Highway 26/89/191, you can turn east on the **Gros Ventre River Road** 5 miles before you reach Jackson and follow the river east into its steep canyon—a few miles past the little town of Kelly you'll leave the park and be in **Bridger-Teton National Forest.** In 1925, a huge slab of mountain broke off of the north end of the Gros Ventre Range on the east side of Jackson Hole, a reminder that nature still has an unpredictable and violent side.

The slide left a gaping open gash in the side of Sheep Mountain, sloughing off nearly 50 million cubic yards of rock and forming a natural dam across the Gros Ventre River half a mile wide. Two years later, the dam broke, and a cascade of water rushed down the canyon and through the little town of Kelly, taking several lives. The town of **Kelly** is a quaint and eccentric community with a large number of yurts and, nearby, the **Teton Science School.** Up in the canyon formed by the Gros Ventre River, there is a roadside display with photographs of the slide area and a short nature walk from the road down to the residue of the slide and **Lower Slide Lake.** Here, signs identify the trees and plants that survived or grew in the slide's aftermath.

5 Organized Tours & Ranger Programs

The **Grand Teton Lodge Company** (☎ **307/543-2811**) runs bus tours of both Grand Teton and Yellowstone from mid-May to mid-October.

Winter and summer, wildlife biologists lead tours of Grand Teton, Yellowstone and forest lands through the ✪ **Great Plains Wildlife Institute,** P.O. Box 7580, Jackson Hole, WY 83002 (☎ **307/773-2623;** www.wildlifesafari.com). With open-roofed vans, rafts, sleighs and on foot, these tours bring visitors closer to the wildlife than they're likely to get on their own, and guests sometimes participate in radio tracking and other research projects. The **Teton Science School,** P.O. Box 68, Kelly, WY 83011 (☎ **307/733-4765;** e-mail tss@wyoming.com), offers summer programs for students and adults that discuss the ecology, geology, and wildlife of the park, as well as workshops in photography and tracking. The **Grand Teton Natural History Association** is a not-for-profit organization that provides myriad information about the park, including information for travelers through its bookstores at visitors centers in and around the park. These materials are available by writing the association at P.O. Drawer 170, Moose, WY 83012 (☎ **307/739-3403;** www.granteton.com/gtnha).

Within the park, there are several interesting ranger programs. These range from a ranger-led, 3-mile hike from the Colter Bay Visitor Center to Swan Lake, to a relaxed evening chatting with a ranger on the back deck of the Jackson Lake Lodge, with the Tetons as a dramatic backdrop and spotting scope for watching moose and birds. There are numerous events during the summer at Colter Bay, South Jenny Lake, and the Moose Visitors Center. Check the daily schedules in the park's paper, the *Teewinot,* which you can pick up at any visitor center.

At Jenny Lake, there are **wildflower walks** led by rangers who can tell you the difference between lupine and larkspur, daily in June and July, and morning and twilight hikes to Hidden Falls (you take the boat across the lake), among other activities.

At Colter Bay, you can climb aboard boat for an afternoon **fire and ice cruise,** during which a ranger will talk about the volcanics, the glaciers, and the fires that have shaped and colored the landscape. There are programs on Indian art and culture, lakeshore strolls with rangers, and evening gatherings at the Colter Bay amphitheater in which rangers teach about park wildlife.

Youngsters 8 to 12 can join **Young Naturalist programs** at Colter Bay or Jenny Lake and learn about the natural world for 2 hours while hiking with a ranger. Signups are at the visitors centers, and the kids will need basic hiking gear.

There are evening campfire gatherings at the Gros Ventre, Signal Mountain, Lizard Creek, and Colter Bay campground amphitheaters. Topics vary.

6

Hikes & Other Outdoor Pursuits in Grand Teton National Park

*I*n addition to water sports on its lakes and rivers, Grand Teton has hundreds of miles of trails with opportunities for every level of hiker. The varied trail system of about 200 miles offers both short, mostly flat trails within shouting distance of the road system, and more demanding trails in the Teton range that escape the crowds and challenge the body.

For a more extensive and more detailed list of trails than what follows here, pick up *Teton Trails* by Katy Duffy and Darwin Wile. It's available from the Grand Teton Natural History Association, P.O. Drawer 170, Moose, WY, 83012 (☎ **307/739-3403**).

1 Day Hikes

The park's many trails vary greatly in length and level of difficulty, so you'll want to consult with rangers at the park. They can update you on everything from bear activity to trail damage (such as damaged bridges) to weather concerns. Rangers may be able to suggest hikes suitable to your expectations and ability; they also conduct various guided walks.

Below is a fairly broad selection of hikes, ranging from easy to difficult. For those who have only a brief time at Grand Teton, here are two suggestions for the "If you can only do one hike" category: the **Signal Mountain Summit Trail** and the **Inspiration Point Trail** in the Jenny Lake region.

You'll find that trails are generally very well marked. Turn to chapter 5 for **maps** of the Colter Bay Area, the Signal Mountain and Jackson Lake areas, and the Jenny Lake Area showing major trails described in this section.

Just remember, if you are planning to hike for more than 30 minutes, be sure and carry a supply of water.

COLTER BAY AREA

A map showing the trails in this area is in chapter 5.

Lakeshore Trail. 2 miles RT. Easy. Access: Trailhead located at the Marina entrance.

This short hike in the Colter Bay area starts at the marina and leads out to pebble beaches on the west side of a point with views across Jackson Lake of the entire Teton range. It's wide and shady, and you can stop to look over the boats moored in the marina; then, at the end of the trail, you get a view across Jackson Lake of the entire Teton range. The views leap out at you when you arrive at the end of the trail; water laps on the shore and, thankfully, you're out of earshot of the visitor center. This 2-mile loop can be completed in about 1 hour of brisk walking.

TRAILS FROM THE HERMITAGE POINT TRAILHEAD

The **Hermitage Point Trailhead** near the marina is the starting point for an interesting variety of trips ranging from 1 to 9 miles. With careful planning, it's possible to start the day with a hike beginning at Colter Bay that leads past **Cygnet Lake** across **Willow Flats** to Jackson Lake Lodge, where you can stop for lunch). Then, after a break, take the path that returns back to Colter Bay in time for the evening outdoor barbecue. All told, that's 9.3 miles round-trip. The numerous trail options here can be confusing, so carry a map.

Hermitage Point Trail—A Loop. 6.5 miles RT. Moderate. Access: There are directional signs near the Swan Lake/Heron Pond Trail Intersection.

It's a 6.5-mile loop from the trailhead through a thickly forested area to the isolated Hermitage Point, a peninsula jutting into Jackson Lake, from which you can look across the bay to the Signal Mountain Lodge. If you're seeking solitude, this is an excellent place to find it, though you should check with rangers before leaving since this is bear country.

Photo Op

Within minutes, the Hermitage Point Trail opens to a broad meadow covered with sagebrush and, later in the summer, blooming wildflowers, offering one of the most spectacular views of Mt. Moran, which is as impressive in its way as the Grand Teton. To avoid retracing your steps past Heron Pond, bear right at the third creek intersection and continue straight ahead to the corrals at Colter Bay—this route adds no distance to the hike.

Heron Pond Trail. 3 miles RT. Easy. Access: Trailhead located at Hermitage Point Trailhead, Colter Bay.

You journey through dense stand of lodgepole pine to this pond, inhabited by beavers most likely to be seen in the early morning. This is bear territory, as well as a home for Canada geese, trumpeter swans and moose. Wildflowers are part of the show in the early summer, look for lupine, gilia, heart leaf arnicas, and the Indian paintbrush. Don't be put off by the fact that the first 200 yards of the trail are steep; after reaching the top of a rise, it levels out and has only moderate elevation gains from that point on. *Note:* Since three trails run through this area, the foliage and terrain for this, the Swan Lake Trail, and Hermitage Point Trail are virtually identical.

Swan Lake Trail. 3.9 miles RT. Easy. Access: Trailhead located at Hermitage Point Trailhead, Colter Bay.

Finding swans at Swan Lake requires a trip to the south end where a small island offers them isolation and shelter for nests. The distance from Swan Lake through a densely forested area to a sign at the Heron Pond intersection is 0.3 mile. Hermitage Point is 3 miles from this junction along a gentle path that winds through a wooded area that's popular with bears. The total circumnavigation from the Colter Bay area is doable in 2 hours.

Willow Flats Trail. 5 miles one way. Easy. Access: Horse corrals at Colter Bay.

An alternative to mountainous, forested trails, this trip from Colter Bay to Jackson Lake Lodge takes you across marshy flats where you'll have an excellent view of the Tetons and a good chance of seeing moose and other wildlife. You begin by skirting the sewage ponds at Colter Bay (sorry), then pick up a trail east to Cygnet Lake. Instead of looping back to Colter Bay, you take a spur that crosses Pilgrim Creek going east across the flats. You can hike in either direction, but drop a car at each end if you don't want to double back on foot.

JACKSON LAKE LODGE AREA

A map showing the trails in this area is in chapter 5.

Christian Pond Trail. 1 mile RT. Easy. Access: The trailhead is some 200 yards south of the entrance to Jackson Lake Lodge, most easily accessed from the Jackson Lake Lodge corrals. It's unmarked, so look carefully.

This trail begins with a half-mile walk through a grassy, wet area to a pond with nesting trumpeter swans and other waterfowl. You can circumnavigate the pond, adding another 3 miles to the trip. In May

Photo Op

A wide-open meadow near the summit of Signal Mountain presents an excellent opportunity to look to the west for photos of both Mt. Moran and the Teton Range. The best time to take those photos is before 11am, when the sun will be mostly at your back, or in the early evening, when the sun will be lower in the sky to the west.

and June this a great wildflower walk, but also prime habitat for bears, so check with rangers before venturing onto the trail. The south end of the pond is covered with little grassy knolls upon which the birds build their nests and roost, and beavers have constructed a lodge here too. In the warmer months, the area is covered with colorful wildflowers. It's a restful sanctuary but one often infested by gnats and mosquitoes.

✪ **Signal Summit Mountain Trail.** 6 miles RT. Moderate. Access: The trailhead is near the entrance to the Signal Mountain Lodge, or you can drive 1 mile up Signal Mountain Road to a pond on the right, and pick up the trail there.

This up-and-down trail gives you a few fine hours of uncrowded trail time with views of the mountains, wildflowers, and, at the end, a grand panorama of the glacially carved valley. After negotiating a steep climb at the beginning of the trail, you'll come upon a broad plateau covered with lodgepole pines, grassy areas, and seasonal wildflowers. Cross a paved road to a lily-covered pond, and just beyond you'll choose two different trails up the mountain—take the right one up (ponds, wildlife, maybe moose and bear) and the left one down (open ridges with views). Both trails offer excellent opportunities to observe the shy, redheaded, pileated woodpecker.

TWO OCEAN & EMMA MATILDA LAKE TRAILS

You can come to these lakes from the east or west: from the west you'd begin at the Grand View Point Trailhead; 1 mile north of Jackson Lake Lodge; or at the Christian Pond Trailhead, just east of Jackson Lake Lodge. From the east, you'd go up Pacific Creek Road, 4 miles east of Jackson Lake Junction on the road to the Moran entrance. There is a pullout for Emma Matilda Lake 2 miles up this road, or you can go a half mile further, take a left on Two Ocean Lake Road, and go to the Two Ocean Lake trailhead parking lot, with trails leading to both lakes.

Emma Matilda Lake Trail. 11.7 miles RT. Easy to moderate. Access: Emma Matilda Lake Trailhead on Pacific Creek Road or trailhead off Two Ocean Lake Road north of Jackson Lake–Moran Road.

Circumnavigating this lake is a pleasant, up-and-down journey with great views of the mountains and a good chance of seeing wildlife. Emma Matilda Lake was named after the wife of Billy Owen, reputedly the first climber to reach the peak of the Grand Teton. The hike winds uphill for a half mile from the parking area to a large meadow favored by mule deer. The trail follows the northern side of the lake through a pine forest 400 feet above the lake, then descends to an overlook where you'll have panoramic views of the Tetons, Christian Pond, and Jackson Lake. The trail on the south side of the lake goes through a densely forested area populated by Englemann spruce and subalpine fir. Be watchful and noisy, because this is bear country. It's possible to branch off onto the Two Ocean Lake Trail along the northern shore of the lake.

○ **Two Ocean Lake Trail.** 5.7 miles RT. Easy. Access: Two Ocean Lake Trailhead on Two Ocean Lake Road, or Grand View Point Trailhead.

Take your time and take a picnic on this delightful, underused trail around Two Ocean Lake. You can start at either end, but I recommend a side-trip up Grand View Point, which will add about 2.5 miles of hiking. You'll be rested for this climb because the walk around the lake is fairly level, and you'll be in a great mood if you've been watching ducks, swans, grebes and loons on the water. The variety of habitat—marshes, lakes, woodlands, and meadows—means you'll see birds, wildflowers, butterflies and possibly beaver, elk, deer and moose. Great views of the Tetons, too, but for the best views you need to take the trip up to Grand View Point, a climb that will take you from lodgepole to fir to a hilltop of arrow-leaf balsam root, with its large, orange flowers. You'll look down on lakes, meadows and volcanic outcrops, and in the distance you'll gaze at the Tetons, the Mount Leidy Highlands and Jackson Lake. It's possible to branch off onto the Emma Matilda Lake Trail at the east end of Two Ocean Lake.

JENNY LAKE AREA

A map showing the trails in this area is in chapter 5.

Amphitheater Lake Trail. 9.6 miles RT. Difficult. Access: Use the Lupine Meadows Trailhead. From the Moose entrance station on Teton Park Road, drive 6.6 miles to the Lupine Meadows Junction and follow signs to the trailhead; if you're coming from Jenny Lake, the trailhead is at the end of a road less than 1 mile south of South Jenny Lake.

Especially for Kids

Youthful visitors (ages 8 to 14) to the park are encouraged to explore and experience Grand Teton as members of the **Young Naturalist** program. To participate, pick up a copy of the Young Naturalist activity brochure at any visitor center, then complete projects outlined in the booklet during your stay. When you present the completed project, and $1, to a ranger at the Moose, Jenny Lake, or Colter Bay visitor center, you'll be awarded a Young Naturalist patch.

There are two trails that most kid could do, both of which are at Jenny Lake. The **Inspiration Point** hike is less strenuous if you take the boat shuttle across Jenny Lake. This reduces the hiking distance to less than a mile; at 7 miles round-trip, the entire Jenny Lake Loop Trail is a bit too long for kids, but the terrain is fairly level and doable if you stick to the portion along the eastern shore.

Here's a trail that can get you up into the high mountains and out in a day—if you're in good shape and acclimated to the altitude; it's a 3,000-foot climb. You'll cross glacial moraines and meadows quilted with flowers, and enter forests of fir and lodgepole and whitebark pine (a bear food—be alert!). Finally you clear the trees and come into an amphitheater of monstrous rock walls topped by Disappointment Peak, with the Grand and Teewinot in view. Surprise Lake and Amphitheater Lake sit in this dramatic setting, with a few gnarled trees struggling to survive on the slopes.

✪ **Cascade Canyon Trail.** 4.5 miles one-way. Moderate to difficult. Access: The trail into Cascade Canyon begins at Inspiration Point.

Cascade Canyon Trail is the most popular trail in the park for knowledgeable hikers. You can begin the hike from South Jenny Lake, but you can also shave 2 miles off each way by riding the boat service across the lake and beginning your hike at the Boat Dock. At this point, you're only a 1 mile steep hike from Inspiration Point (see the "Hidden Falls & Inspiration Point Trail" below), which is as far as many visitors ever get. From here, you make a brief steep climb to the glacially rounded canyon, where the trail levels out and you're in a wonderland of wildflowers and waterfowl and busy pikas. On a nice day, the warblers will be singing and you may see moose and bear.

If you want to go further, you have two choices when you reach forks of North and South Cascade Canyon: follow the South Fork to Hurricane Pass, or the North Fork to Lake Solitude. These are overnight trips for most mortals, so you'll need camping gear and backcountry permit.

A less taxing alternative to the Cascade Canyon trip mentioned above is a detour to **Moose Ponds,** which begins on the Inspiration Point trail. The ponds, located 2 miles from either west or east boat docks, are near the south end of the lake, and are alive with birds. The area near the base of Teewinot Mountain, which towers over the area, is populated with elk, mule deer, black bears, and moose. The trail is flat (at lake level), short, and easy to negotiate in 1 to 1.5 hours. The best times to venture forth are in early morning and evening.

Hidden Falls & Inspiration Point Trail. 1.8–5.8 miles RT. Moderate. Access: Trailheads at East Shore Boat Dock or at the West Shore Boat Dock of Jenny Lake (if you take the boat shuttle).

Many people cross Jenny Lake, either by boat or on foot around the south end, and then make the short, forest-shaded uphill slog to **Hidden Falls** (less than 1 mile of hiking if you take the boat; 5 miles RT if you walk around), which tumbles down a broad cascade. Some think that's enough, and don't go another steep half mile to **Inspiration Point.** Up there you get a great view of Jenny Lake below, and you can see the glacial moraine that formed it. If you're only going to these two overlooks, we recommend a relaxed and easy hike around the south end of the lake.

Whichever route you take to Inspiration Point, start early in the day so as to avoid the crowds. Then pace yourself. And once you've reached Inspiration Point, what's to stop you from proceeding on to Cascade Canyon?

Jenny Lake Loop Trail. 6.6 miles RT. Easy to moderate. Access: Trailhead at East Shore Boat Dock.

Another lake to circumnavigate, following the shore. You can cut it in half by taking the Jenny Lake Boat Shuttle from the East Shore Boat Dock to the West Shore Boat Dock. The lake, which is 2.5 miles long, sits in a pastoral setting at the foot of the mountain range, so it presents excellent views throughout the summer.

Warning: This is one of the most popular spots in the park; to avoid crowds travel early or late in the day. The trails to Hidden Falls, Inspiration Point, and the Moose Ponds branch off of this trail on the southwest shore of the lake. The trails to String and Leigh lakes branch off this trail on the north shore of Jenny Lake.

Leigh Lake Trail. 7.4 miles RT. Easy. Access: The trailhead is located adjacent to the String Lake Picnic Area.

This trail begins at String Lake, which is, well, a stringy lake connecting Leigh and Jenny lakes. The trail for Leigh Lake is well marked, relatively flat, and goes through a forested area that is always within sight of the lake. Picnickers willing to expend the energy necessary to hike roughly 0.9 mile from the String Lake Picnic Area to the end of the lake will find themselves eating in a less congested area with spectacular views of Mt. Moran. The trail continues along the shore of Leigh Lake but is rather uninteresting. A better option, if time allows, is to return to the picnic area, cross the String Lake inlet, and explore the western edge of Jenny Lake along the trail that circumnavigates the lake (see the "Jenny Lake Loop Trail" described above).

String Lake Trail. 1.8 miles. Easy. Access: Trailhead is located at the Leigh Lake Trailhead.

This easy hike along the eastern shore of String Lake has two things going for it: It provides easy access to Leigh Lake, and it's in a forest that is a better alternative for picnics than the crowded picnic area. You'll wander in the shade of a pine forest along the shore with excellent views of Mt. Moran above. However, because this is a heavily trafficked area, you should not count on seeing much wildlife, if any. This is also the starting point for a more ambitious trip up Paintbrush Canyon.

Taggart & Bradley Lakes Trail. 5.0 miles RT. Moderate. Access: The trailhead is well marked and located west of Teton Park Road, approximately 6 miles south of Jenny Lake.

Want to get away from the crowds on Jenny Lake trails? Just down the road from South Jenny is the trailhead to Taggart and Bradley lakes, named for two members of the 1872 Hayden expedition. This hike winds through a burned-out area in the midst of recovery to a lake that was created by glacial movements. The hike from the parking lot to the lake (where you can fish from the shore), is only 1.6 miles along the southern (left) fork of the trail. Swimming in these cold waters is not recommended. From the lake, you can return by the same trail or continue north to **Bradley Lake** for a round-trip of 5 miles. This route adds 1.8 miles to the trip, and the elevation gain is 467 feet, but the payoff is that at its highest point the trail overlooks all of Taggart Lake and the stream flowing from it. Like other hikes in Grand Teton, this one is best made during the early morning or early evening hours when it's cooler and there's less traffic.

FURTHER AFIELD: SOUTHEAST OF MOOSE

Though it is situated near Kelly, outside the park boundaries, the Gros Ventre Slide area is both an interesting hiking area and historical site. You can get to the slide area by traveling east from the Gros Ventre Junction on U.S. 89, 6 miles north of Jackson; alternately, 1 mile north of the Moose Junction on U.S. 89, take the Antelope Flats Road to the second right turn; then take the second left. There will be a sign.

It was at this spot in June 1925 that the side of Sheep Mountain broke loose and created one of the largest earth movements ever observed. Nearly 50 million cubic yards of sandstone formed a dam 225 feet high and 0.5-mile wide across the Gros Ventre River. Then, 2 years later, the upper 60 feet of the dam gave way, creating a raging river that flooded the town of Kelly 3.5 miles downstream. Informational brochures and trail maps of the interpretive trail here, which is in the Bridger-Teton National Forest, are available from the U.S. Forest Service.

You can stop in at the Forest Service Information Center at 340 N. Cache in downtown Jackson (☎ **304/739-5500**) where you can pick up all the information you'll need to hike in this area.

2 Exploring the Backcountry

Grand Teton may seem small compared to Yellowstone, but there are more than 200 miles of trails in the backcountry, and good opportunities for solitude and adventure. Like Yellowstone, you have to have a permit from the Park Service to sleep in the backcountry—the permits are free, and serve more to keep track of campers and make sure no one area is overused. Here, the permits are for camping above 7,000 feet in one of several camping "zones," where you can make some choices of sites.

For **general information** on backpacking and safety, see chapter 2.

INFORMATION BEFORE YOU GO   For background information, write for the Grand Teton **Backcountry Camping** brochure, P.O. Drawer 170, Moose, WY 83012.

BACKCOUNTRY PERMITS   As in Yellowstone, you are required to secure a backcountry permit from the Park Service in order to use an overnight campsite; again, the good news is that for now the permits are free; the bad news is that reservations are not. The permit is valid only on the dates for which it is issued. There are two methods of securing permits: They may be picked up the day before you commence your trip, or you can make a reservation for a permit in advance of your arrival, for a $15 fee. Reservations are only accepted from January 1 to June 1; it's wise to reserve a camp area if you're going in July or August.

Warning: The reservation is just that, a reservation; upon your arrival at the park, you'll need to secure the permit. Permits are issued in Grand Teton at the Moose and Colter Bay visitor centers and the Jenny Lake Ranger station; reservations may be made by writing the **Permits Office,** Grand Teton National Park, P.O. Drawer 170, Moose, WY 83012, or faxing 307/739-3438. While a special fishing permit is required in Yellowstone, only a **Wyoming fishing license** is required in Grand Teton.

WHEN TO GO   Remember that this region has a short summer, and virtually no spring. While the lower elevation areas of the park are open in May, some of the high country trails may not be clear of snow or high water before late June. Look in the *Backcountry Camping* brochure for approximate dates when specific campsites will be habitable.

MAPS   Topographic maps of Grand Teton are available from the U.S. Geological Survey and Trails Illustrated, as is the **Grand Teton Hiking and Climbing** map, which includes maps of Granite and Moran canyons and a trip planner; it is available from the **Grand Teton Natural History Association,** P.O. Drawer 170, Moose, WY 83012 (☎ **307/739-3403**).

THE BACKCOUNTRY IN GRAND TETON   The premier backcountry activity in Grand Teton is not hiking but rather **mountain-climbing,** which you should not attempt alone unless you are an expert. For a complete discussion of mountaineering possibilities and outfitters in Grand Teton National Park, see "Climbing," later in this chapter.

Perhaps the most popular backcountry trail in Grand Teton is the 19.2-mile ✪ **Cascade Canyon Loop.** The loop starts on the west side of Jenny Lake, winds northwest 7.2 miles on the **Cascade Canyon Trail** to Lake Solitude and the Paintbrush Divide, then returns on the 10.3-mile-long **Paintbrush Trail** past Holly Lake, tucked into a cirque including Mount Woodring. Despite its shortness, it is one of the most rigorous hikes in either park because of gains in elevation—more than 2,600 feet—rocky trails, and switchbacks through scree that can become slippery, especially in years when snow remains until the middle of summer on the north-facing side of Paintbrush Divide.

Rangers recommend the hike for several reasons, the most noteworthy of which is unsurpassed scenery. Moose and black bears are in this part of the park, so hikers are cautioned to be diligent about making noise. You may also see harlequin ducks, since they nest near the trail in Cascade Creek. You'll also see many other birds, myriad types of wildflowers, and large stands of whitebark pine trees.

Though it adds 5.1 miles to the trip (one-way), a detour west from the Cascade Canyon Trail to **Hurricane Pass** will reward you with a view from the foot of **Schoolroom Glacier.** If you're feeling spunky, head west into the Jedediah Smith Wilderness on a trail that eventually crosses into Idaho. If you're feeling *particularly* spunky, you can actually continue this trek to Alaska.

If you're unable to complete the hike in 1 day, you can trek 7.2 miles on the Cascade Canyon Trail to **Solitude Lake** and return via the same trail. If you can afford a 2-day trip, camping zones are 6 miles west of the trailhead on the Cascade Canyon Trail and 8.7 miles northwest on the Paintbrush Canyon Trail at Holly Lake. Be sure and get a reservation.

Perhaps the quickest way to get up high in these mountains for a backcountry foray is to hitch a ride up **Rendezvous Mountain** on the Jackson Hole Ski Resort Tram. This puts you at 10,450 feet in **Bridger-Teton National Forest,** just south of the park, and ready to embark north toward the park's Middle Fork Cutoff. From here, you can head down into Granite Canyon to Phelps Lake, or go north along the **Teton Crest Trail** to Fox Creek Pass (over 8 difficult miles from the tram) and **Death Canyon** and beyond.

If you are hardy enough to make it to **Death Canyon Shelf,** a wildflower-strewn limestone ledge that runs above Death Canyon toward **Alaska Basin,** you'll have an extraordinary high altitude view of the west side of the Tetons' biggest peaks. If you are on an extended backcountry trip, you can continue north to Hurricane Pass, where you can come back down to the valley floor by way of Cascade Canyon.

This kind of backcountry trip is really an expedition, and requires skill and experience. Go over any such plans with park rangers, who can help you evaluate your ability to take on such a challenge.

3 Other Activities

In addition to the activities listed here, check out some of the other options in the Jackson area that are listed in chapter 8.

BIKING   Unfortunately, bikes are banned from hiking trails in the park, and on the paved roads below the problem is safety—there are huge RVs careening about, and some roads have only narrow shoulders. Teton Park Road has been widened somewhat, but traffic is heavy here; road bikers should try **Antelope Flats,** beginning at a trailhead 1 mile north of Moose Junction and going east. Sometimes called **Mormon Road,** this paved route crosses the flats below the Gros Ventre Mountains, past old ranch homesteads and the small town of Kelly. It connects to the unpaved **Shadow Mountain Road,** which actually goes outside the park into national forest, climbing through the trees to the summit. Total distance is 7 miles and the elevation gain is 1,370 feet, and you'll be looking at Mt. Moran and the Tetons across the valley.

Mountain bikers have a few more options: Try **Two-Ocean Lake Road** (reached from the Pacific Creek Road just north of Moran Junction) or the **River Road,** a 15-mile dirt path along the Snake River's western bank (bison use it, too, and you'd be smart to yield). Ambitious mountain bikers may want to load their overnight gear and take the **Grassy Lake Road,** once used by Indians, west from Flagg Ranch on a 50-mile journey to Ashton, Idaho.

A map that shows bicycle routes, *Grand Teton Bicycling,* is available from the Park Service at visitor centers, or at **Adventure Sports,** at Dornan's in the town of Moose (☎ **307/733-3307**), which is inside the boundaries of Grand Teton National Park. You can also rent mountain bikes here, $24 for a full day, $15 half day.

BOATING   Boaters have more choices in Grand Teton than they do in Yellowstone. Motorboats are permitted on Jenny, Jackson, and Phelps lakes. Bigger boats, even a few yacht-sized vessels, find room on Jackson Lake, where powerboats pull skiers, sailboats move noiselessly in summer breezes, and fishers ply the waters. Those who venture on the big lake need to be aware that the weather can change suddenly, and late afternoon lightning is not uncommon; sailors should be particularly wary of the swirling winds that accompany thunderstorms. **Scenic cruises** of Jackson Lake, as well as twice-a-week floating steak-fry cruises, are available daily at the **Colter Bay** marina from May through September.

If you bring your own boat, you must register it: For nonmotorized craft, it's $5 for 7 days, or $10 for a year permit; motorized skippers pay $10 for 7 days and $20 for an annual permit, which you can buy at any visitors center. Boat and canoe rentals, tackle, and fishing licenses are available at Colter and **Signal Mountain** (rental fees of $16 per hour for motorboats include permits). For shuttles to the west side of Jenny Lake, and for cruises, call **Teton Boating Company** (☎ 307/733-2703).

Motorized boats are allowed on Phelps, Jackson and Jenny Lakes, but on Jenny Lake the motor can't be over 8 horsepower. Only human-powered vessels are permitted on Phelps, Emma Matilda, Two Ocean, Taggard, Bradley, Bearpaw, Leigh, and String lakes. Rafts, canoes, dories, and kayaks are allowed on the Snake River within the park. No boats at all are permitted on Pacific Creek or the Gros Ventre River.

Scenic cruises of Jackson Lake are conducted daily, and floating cruises are twice-weekly, both leaving from the **Colter Bay Marina** from May through September. You'll travel to Elk Island, where they cook up steaks and trout. It takes about 3 hours altogether. Cruises cost $11 for adults, $6 for children ages 3 to 11; dinner cruises are $35 for adults, $23 for children.

Additionally, you can rent kayaks and canoes at **Adventure Sports** at Dornan's in the town of Moose (☎ 307/733-3307), which is in the boundaries of Grand Teton National Park. Rentals run $30 per day, $20 for a half day.

CLIMBING   The search-and-rescue volunteers are busy these days at Grand Teton. Every year there are rescues of climbers who fall or get trapped on Teton rock faces, and many years there are fatalities. Yet the peaks have a strong allure for climbers, even inexperienced ones, perhaps because you can reach the top of even the biggest ones in a single day, but not easily. The terrain is mixed, with snow and ice year-round—knowing how to self-arrest with an ice axe is a must—and the weather can change suddenly. The key is to get good advice, know your limitations, and if you're not already skilled, take some lessons at the local climbing schools (see paragraph below). If you go without a professional guide, you should have experienced companions who know the mountain.

Climbers who go out for a day do not have to register or report to park officials, so they should be sure and tell friends where they're going and when they'll be back. Overnight climbers must pick up a free permit. Climbing rangers who can lead rescue efforts are on duty at the **Jenny Lake Ranger Station** (☎ 307/739-3343) at South Jenny Lake from June until the middle of September. The American Alpine Club provides cheap dormitory beds for climbers at the Grand Teton Climbers' Ranch (Climbers' Ranch, Moose, WY

83012). Guided climbs of Grand Teton are offered by **Jackson Hole Mountain Guides** (☎ **307/733-4979**) and **Exum Mountain Guides,** in Moose (☎ **307/733-2297**). Those who need to practice their moves on a rainy day should try the **Teton Rock Gym,** 1116 Maple, Jackson, WY 83001 (☎ **307/733-0707**).

The **Jenny Lake Ranger Station,** which is open only in summer, is the center for climbing information; climbers are encouraged to stop in and obtain information on routes, conditions, and regulations.

FISHING The lakes and streams of Grand Teton are popular fishing destinations, loaded with lively cutthroat trout, whitefish, and mackinaw (lake) trout in Jackson, Jenny and Phelps Lake. Jackson has produced some monsters weighing as much as 50 pounds, but you're more likely to catch fish under 20 inches, fishing deep with trolling gear from a boat during hot summer months.

The Snake River runs for about 27 miles in the park, and has cutthroat and whitefish up to about 18 inches. It's a popular drift boat river for fly-fishermen. If you'd like a guide who knows the holes, try **Jack Dennis Fishing Trips** (☎ 307/733-3270), **Solitude Float Trips** (☎ 307/733-2871), **Westbank Anglers** (☎ 307/733-6483), which is another full-service fly shop that sells gear and organizes trips in Jackson Hole, or **Fort Jackson Float Trips** (☎ 800/735-8430). As an alternative, stake out a position on the banks below the dam at **Jackson Lake,** where you'll have plenty of company and just might snag something. You'll need a Wyoming state fishing license (nonresident $6 for one day, $65 for season; $15 for ages 14 to 18, no license for under 14), and you'll have to check creel limits, which vary from year to year and place to place. There aren't fishing guide books devoted specifically to Grand Teton, but there's good information on the park's lakes and streams in *Fishing Wyoming,* by Kenneth Graham (Falcon Press, Helena, Mont.).

FLOAT TRIPS The upper end of the Snake River in the park can be deceptive—its smooth surface runs fast during the spring, and there are deadly snags of fallen trees and other debris. Without a local guide or past experience you might want to think twice about dropping your personal raft in. Check in with rangers, and let them discourage you if they think your skills may not match the river. There are plenty of commercial-rafting outfitters, who will help you get acquainted, listed below. If you want white water, there are a dozen commercial outfitters offering white-water trips down Snake River Canyon, outside the park (see chapter 8 in the Jackson section).

The park's 27-mile stretch of river is wonderful for wildlife, with moose, eagles and other animals coming to the water's edge. There are many commercial float operators in the park, They mostly run trips from mid-May to mid-September (depending on weather and river flow conditions). These companies offer 5- to 10-mile scenic floats, some with early-morning and evening wildlife trips. Try **Triangle X-Osprey Float Trips** (☎ 307/733-5500), **Barker-Ewing Float Trips** (☎ 800/365-1800), **Grand Teton Lodge Company** (☎ 307/543-2811); **Signal Mountain Lodge,** in Grand Teton National Park, P.O. Box 50, Moran, WY 83013 (☎ 307/543-2831); and **Flagg Ranch Float Trips** (☎ 307/543-2861). Scenic float trips cost about $35 for adults, with discounts for children under 12.

HORSEBACK RIDING   Horseback riding is as popular in Grand Teton as it is in Yellowstone. The **Grand Teton Lodge Company** offers tours from stables next to the visitor centers at Colter Bay and Jackson Lake Lodge. Choices are 1- and 2-hour guided trail rides daily on tame animals. An experienced rider may find these tours too tame; wranglers refer to them as "nose-and-tail" tours. The names of several other companies that organize horseback trips are in chapter 8 in the Jackson section.

4   Winter Sports & Activities

Park facilities pretty much shut down during the winter, except for a skeleton staff at the Moose Visitors Center, and the park shows no signs of becoming the winter magnet for snowmobilers or backcountry skiers that Yellowstone is. That may be just as well— you can enjoy some quiet, fun times in the park without the crowds.

WINTER ROAD CONDITIONS   **Teton Park Road** opens to conventional vehicles and RVs around May 1. The **Moose–Wilson Road** opens to vehicles about the same time. Park roads close on November 1 for the winter season. They are open to snowmobilers after mid-December.

SPORTING GOODS & EQUIPMENT RENTALS   Jackson has enough sporting equipment places to keep everyone in Wyoming outfitted. The **Jack Dennis Outdoor Shop** on the south side of Town Square (☎ **307/733-3270**) has all the skis and outdoor clothing you can possibly need. **Teton Mountaineering,** 170 N. Cache (☎ **307/733-3595**), is the equipment shop for the knowledgeable and advanced skier or ice-climber; **Hoback Sports,** 40 S. Millward (☎ **307/733-5335**), is the fast food dispenser of ski shops and has one other location at the Snow King (☎ **307/ 733-5200**). **Skinny Skis,** at 65 W. Deloney off Town Square (☎ **307/733-6094**), is a year-round specialty sports shop and has excellent equipment. For a great supply of seconds (same quality of material as "firsts"), stop at **Moosely Seconds** in Moose (☎ **307/ 733-7176**).

CROSS-COUNTRY SKIING   You can ski flat or steep in Grand Teton; the two things to watch out for are hypothermia and avalanches. As with climbing, know your limitations, and make sure you're properly equipped. Check with local rangers and guides for trails that match your ability. Among your options are the relatively easy **Jenny Lake Trail,** starting at the Taggart Lake Parking Area, about 8 miles of flat and scenic trail that follows Cottonwood Creek. A more difficult ski is the **Taggart Lake-Beaver Creek Loop,** a 3-mile route that has some steep and icy pitches coming back. About 4 miles of the **Moose-Wilson Road**—the back way to Teton Village from Moose—is unplowed in the winter, and is an easy trip through the woods. You can climb the windy unplowed road to the top of **Signal Mountain**—you may encounter snowmobiles—and have some fun skiing down. There is an easy ski trail from the Colter Bay Ranger Station area to **Heron Pond**—about 2.6 miles, with a great view of the Tetons and Jackson Lake. Get a ski trail map from the visitors centers.

Skiers who come to Jackson Hole are usually after the hard, steep stuff at the Jackson Hole Ski Resort, but there's a growing contingent of backcountry telemark skiers, who ski off Teton Pass and out of the ski resort boundaries.

SNOWMOBILING   Snowmobiling is another popular winter option. The main roads in Grand Teton are groomed, providing access to trails in the nearby **Bridger-Teton National Forest,** the area to the immediate east of Grand Teton National Park, and to the **Continental Divide Trail,** which runs 320 miles through the Rockies.

For snowmobile rentals **in Jackson,** contact **Leisure Sports** (☎ **307/733-3040**), **BEST Adventures** (☎ **307/733-4845**), and **Wyoming Adventures** (☎ **800/637-7147**). Snowmobile rentals cost about $110 per day, with an extra charge for a second rider.

During winter, **Flagg Ranch Resort** (see chapter 7) is a base for snowmobiling in the southern reaches of Yellowstone, but given its isolation from the rest of Grand Teton during these months, we don't recommend you consider basing yourself there.

7

Where to Stay & Dine in the Parks

*T*he first, best step you can take in planning a trip to the parks is to carefully examine a park map (see our maps in chapter 3 and in chapter 5). Though the parks, Grand Teton in particular, are small enough that you can get practically anywhere in a day, you'll want to be acquainted with the locations of the park attractions you want to see and their accommodations possibilities. For instance, if you want to see Old Faithful at all different hours of the day and night, or if you want to bike the Lonesome Geyser Trail, try to get a room at the Old Faithful Inn or the new Snow Lodge. If you find big bodies of water soothing, check in at the Lake Hotel or Colter Bay.

Review any excursions you might want to make outside the park, too. You might want to stay near the appropriate entrance, or even get a room in one of the gateway towns.

Keep in mind that the characteristics of the lodgings vary considerably, and request specific information about the type of rooms available before making a reservation. If you are bedding down in one of the historic hotels or cabins in the parks, be aware that they offer fewer modern conveniences than your typical commercial motel.

One final bit of advice: Try to spend at least one night within park boundaries. When the sun dips below the horizon, you will see a summer sky (weather permitting) that sparkles more brightly than in the gateway cities, and you'll hear coyotes and other wildlife. And you will discover that the hours just after daybreak are an ideal time for exploring; paths are empty, animals go about their early morning routines oblivious to visitors, and the silence is deafening.

1 Lodging in Yellowstone National Park

To book a room within Yellowstone, you need to contact **Yellowstone National Park Lodges,** P.O. Box 165, Yellowstone National Park, WY 82190 (☎ **307/344-7311**). Yellowstone accommodations are normally open from early summer to late October.

Yellowstone National Park Lodges' winter season begins in mid-December and runs through mid-March, offering snowmobilers and cross-country skiers accommodations and meals at either Mammoth Hot Springs or Old Faithful Snow Lodge. More exact openings and closings are given in the individual listings below.

It's easier to find a vacant room before June 15 and after September 15. The more popular lodges and campgrounds in the parks are typically fully booked during the peak season, so reservations should be made at least 6 months in advance. But there is no "off-season" in Yellowstone, so don't expect to find reduced rates at any time of the year.

If you want television, air conditioning and other modern amenities typical of American hotels, stay in a gateway town rather than in the park. It's not just that some of the inns are close to a century old, it's a style of management that the park has encouraged. Though some of the park lounges now have televisions, and telephones have been added to many rooms, the park and its concessionaires still provide a more old-fashioned type of vacation. Most of the accommodations do have heat, though in some cases—the cabins at Roosevelt and the tent cabins at Colter Bay—it's a wood stove.

MAMMOTH HOT SPRINGS AREA

5 miles from the Gardiner (north) entrance to Yellowstone.

This area is open year-round, and houses the park headquarters. It's a short drive from the park's north entrance, and you can often find rooms here as it's not a very popular place to stay. Nonetheless, it does have much to offer: the park's best visitor center; colorful, travertine limestone terraces; a historic hotel with one of the park's better restaurants; and a campground.

Mammoth Hot Springs Hotel and Cabins. P.O. Box 165, Yellowstone National Park, WY 82190. ☎ **307/344-7311.** Fax 307/344-7456. www.travelyellowstone.com. 224 units. $48–$83 double; $245 suite; $55–$88 cabin (sleeps up to 4). AE, CB, DC, DISC, MC, V.

Below the steaming, stair-stepping terraces of Mammoth Hot Springs, only 5 miles from the north entrance, is the only hotel open during both summer and winter seasons on the northern side of the park. The peaceful scene here, where elk often graze the strips of lawn around the hotel, is somewhat quickened by the flow of tourists stopping by the park headquarters and stores. The hotel itself is less distinguished than the Lake Hotel or the Old Faithful Inn, but its dormer windows and wood floors are attractive, and the high-ceilinged lobby is comfortable and relatively quiet, particularly the adjacent **Map Room,** with its overstuffed sofas and huge windows. The only high-end accommodations are the suites. Standard rooms and cabins are arranged around three grassy areas, where the resident elk often graze. Rooms offer minimal but apt appointments and various bed arrangements; if you require a tub be sure and request one when you make your reservation; otherwise, you could get a cramped, old-fashioned shower stall. The cabins here are cottage-style buildings, some with private hot tubs and sundecks. A formal dining room and a fast-food restaurant are both located in a separate building; nearby amenities include a medical clinic, grocery store, stables, and a filling station. In the winter, Mammoth is a take-off point for cross-country skiing and visits by tour bus to the wildlife-rich Lamar Valley.

CANYON VILLAGE AREA

40 miles from the West Yellowstone (west) entrance; 38 miles from the Gardiner (north) entrance.

This is one of the busiest areas in the park because the Grand Canyon of the Yellowstone is, like Old Faithful, on everyone's itinerary. Accommodations here are in modestly priced motel units or a large campground, and there are restaurants and coffee shops that fit most palates and pocketbooks, as well as a visitor center, general store, and post office. With the many amenities available here, it doesn't matter that it's 40 miles from the nearest gateway town.

Canyon Lodge and Cabins. In Canyon Village (P.O. Box 165), Yellowstone National Park, WY 82190. ☎ **307/344-7311.** www.travelyellowstone.com. 609 units. $105 double; $51–$101 cabin (sleeps up to 8). AE, CB, DC, DISC, MC, V. Open June 4–Sept 12.

This is one of the newer facilities in the park, but it can't escape the retro-1950s atmosphere of sprawling, crowded Canyon Village. The lodge is a half mile from the Grand Canyon of the Yellowstone and Inspiration Point, so you can leave the car and walk to one of the most popular spots in the park. Completed in 1993, the lodge offers tastefully appointed motel-style accommodations in the three-story building, and in cabins that are scattered throughout the village. You won't find any surprises in the motel units, which have various sleeping configurations designed to accommodate the needs of couples as well as families. The cabins are single-story duplex and fourplex structures with private bathrooms that are among the largest in the park. They're much nicer than their "rustic" counterparts in other centers, but given the sheer number of units involved, this wouldn't be the place to "get away from it all." The newly opened Dunraven Lodge is tasteful and simple and nicely backed up against forest, away from the traffic of the village.

TOWER-ROOSEVELT AREA

23 miles from the Gardiner (north) entrance; 29 miles from the northeast entrance.

This is a throwback to the early days of car-camping in Yellowstone: no big complex of shops and services, and not a lot of amenities either. It feels out of the way and uncrowded, which is worth a lot, and the lodge is well connected to hiking trails and the beautiful corridor of the Lamar Valley and River that runs to the northeast entrance.

Roosevelt Lodge Cabins. P.O. Box 165, Yellowstone National Park, WY 82190. ☎ **307/344-7311** for reservations. 80 cabins (62 without private bathroom, 6 with toilet/sink but no shower). $40–$77 cabin (sleeps up to 4). AE, CB, DC, DISC, MC, V.

This is considered the park's family hideaway, a low-key operation with primitive cabins, horseback rides, and a lodge restaurant that's more like a big ranch house. The bare-bones cabins are called Roughriders, and they're furnished with two simple beds, clean linens, a writing table, and a wood stove. The Frontier cabins are a better option as they have their own bathrooms and showers. The lodge is a rugged but charming stone edifice with a long, deep porch outfitted with rockers so guests can converse with each other, nature, or the squirrels that scurry about. Inside, you'll find a registration desk, a dining area with a massive fireplace—burning gas with fake logs, sadly—and a lounge, also festooned with a fireplace and furnished with overstuffed furniture and a player piano. Stagecoach rides, horseback trips, and Western trail cookouts give this place a cowboy flavor, and it's a less pushy, crowded scene than other park villages.

LAKE VILLAGE AREA

27 miles from the east entrance; 56 miles from the west Yellowstone (west) entrance; 43 miles from the south entrance.

More even than the Old Faithful Inn, this lodge on the lake has the feel of an old-fashioned resort. In addition to providing access to the lake's recreational opportunities and the nearby hiking trails, there are accommodations in a historic hotel, motel and cabin units, and lakeside camping sites. The food at the hotel is as good as any in the park, though low-priced alternatives are in the neighborhood.

Lake Lodge Cabins. On Lake Yellowstone (P.O. Box 165), Yellowstone National Park, WY 82190. ☎ **307/344-7311.** www.travelyellowstone.com. 186 cabins. $48–$101 double. AE, CB, DC, DISC, MC, V. Open June 10–Sept 12.

These cabins surrounding Lake Lodge stand near the lake just around the corner north of the Lake Yellowstone Hotel. The lodge is an old Western longhouse fronted by a porch with rockers that invite visitors to sit and gaze out across the waters. The floors inside the lodge gleam like a gymnasium, which is what the building brings to mind. Two small rock fireplaces contribute the only ambience to the room, which has virtually no seating. The centerpiece is the reception desk, which is located next to an undernourished gift shop. A small bar area and a cafeteria serve drinks and inexpensive meals. Accommodations are in well-preserved, clean, freestanding cabins near a trout stream that threads through a wooded area. The cabins come in two grades: Western cabins provide electric heat, paneled walls, two double beds, and combination bathrooms, while Frontier cabins are smaller and sparsely furnished, with only one double bed each and small shower-only bathrooms. There are nature walks around the lodge, but this is a trout spawning area, so access is usually restricted early in the summer when grizzlies come looking for spawning trout.

✪ **Lake Yellowstone Hotel and Cabins.** On the north side of the lake (P.O. Box 165), Yellowstone National Park, WY 82190. ☎ **307/344-7311.** www.travelyellowstone.com. 297 units. $96–$143 double; $77 cabin (sleeps up to 4); $373 parlor suite. AE, CB, DC, DISC, MC, V. Open May 14–Oct 3.

The ionic columns, dormer windows, and deep porticos of this yellow frame building will carry you back to the Victorian era, an illusion only strengthened when you find yourself sipping a drink in the huge sunroom overlooking the lake while someone plays the piano. The facility was completely restored in the early 1990s, and its better rooms are the park's most comfortable and roomiest. Accommodations are in three- and four-story wings in the hotel, in a motel-style annex, and in cabins. The upper-end rooms here have stenciled walls and traditional spreads on one queen or two double beds. The freestanding cabins, a desirable low-priced alternative, are decorated with knotty-pine paneling and furnished with double beds and a writing table. *Note:* If you take a cabin, request a single rather than a duplex, since walls are paper thin.

Only the bar here leaves something to be desired: Guests are served from what looks like a temporary set-up by the dining room entrance. The dining room has rattan furniture and is big enough to feed the busloads that arrive at mealtimes. A take-out delicatessen on the first floor serves ordinary finger food at a snail's pace.

GRANT VILLAGE AREA

22 miles from the south entrance; 47 miles from the West Yellowstone (west) entrance.

Though it's the nearest "village" to the south entrance, this fairly recent addition lacks character. Nevertheless, it's by the south end of beautiful Lake Yellowstone and has a good visitors center and access to various sights.

Grant Village. On the West Thumb of Yellowstone Lake (P.O. Box 165), Yellowstone National Park, WY 82190. ☎ **307/344-7311.** www. travelyellowstone.com. 300 units. $83–$96 double. AE, CB, DC, DISC, MC, V. Open May 28–Oct 3.

The southernmost of the major overnight accommodations in the park, Grant Village was completed in 1984 and is one of the more contemporary choices in Yellowstone. It hasn't got a lot of life, architecturally: The lodge consists of six ordinary looking, motel-type two-story chalets set back from the water's edge, as well as a reception area and gift shop that are in a separate building near the village entrance. Rooms are tastefully furnished, most outfitted with light wood furniture, track lighting, electric heat, and laminate counters. Nicer (and more expensive) rooms have lake views, mullioned windows, and one queen or one or two double beds. Midrange rooms are set farther back from the lake and overlook drab grounds that seem as if construction was completed only recently. Grant Village is isolated from other park centers, so you're likely to drink in its tiny lounge and eat in one of its two restaurants overlooking the lake. Other guest services located here include a laundry facility, service station, and convenience store.

OLD FAITHFUL AREA

30 miles from the West Yellowstone (west) entrance; 39 miles from the south entrance.

Ignore the crowds. Block out the frenzied pace. At the Old Faithful area you'll spend a night in the midst of the most famous geyser basin in the world. You'll also have more choices of rooms, restaurants, and services—including a visitor center, gas station, and Hamilton store—than anywhere else in the park. From a logistical point of view, you'll have excellent access to attractions in every direction.

✪ **Old Faithful Inn.** P.O. Box 165, Yellowstone National Park, WY 82190. ☎ **307/344-7311.** Fax 307/344-7456. www.travelyellowstone.com. 359 units (more than half with private bathroom). $52–$242 double; $325 suite. AE, CB, DC, DISC, MC, V. Open May 1–Oct 17.

When Robert Ringer designed the Old Faithful Inn almost a century ago, he found the perfect blend of rustic and regal, a grand building that blends beautifully with the native timbers and rock. There are three hotels within viewing distance of the geyser, including a very nice new one, but this is the crown jewel of Yellowstone's man-made wonders. Seven stories tall with dormers peaking from a shingled, steep-sloping roof, it looks like a lodgepole jungle gym inside—and indeed, you can climb the stairs to its internal balconies, and, with permission, ascend to a widows' walk and crows' nest. Only 30 miles from the west entrance and 40 miles from the south entrance, this is the first place visitors think of when they want a bed for the night, so make reservations far ahead during the busy summer months. The dining room is warmed on cool evenings by a fieldstone fireplace. Like other park properties, this lobby also houses a busy fast-food outlet that serves light meals, and there is a bar, and a gift shop. Guest rooms are in the main building, and in wings that flank the main lodge. Original rooms are well appointed with conservative fabrics and park-theme art, but may not have private bathrooms; the wing rooms offer better facilities and more privacy.

Old Faithful Lodge Cabins. P.O. Box 165, Yellowstone National Park, WY 82190. ☎ **307/344-7311.** www.travelyellowstone.com. 122 cabins (40 without private bathroom). $32–$58 double. AE, CB, DC, DISC, MC, V. Open May 21–Sept 19.

The cabins that once littered the landscape around the world's most famous geyser were hauled off years ago, but there are still some leftovers in the area, and they offer an inexpensive lodging option. Rent one of the budget cabins, which are just slightly less flimsy than tents, and you'll get basic beds and sinks, and a sense of what it was like to visit Yellowstone half a century ago. Showers and rest rooms are a short walk away. Frontier Cabins are the best units, adding a private bathroom to other amenities. You're within a short walk of a cafeteria and a snack bar. The lodge is perhaps the busiest spot in the geyser area, featuring several snack shops and a huge cafeteria dishing up varied fast food. Just off the lobby is one of the largest gift shops in the park and an old gymnasium that occasionally hosts square dancing and movies.

Camping in Yellowstone **141**

Old Faithful Snow Lodge and Cabins. Old Faithful, P.O. Box 165, Yellowstone National Park, WY 82190. ☎ **307/344-7311.** Fax 307/344-7456. www.travelyellowstone.com. 134 units. $121 double; $101 cabin. AE, CB, DC, DISC, MC, V.

If your last visit to Yellowstone included a stay at the Old Faithful Snow Lodge, put the memory out of your mind. The old dormitory-style lodge was torn down in 1998, and this new, award-winning place could aptly be called the *New* Faithful Snow Lodge. The big beam construction and high ceiling in the lobby echo the Old Faithful Inn, and a copper-lined balcony curves above the common area, where guests can relax in wicker furniture. The rooms are spacious and comfortable (still no TVs!), and a spacious dining room shares a two-sided fireplace with a lounge.

2 Camping in Yellowstone

Camping at Yellowstone's 12 developed campgrounds can be a happy affair, with the stars overhead, the scent of pine, and friendly neighbors from all over the world. The campgrounds are spaced throughout the park.

For those who carry their tents on their backs and want no neighbors other than their hiking buddies, there's plenty of room out there. Some areas in the Yellowstone backcountry are delicate habitat—the southeast arm of Yellowstone Lake is an example—and visitors must camp in designated areas for a limited time only. This in no way diminishes the sense of being in a true wilderness. Check with the **Yellowstone Backcountry Office** (☎ 307/ 344-2160) for rules, reservations, and advice.

GETTING A CAMPSITE The National Park Service has shifted management of five major campgrounds to Yellowstone National Park Lodges, which means, predictably, higher fees, but also allows you to make reservations ahead of arrival. The other seven campgrounds still managed by the park are available only on a first-come, first-served basis. These lower cost campgrounds are at Indian Creek, Lewis Lake, Mammoth, Norris, Pebble Creek, Slough Creek, and Tower Fall. I happen to like the Norris campground, and Slough Creek, which tends to be available when others are full. Check with rangers about campsite availability when you enter the park; generally, you need to arrive early to get a site—some campgrounds are fill up as early as 8am.

Yellowstone National Park Lodges operates larger, busier campgrounds at Bridge Bay, Canyon, Grant Village, Madison, and

Fishing Bridge. Some like Bridge Bay are rather barren of trees unless you get a site on the fringes. Opening dates (see chart below) vary with weather and road conditions so it's wise to double-check availability of specific camping areas. Reservations can be made by calling ☎ **307/344-7311,** or by writing Yellowstone National Park Lodges, P.O. Box 165, Yellowstone National Park, WY 82190.

REGULATIONS　You can only set up your tent in designated areas and stays are limited to 14 days between June 15 and Labor Day, and to 30 days the rest of the year, except at Fishing Bridge, where there is no limit. Check-out times for all campgrounds is 10am. Quiet hours are strictly enforced between the hours of 8pm and 8am. No generators or loud music are allowed during these hours.

THE CAMPGROUNDS　For exact information on prices, opening dates, and amenities, please refer to the chart, "Amenities for Each Campground: Yellowstone National Park," in this section.

These are campgrounds, not motels, so the **amenities** are sparse, but some have laundry facilities, showers, bathrooms and potable water, which are luxuries to campers who've experienced the world's more primitive campgrounds.

In the northeast area of the park, the **Tower Fall campground** is near a convenience store, restaurant, and gas station at Tower Lodge, 19 miles north of Canyon Village and 18 miles east of Mammoth. **Slough Creek campground** is in a remote section of the Lamar Valley near the northeast entrance; the good news is there are fewer people, good fishing, and the possibility of wolf sightings; the bad news is that rest room facilities are in pit toilets.

Canyon campground is the busiest in the park, so generally requires an early check in. Sites are assigned by rangers, and are in a heavily wooded area; the store, restaurants, visitor center, and laundry at Canyon Center are nearby.

Because it's in an area of spring bear activity, attempts have been made over the years to close the RV park at **Fishing Bridge.** It's still open, but sometimes its opening is delayed, and only hard-sided camping vehicles are allowed here.

Bridge Bay is located near the shores of Yellowstone Lake, so you get tremendous views, especially at sunrise and sunset. Unfortunately, though surrounded by the forest, the area has been clear cut, so there's no privacy except around the perimeter. It's close to boat-launching facilities and the boat rental operation.

Amenities for Each Campground: Yellowstone National Park

Campground	Total Sites	RV Hookups	Dump Station	Toilets	Drinking Water	Showers	Fire Pits/Grills	Laundry	Public Phone	Reserve	Fees	Open
Inside the Park												
Bridge Bay*	430	No	Yes	Yes	Yes	No	Yes	No	Yes	Yes	$15	Late May–Sept
Canyon*	272	No	Yes	Yes	Yes	Yes	Yes	Yes	Yes	Yes	$15	June–Sept
Fishing Bridge* Day	341	Yes	Yes	Yes	Yes	Yes	Yes	Yes	Yes	Yes	$26	Late May–Labor
Grant Village*	425	No	Yes	Yes	Yes	Yes	Yes	Yes	Yes	Yes	$15	Late May–Sept
Indian Creek	75	No	No	Yes	Yes	No	Yes	No	No	Yes	$10	June–Sept
Lewis Lake	85	No	No	Yes	Yes	No	Yes	No	No	No	$10	Mid-June–Nov
Madison*	280	No	Yes	Yes	Yes	No	Yes	No	Yes	Yes	$15	Late May–Nov
Mammoth	85	No	No	Yes	Yes	No	Yes	No	Yes	No	$12	Year-round
Norris	116	No	No	Yes	Yes	No	Yes	No	Yes	No	$12	Mid-May–Sept
Pebble Creek	36	No	No	Yes	Yes	No	Yes	No	No	No	$10	Mid-June–Sept
Slough Creek	29	No	No	Yes	Yes	No	Yes	No	No	No	$15	Late May–Nov
Tower Fall	32	No	No	Yes	Yes	No	Yes	No	No	No	$10	Mid-May–Late Sept
Near the Park												
Bakers Hole	72	No	No	Yes	Yes	No	Yes	No	Yes	Yes	$10	Late May–Sept
Lonesomehurst	26	No	No	Yes	Yes	No	Yes	No	No	Yes	$10	Late May–Sept
Rainbow Point	85	No	No	Yes	Yes	No	Yes	No	Yes	Yes	$10	Late May–Sept

*Reserve through Yellowstone National Park Lodges.

Fishing Bridge, Bakers Hole, and Rainbow Point accept hard-sided vehicles only.

Madison is in a wooded area just south of the river, a popular spot with good access to fishing and hiking. **Norris** is one of the park's better camping areas, with attractive, wooded locations in the heart of the park, close to wildlife activity and the Gibbon River. These camp areas seem less like outdoor motels than the big camp-grounds on the park's east side.

3   Camping Near Yellowstone

There are three National Forest Service campgrounds in the **West Yellowstone** area, all located in the Gallatin National Forest (see "Amenities for Each Campground: Yellowstone National Park" in the previous section for amenities, prices, and opening dates). Bakers Hole and Rainbow Point accommodate RVs only; Lonesome-hurst accommodates RVs and tent campers. They are all convenient to the park entrance at West Yellowstone. For reservations, call ☎ **800/280-2267. Bakers Hole,** just 3 miles north of West Yellowstone on U.S. 191, is popular and has only 72 sites, so reserve early. Only RVs are accepted, but there are no hookups. **Lonesomehurst,** 8 miles west of the park on U.S. 20, then 4 miles north on Hebgen Lake Road, is only one-third the size of Bakers Hole and fills up quickly in summer, so reservations are also strongly ad-vised. It has tent and RV sites. **Rainbow Point** is reached by driving 5 miles north of West Yellowstone on U.S. 191, then 3 miles west on Forest Service Road 610, then north for 2 miles on Forest Service Road 6954. It accommodates only RVs, but there are no hookups.

In addition, there are a few RV parks in the town of West Yellowstone. While these parks have full utility hookups and are designed for hard-sized vehicles, if there's space left over and you're willing to pay the price for a utility hookup that you won't be able to fully utilize, an owner of an RV park may allow you to pitch your tent. **The Hideaway RV Campground,** at the corner of Gibbon Street and Electric Avenue (☎ **406/646-9049**), has cable TV hook-ups, for those who simply cannot bear to live without their favor-ite TV programs, and is open May through October. **The Yellowstone Park KOA** (☎ **406/646-7606**) is 6 miles west on U.S. 20 and offers a pool, a hot tub, and a game room for kids. It stays open May through September.

4   Dining in Yellowstone

Maybe I'm just paranoid about corporate concessionaires, but I'm sensing a certain sameness creeping into the menus at the restaurants in Yellowstone's major hotels. The dining rooms at Mammoth Hot Springs Hotel, Old Faithful Inn, and Lake Yellowstone Hotel each have a distinctive ambience, but the cuisine seems less distinguishable than it did a few years ago. Nevertheless, you should plan a visit to one or more of these big halls, the prices are decent, the atmosphere is festive and just elegant enough that you might want to dress up a bit for dinner—put on socks perhaps, and a shirt with a collar. Reservations are recommended, but not required.

If you're not up for restaurant dining, but you're tired of using your camp stove, there is counter-style fast-food service at the **Hamilton General Stores** and snack shops and cafeterias in the villages at Canyon, Mammoth, Grant Village, the Yellowstone Lake Lodge, and at Old Faithful.

MAMMOTH HOT SPRINGS

You'll find the **Terrace Grille** at the opposite end of the building in which Mammoth Hot Springs Hotel Dining Room is located. Here the typical restaurant fare is served in a less formal and less pricey dining room, but no reservations can be made.

Mammoth Hot Springs Hotel. At Mammoth Hot Springs. ☎ **307/344-7901.** www.travelyellowstone.com. Dinner reservations required. Breakfast $2–$6; lunch $6–$9; dinner $8–$21. AE, DC, DISC, MC, V. Summer daily 6:30–10am, 11:30am–2pm, and 5:30–10pm. STEAK/SEAFOOD.

At Mammoth, the breakfast buffet features scrambled eggs, French toast, and muffins. Delicious omelettes are served with home fries and toast. The midday repast is an array of sandwiches, including teriyaki chicken breast, a grilled vegetarian sandwich, and grilled German bratwurst. Dinner is a bit more substantial, and bears a predictable similarity to its counterparts at other park hotels. The specialty is shrimp and scallops served over linguine and topped with a curry sauce.

CANYON VILLAGE AREA

Like restaurants in the other park centers, the eating options at Canyon Village consist of three choices: a casual, soda fountain–style restaurant, a fast-food cafeteria, and a conventional dining room.

The **Canyon Glacier Pit Snack Bar,** which is operated by Hamilton Stores, is in the same building as the convenience store and souvenir shop. Seating is on stools in the fashion of a '50s soda fountain; expect a wait of up to 30 minutes during peak hours. Breakfast consists of egg dishes, lunch is soup and sandwiches, and dinner is traditional Western food. Hours are daily 6:30am to 10pm from May 18 to September 24.

The **Canyon Lodge Cafeteria** is a fast-food alternative managed by Yellowstone National Park Lodges and is across the parking lot in the Canyon Lodge area. Hours are the same as at the snack bar, and the menu bears some striking similarities—but you may get through the cafeteria line faster than you would get a stool at the soda fountain. The cafeteria is open from June 1 to September 8.

Canyon Lodge Dining Room. Canyon Village. ☎ 307/344-7901. Reservations required. Breakfast $2–$6; lunch $5–$7; dinner $12–$17. Open daily June to mid-Sept 6:30–10:30am, 11:30am–2pm, and 5:30–10pm. AC, DC, DISC, MC, V. STEAK/SEAFOOD

The spacious dining area has the same 1950s feel that infects most of Canyon Village, and when it fills up, it's noisy. The salad bar is long and loaded, but otherwise the fare is similar to that at the other park restaurants: steak, chicken, fish and pasta. The crowds can be large, but there is a relaxed and unhurried feel to the place that you don't find at some of the park's other busy points. The dining room is kid friendly.

TOWER-ROOSEVELT AREA

Roosevelt Lodge. At Tower Junction. ☎ **307/344-7901.** www. travelyellowstone.com. Reservations recommended. Breakfast $4–$7; lunch $6–$12; dinner $8–$21. AE, CB, DC, DISC, MC, V. Summer daily 7am–10am, 11:30am–3pm, and 5–9pm. STEAK/SEAFOOD.

This is supposed to be the cowboy alternative to the fancier cuisine served at the bigger park hotels, but it's really not that special. Like the aging cabins that take you back to the early days of auto camping, Roosevelt's dining area is simple and sparse, a collection of tables that takes up one side of the lodge's big lobby. They boast that Roosevelt beans are prepared locally, but the food is mostly bland and tastes like the variety that grows in large tin cans. You choose from a short list of entrees and select three side dishes. Better idea: Join Roosevelt's Old West Dinner Cookout, and ride by horse or wagon through the Pleasant Valley to a chuck wagon dinner that includes cornbread, steak, watermelon, those famous beans, and apple crisp. It costs $39 to $50 for an adult, depending on the route of your horseback ride, or $32 if you go by wagon. Children pay less.

YELLOWSTONE LAKE

For the eat-on-the-run traveler, a **deli** in the Lake Yellowstone Hotel serves lighter fare in an area that is slightly larger than a broom closet from 11am to 9pm. Just down the road, the **Hamilton store** offers three meals in a section of the store that is shared with tourist items; the best bet here is breakfast or a burger. It's open from 7am to 9pm. Inexpensive meals are served cafeteria-style at the **Yellowstone Lake Lodge and Cabins** from 7am to 8pm. All hours listed here are from mid-May to early October.

✪ **Lake Yellowstone Hotel.** On the north side of the lake. ☎ **307/ 344-7901.** www.travelyellowstone.com. Dinner reservations required. Breakfast $4–$6; lunch $5–$7; dinner $8–$21. AE, DC, DISC, MC, V. Open daily mid-May to early Oct 6:30–10am, 11:30am–2:30pm, and 5:30–10pm. PASTA/STEAK/ SEAFOOD.

This is one of most pleasant places to eat in Yellowstone, with a view of the lake stretching south from a big, high-ceilinged dining room that doesn't feel crowded even when it's full. Once again, Yellowstone National Park Lodges serves you. Among the variations here are a generous breakfast buffet with alternatives including a tasty traditional country pan breakfast of bacon, eggs, and home fries; a Southwestern pan breakfast seasoned with chiles and salsa; and huevos rancheros. There's also a wide selection of fresh fruit, juices, pastries, and cereals. The dinner menu is equally inviting. Appetizers include duck quesadillas and spanikopitas (a Greek pastry stuffed with spinach and cheese), while entrees include breast of duck, fettuccine with smoked salmon, and several beef dishes.

GRANT VILLAGE

The casual choice here is the **Lake House,** footsteps away from the Grant Village restaurant. It specializes in less expensive fish entrees, as well as burgers and beer. Meals are served from 5:30 to 9pm late May to early October. No reservations.

Grant Village. At Grant Village. ☎ **307/344-7901.** www.travelyellowstone. com. Dinner reservations required. Open June–Sept. Breakfast $4–$6; lunch $6– $9; dinner $11–$21. AE, CB, DISC, MC, V. Summer daily 6:30–10am, 11:30am– 2:30pm, and 5:30–10pm. STEAK/SEAFOOD.

Breakfast and lunch at the Grant Village restaurant are much like the other restaurants in the park, though the chef occasionally surprises diners with interesting items that stray from the norm. Lunch may include panfried trout covered with toasted pecans and lemon butter, Wyoming Cheese steak, and a one-third-pound gourmet burger. The dinner menu ranges from honey-lemon chicken to swordfish with lemon dill butter to blackened prime rib. Quality and ambience here are comparable to the better dining rooms at the major park hotels.

OLD FAITHFUL AREA

Choices abound here. For quick and inexpensive, there is the **Old Faithful Inn** cafeteria serving lunch and dinner in a fast-food environment that fits the mood of a crowd on the move; an ice-cream stand in the lobby is your best choice for dessert. The **Hamilton Store** also has a lunch counter.

✪ **Old Faithful Inn.** Near Old Faithful. ☎ **307/545-4999.** Dinner reservations required. Breakfast buffet $7; lunch $5–$9; dinner $9–$22. AE, DC, DISC, MC, V. Open daily May–mid-Oct 6:30–10am, 11:30am–2:30pm, and 5–10pm. STEAK/SEAFOOD.

There's nothing wrong with the food here, but it pales beside, or beneath, the gnarled log architecture of this distinguished historic inn. Once again, this is Yellowstone National Park Lodges fare, similar to other park restaurants. Breakfast is strictly buffet, but there's a lot to choose from. The dinner menu is fairly long, with four cuts of prime rib, fish dishes, roasted Cornish game hen, and pastas including a fettuccini with artichoke hearts, mushrooms, and olives. They also serve a tasty broiled Mexican Caesar salad. Just to enjoy the inn's ambience a bit longer, you should have at least one dinner here.

Old Faithful Snow Lodge. Near Old Faithful (east of Inn). ☎ **307/344-7901.** No reservations. Breakfast $4–$7; lunch $5–$9; dinner $9–$16. AE, DC, DISC, MC, V. Open May to mid-Oct and mid-Dec to mid-Mar daily 6:30 to 10am, 11:30am to 2:30pm, and 5 to 10pm. STEAK/SEAFOOD.

In the well-designed new snow lodge, this spacious restaurant provides an alternative to the Old Faithful Inn dining room. It's a little quieter, a little less expensive, and a little less formal, which is reflected in a menu heavy on burgers and salads. It still has some Yellowstone National Park Lodges stalwarts on the menu—teriyaki chicken and London broil—and, again in contrast to the Inn, there is a breakfast menu that goes beyond buffet. It's a huge improvement over the cramped restaurant of the old Snow Lodge; if you come in winter, check out the cozy lounge connected by a two-sided fireplace.

5 Lodging in Grand Teton National Park

The three concessionaires that operate lodgings within Grand Teton provide a range of accommodations that can suit any wallet or taste, but not every schedule. We say fairly often in this guide that the shoulder seasons of fall and spring are the best times to have the parks to yourself, but these are not the easiest times to find a room at the inn. If you come in early May, you'll find padlocks on the doors everywhere but at Flagg Ranch, which technically isn't in Grand Teton anyway, but on the John D. Rockefeller Jr. Memorial Parkway. Likewise by mid-October, you'll be bunking in Jackson.

You can get information about or make reservations for Jackson Lake Lodge, Jenny Lake Lodge, and Colter Bay Village through the **Grand Teton Lodge Company,** Box 240, Moran, WY 83013 (☎ **307/543-2811;** www.gtlc.com). For Signal Mountain Lodge, contact **Signal Mountain Lodge Co.,** Box 50, Moran, WY 83013 (☎ **307/543-2831;** www.signalmtnlodge.com). Reservations at **Flagg Ranch** are made though Flagg Ranch, Box 187, Moran, WY 83013 (☎ **800/443-2311**).

Rooms in Grand Teton National Park properties have telephones, but no televisions or air-conditioning. You'll find televisions in the lounge areas at the Jackson Lodge, Signal Mountain Resort, and Flagg Ranch.

FLAGG RANCH VILLAGE AREA

2 miles from the south entrance to Yellowstone; 5 miles from the northern boundary of Grand Teton.

Like Grant Village in Yellowstone, Flagg Ranch offers travelers the full gamut of services: cabins, tent and RV sites, an above-average restaurant, and a gas station. It's also a popular jumping-off spot for snowmobilers during winter months. However, since it's situated in a stand of pines in the middle of nowhere, there's not much to do in the immediate vicinity except watch the Snake River roll by.

Flagg Ranch Resort. P.O. Box 187, Moran, WY 83013. ☎ **800/443-2311** or 307/543-2861. www.flaggranch.com. 92 cabins, 171 RV sites. TEL. $131 cabin (sleeps up to 4). Lower rates off-season. AE, DISC, MC, V.

A few years ago this resort just outside Yellowstone National Park was showing its age—the sort of place a hunter would rent a drafty room to collapse in after a few days in the woods. Not anymore: It's all fixed up, transformed into an all-seasons resort on the Snake River with log-and-luxury ambience. The newest accommodations are duplex and fourplex log cabins constructed in 1994 that feature king-size beds, spacious sitting areas with writing desks and chests of drawers, wall-to-wall carpeting, and bathrooms with tub-shower combinations and separate vanities.

The only livestock on the ranch these days are the herds of snow-mobiles that gather here in the winter to warm up before entering Yellowstone. In the summer, there are float trips, horseback rides, and excellent fishing in Polecat Creek or the Snake River. The new lodge is a locus of activity, with its double sided fireplace, fancy dining room, gift shop, espresso bar and pub with large-screen television, convenience store, and gas station. A campground and RV facility are situated on the grounds amid a stand of pine trees.

COLTER BAY VILLAGE AREA

11 miles from the park's northern boundary; 10 miles from the Moran (east) entrance.

The village provides an excellent base of operations for visitors who want to hike or enjoy the lake. It encompasses two restaurants, one snack bar, a visitor center, amphitheater, museum, general store, post office, sporting-goods shop, and laundry facilities. Scenic cruises and boat rentals can be arranged at the marina. The village operates from mid-May to late September.

✪ **Colter Bay Village.** P.O. Box 240, Moran, WY 83013. ☎ **800/628-9988** or 307/543-2855. www.gtlc.com. 166 units. $31–$116 log cabin; $30 tent cabin. AE, DC, MC, V. Open mid-May to late Sept.

You might call this the people's resort of Grand Teton. Its simpler lodgings, lower prices, and a lively, inclusive atmosphere seem particularly suited to families. Situated on the eastern shore of Jackson Lake, 35 miles north of Jackson, Colter Bay Village is a full-fledged recreation center. Guest accommodations are in roughly built log cabins perched on a wooded hillside; they are clean and simply furnished with area rugs on tile floors, beamed ceilings, and copies of pioneer furnishings—chests, oval mirrors, and extralong bedsteads with painted headboards. The simple bathrooms have stall showers, and some singles share bathrooms. If you want to take a trip back to the early days of American auto-travel, when car-camping involved unwieldy canvas tents on slabs by the roadside, you can spend an inexpensive night in "tent cabins." Bring your sleeping bags and sleep on squeaky bunks, and stop that giggling because there's another tent nearby with equally thin walls and small children trying to settle down. The shared shower/bathroom is just down the road. There's also an RV/trailer park.

Jackson Lake Lodge. P.O. Box 240, Moran, WY 83013. ☎ **800/628-9988** or 307/543-2811. www.gtlc.com. 385 units. TEL. $110–$190 double; $135–$198 cottage (sleeps up to 5); $355–$500 suite (sleeps up to 4). AE, DC, MC, V. Open mid-May to mid-Oct.

Much the way Old Faithful Inn or the Lake Hotel capture historic eras of Yellowstone tourism, Jackson Lake Lodge epitomizes the architectural milieu of the period when Grand Teton became a park. Unfortunately, that era was the 1950s, an era of right angles, flat roofs and big windows. Still, the lodge is popular, particularly for its wonderful setting overlooking Willow Flats, the lake in the distance, and towering over it, without a stick in the way, the Grand Teton and Mount Moran. You don't even have to go outside to see this impressive view—the lobby has 60-foot tall windows. Add to that a good restaurant, comfortable rooms, and easy access from Jackson, only 35 miles away. Guest rooms are in the three-story main lodge and in cottages scattered about the property, some of which have large balconies and mountain views. Lodge rooms are spacious and cheery, and most offer double beds, electric heat, and newly tiled bathrooms.

There is a large outdoor swimming pool, a cocktail lounge, full-course dining in the Mural Room, and lighter fare at the Pioneer Grill. Upscale shops selling Western clothing and jewelry are on the main level. At the tour desk you can arrange just about anything, from rafting to riding horses to taking a bus tour up to Yellowstone.

SIGNAL MOUNTAIN AREA

15 miles from the north entrance; 9 miles from the Moran (east) entrance.

Signal Mountain Lodge. P.O. Box 50, Moran, WY 83013. ☎ **307/543-2831.** www.signalmtnlodge.com. 80 units (each sleeps up to 6). TEL. $85–$180 double. AE, DISC, MC, V. Open May–Oct.

Signal Mountain has a different feel, and different owners, from the other lodgings in Grand Teton, adding to the sense that any place you choose to stay in this park is going to give you a fairly unique atmosphere. What they all have in common is the Teton view, and this lodge, located right on the banks of Jackson Lake, may have the best. For one, it's got lakefront retreats that you can really inhabit, with stoves, refrigerators, and fold-out sofa beds for the kids. Other accommodations, mostly free-standing cabins, come in a variety of flavors, from motel-style rooms in four-unit buildings set amid the trees to family bungalows with decks, some enjoying beach frontage. There's also a full-size house large enough for a family reunion. The carpeted cabins feature handmade pine furniture, electric heat, covered porches, and tiled bathrooms; some have fireplaces.

The recently refurbished registration building has a small TV viewing area, a gift shop, and outdoor seating on a deck overlooking the lake. A restaurant and coffee shop that serve average food share a separate building with a small lounge and gift shop. Recreational options include cycling, rafting, waterskiing, and fishing, but note that boat rentals are expensive here. A convenience store and gas station are on the property.

JENNY LAKE AREA

28 miles from the northern boundary; 17 miles from the Moran (east) entrance; 16 miles from the Moose entrance.

Jenny Lake Lodge. Box 240, Moran, WY 83013. ☎ **800/628-9988** or 307/ 543-3300. www.gtlc.com. 37 units. $380 double; $515–$535 suite. Rates include breakfast and dinner and activities. AE, DC, MC, V. Open June to mid-Oct.

Though it's located 20 miles from Jackson Airport, this small resort prides itself on its seclusion and tranquility. It also has an award-winning restaurant and the individual attention that you expect at these kinds of prices. The Lodge is a hybrid of mountain lake resort and dude ranch, with activities like horseback- and bike-riding. Accommodations are in rustic, pitched-roof log cabins fronted by a long, pillared porch. Each cabin has been named for a resident flower and most have forest views, some can see the lake. The luxurious interiors contain bright braided rugs, dark wood floors, beamed ceilings, log furniture with cowhide upholstery, and tiled combination bathrooms. Rooms have one queen, one king, or two double beds. No televisions, of course.

The lodge functions primarily as a dining establishment. Sofas are clustered around a fireplace to create a beautifully cozy sitting area, and the dining room is tastefully decorated with original works created by local artists; a classical guitarist often accompanies the outstanding gourmet meals. Catering to an older, affluent clientele, the style here is an odd mixture of peaceful rusticity and occasional reminders of class and formality (diner jackets are "appreciated").

6 Camping in Grand Teton

Since Grand Teton is so much smaller than its counterpart to the north, distances between campgrounds are reduced substantially. As a consequence, selecting a site in one of the five National Park Service campgrounds within the park becomes a matter of preference (rather than geography) and availability. Five campgrounds in Grand Teton are operated by the National Park Service; these are at Gros Ventre, Jenny Lake, Signal Mountain, Colter Bay, and Lizard Creek. Two other campgrounds, the Colter Bay Trailer Village and the Flagg Ranch campground, are operated by park concessionaires and are the only campgrounds with RV hookups (Flagg Ranch has sites suitable for RVs as well as tents, while the Colter Bay Trailer Village is only for RVs). The only sites in the park where RVs are not allowed are those at Jenny Lake, which has a tent-only campground.

GETTING A CAMPSITE   Campgrounds operate on a first-come, first-served basis, but reservations are available to groups of 10 or more by writing **Campground Reservations,** Grand Teton National Park, Moose, WY 83012. You can get recorded information on site availability by calling (☎ **307/739-3603**). Reservations for **trailer sites** at Colter Bay campground may be made by contacting the **Grand Teton Lodge Co.,** P.O. Box 240, Moran, WY 83013 (☎ **307/543-2855**). Additionally, **Grand Teton Campground** is a concessionaire-operated campground located in the **Flagg Ranch** complex on the John D. Rockefeller, Jr., Memorial Parkway. The area has 93 sites with utility hookups, 74 tent sites, showers, and launderette. For reservations, contact Flagg Ranch, P.O. Box 187, Moran, WY 83013 (☎ **800/443-2311**).

THE CAMPGROUNDS   For exact information on prices, opening dates, and amenities, please refer to the chart, "Amenities for Each Campground: Grand Teton National Park," in this section. Note that where campgrounds accommodate RVs, they are not given a separate section from tent-campers.

All the park-run campgrounds but Jenny Lake can accommodate tents, RVs, and trailers, but there are no utility hookups at any of them. **Jenny Lake Campground,** a tents-only area, is situated in a quiet, wooded area near the lake. You have to be here first thing in the morning to get a site.

The largest campground, **Gros Ventre,** is the last to fill, if it fills at all—probably because it's located on the east side of the park, a few miles from Kelly on the Gros Ventre River Road. If you arrive late in the day and you have no place to stay, go here first.

✪ **Signal Mountain Campground,** with views of the lake and access to the beach, is another popular spot that fills first thing in the morning. It overlooks Jackson Lake and Mt. Moran, as well as a pleasant picnic and boat launch. There's a store and service station nearby.

Colter Bay Campground and Trailer Village has access to the lake but is far enough from the hubbub of the village to offer a modicum of solitude; spaces are usually gone by noon.

Lizard Creek Campground, at the north end of Grand Teton National Park near Jackson Lake, offers an aesthetically pleasing wooded area near the lake with views of the Tetons, bird-watching, and fishing (and mosquitoes; bring your repellent). It's only 8 miles from facilities at Colter Bay and its sites fill by 2pm.

Amenities for Each Campground: Grand Teton National Park

Campground	Total Sites	RV Hookups	Dump Station	Toilets	Drinking Water	Showers	Fire Pits/ Grills	Laundry	Public Phone	Reserve	Fees	Open
Inside the Park												
Colter Bay	350	No	Yes	Yes	Yes	Yes	Yes	Yes	Yes	No	$12	Mid-May–Late Sept
Colter Bay Trailer Village	112	Yes	Yes	Yes	Yes	No	Yes	Yes	Yes	Yes	$29	Mid-May–Late Sept
Gros Ventre	360	No	Yes	Yes	Yes	No	Yes	No	Yes	No	$12	Early May–Oct
Jenny Lake*	49	No	No	Yes	Yes	No	Yes	No	Yes	No	$12	Late May–Late Sept
Lizard Creek	60	No	No	Yes	Yes	No	Yes	No	Yes	No	$12	Early Jun–Early Sept
Signal Mountain	86	No	Yes	Yes	Yes	No	Yes	No	Yes	No	$12	Mid-May–Oct
Near the Park												
Flagg Ranch	165	Yes	Yes	Yes	Yes	Yes	Yes	Yes	Yes	Yes	$19/$25	Mid-May–Late Sept
Snake River Park KOA	80	Yes	Yes	Yes	Yes	Yes	Yes	Yes	Yes	Yes	$27/$35	Mid-Apr–Mid-Oct
Teton Village KOA	148	Yes	Yes	Yes	Yes	Yes	Yes	Yes	Yes	Yes	$26/$343	May–Mid-Oct
Wagon Wheel	12	Yes	Yes	Yes	Yes	Yes	Yes	Yes	Yes	Yes	$15	Mar–Oct

*Tents only are allowed here

7 Camping Near Grand Teton

There are several places to park the RV or pitch a tent around Jackson Hole, and a few of them are reasonably priced and not too far away from the park. Most charge around $20 per night, though prices seem to change at the drop of a hat, just like local motel prices. Some of your best bets are either out of Jackson or way out of Jackson. See the chart "Amenities for Each Campground: Grand Teton National Park" for amenities, prices, and opening dates.

In Jackson, the **Wagon Wheel Campground** (☎ 307/733-4588) is about 5 blocks north of Town Square at the Wagon Wheel Motel. The **Teton Village KOA** (☎ 307/733-5354) is 12 miles northwest of Jackson. Also away from the crowds, the **Snake River Park KOA Campground** is on U.S. 89, 10 miles south of town (☎ 307/733-7078).

8 Dining in Grand Teton

Just as in Yellowstone, there are not enough places at the table to serve all the travelers in Grand Teton during the busiest meal times of July and August. But there is more variety here, from fast food to bar food to a more varied choice of gourmet meals than you'll find up north. Since there is more than one concessionaire operating the full-service dining rooms, there is no central number for making reservations. In the less formal places, you can expect the same kinds of waits as you would in Yellowstone, and the same rules apply: Come during the off hours if you want to avoid the crowds. It's the only way.

NEAR THE NORTHERN BOUNDARY

In addition to Flagg Ranch, fast food is available at **Leek's Marina,** which is located inside the park, a few miles north of Colter Bay.

Flagg Ranch. John D. Rockefeller, Jr., Pkwy., Moran. ☎ **800/443-2311.** Breakfast $2–$6; lunch $4–$9; dinner $10–$20. AE, DISC, MC, V. Summer hours daily 7am–1:30pm, 5–9:30pm. TRADITIONAL AMERICAN.

The food at this oasis is better than what is typically found in what most refer to as a "family restaurant," and servings are generous. The dinner menu includes fish, chicken, and beef dishes, as well as home-style entrees like ranch beef stew and chicken pot pie. The ambience is nice as well; during both winter and summer months wooden chairs and tables with colorful upholstery liven up this newly constructed log building.

COLTER BAY

John Colter Chuckwagon/Cafe Court Pizza and Deli. Across from the visitor center and marina in Colter Bay Village. ☎ **307/543-2811.** Breakfast $3–$6; lunch $5–$8; dinner $6–$14. DISC, MC, V. Daily 6am–10pm. Closed Oct–Apr. DELI/COMFORT FOOD.

These are the two sit-down restaurants in the village (though there's also a snack shop in the grocery store). Three meals are served daily during the summer months. The **Deli** serves sandwiches, chicken, pizzas, salads, and soup, with prices that range from $4.50 for an individual pizza to $12.99 for a chicken dinner. The **Chuckwagon's** breakfast menu features a huge and quite wonderful all-you-can-eat buffet. Lunch is soup, salad, and hot sandwiches; dinner is a buffet with a nightly special each evening. Among the dinner entrees are trout, lasagna, pork chops, beef stew, and New York strip steaks. The ambience is very casual and straightforward, as these restaurants mostly cater to families.

JACKSON LAKE JUNCTION

The casual dining choice at the Jackson Lake Lodge is the **Pioneer Grill,** complete with 1950s atmosphere and requisite soda fountain. Entrees are light and less expensive than those at The Mural Room (see below), and a takeout menu is available. The restaurant serves three meals and is alone in offering a children's menu. The **Blue Heron** cocktail lounge is one of the nicest spots in either park to enjoy a cocktail. The lounge here offers the same views as the dining room, as well as live entertainment.

✪ **Aspen's Dining Room/Cottonwood Café.** Signal Mountain Resort. ☎ **307/543-2831.** Breakfast $4–$6; lunch $6–$8; dinner $8–$21. AE, DISC, MC, V. Summer, daily 7–10am, 11:30am–2:30pm, and 5:30–10pm. COMFORT FOOD.

There are actually two restaurants here, both serving delicious food in the friendliest style in the park. The fine dining room and lounge is **Aspen's,** whose top-notch fare is supplemented by the Cottonwood Café's sandwiches and Mexican entrees. Dishes at Aspen's include chicken pot pie, pasta, and veal saltimbocca. When the bargain-hunting folks who work for the park's concessionaires head out for dinner, though, chances are good they'll land here and order Nachos Supreme from Cottonwood Café's bar menu. This nutritionist's nightmare—melted cheddar and Jack cheese with spicy beef or chicken served on a bed of corn chips topped with sour cream—will satisfy the appetite of two adults. Since the bar has one of three televisions in the park and is equipped with cable for sports nuts, the crowd tends to be young and noisy. As an alternative, snacks are served on the deck overlooking the lake.

The Mural Room. Jackson Lake Lodge. ☎ **800/628-9988.** Breakfast buffet $8; lunch $6–$9; dinner $16–$22. AE, MC, V. Summer daily 7–9:30am, noon–1:30pm, 6–9:30pm. BEEF/WILD GAME.

Jackson Lake's main dining room is quiet and fairly formal, catering to a more sedate crowd as well as corporate groups; it's also more expensive than other park restaurants. The floor-to-ceiling windows provide stellar views across a meadow that is moose habitat, to the lake and the Cathedral Group. Walls are adorned with hand-painted Western murals. Dinner may be a grand, five-course event that includes a shrimp cocktail, French onion soup, and Caesar salad, followed by an entree of Idaho trout, buffalo strip loin, vegetable lasagna, or rack of lamb. In addition to the main dining room, a **coffee shop** serves breakfast and lunch in an informal setting.

JENNY LAKE

Jenny Lake Lodge Dining Room. Jenny Lake Lodge. ☎ **307/543-3300.** Reservations required. Jackets required for men. Fixed-price dinner $41.50 for nonguests. AE, MC, V. Summer daily 7:30–9am, noon–1:30pm, and 6–9pm. CONTINENTAL.

The finest meals in either park are served here, where a Cordon Bleu chef creates culinary delights for guests (who have included on occasion a U.S. president). All three daily meals are appetizing, but the six-course dinner is the bell-ringer. Guests choose from appetizers like chilled lobster salad, smoked sturgeon ravioli, or buffalo mozzarella and plum tomato salads; and entrees such as grilled salmon, rack of lamb, or prime rib of buffalo. Desserts are equally decadent. Price is no object, at least for guests, since meals are included in the room charge.

8

Gateways to Yellowstone & Grand Teton National Parks

*S*ince the park can be accessed from all four points of the compass, one of the biggest decisions facing you will be where to commence your journey and to base yourself while you're in the area (if you chose not to stay in one of the parks themselves).

1 West Yellowstone, Montana

At the west entrance of Yellowstone National Park.

Yellowstone's west entrance is a tourist Mecca, chock-full of accommodations, restaurants, attractions, souvenir shops, and outposts that help round out an enjoyable vacation. The personality of the town has changed since the popularity of snowmobile excursions increased winter traffic on Yellowstone's trails; it now offers more, and better, year-round facilities.

Originally called Riverside, then Yellowstone, the name was officially changed to West Yellowstone in 1920 when Gardiner residents grudgingly complained that people would assume that the town was the park.

Despite the large numbers of tourist-oriented businesses that have sprung up over the years and the increasingly large crowds to whom they cater, somehow West Yellowstone has managed to retain a personality that is distinctly Montanan. Summer breezes make shopping and strolling its streets a pleasant alternative to spending the day in the car, and there are plenty of treasures (some tacky, some trendy) to keep you interested.

ESSENTIALS

GETTING THERE   For information on air service and car rentals, see "Getting There" in chapter 2. To drive to West Yellowstone from Bozeman (91 miles), take U.S. Highway 191 south to its junction with U.S. 287 and head straight into town. From Idaho Falls, take Interstate 15 north to U.S. Highway 20, which takes you directly into West Yellowstone, a 53-mile drive.

VISITOR INFORMATION Contact the **West Yellowstone Chamber of Commerce,** 100 Yellowstone Ave. (P.O. Box 458), West Yellowstone, MT 59758 (☎ **406/646-7701**).

GETTING OUTSIDE

Yellowstone is probably what brings you here, but outside the park border in the Targhee and Gallatin national forests on the west side, there is plenty of wilderness, trout streams and wildlife.

The area around West Yellowstone ranks among the best **fishing** locales in all of Montana. Come winter, **snowmobiling** and **snowcoach tours** are huge draws for West Yellowstone. For more information on all of these activities, see chapter 4.

Every major hotel and motel in town offers snowmobile packages that include a room and a sled rental, just be sure to book well in advance. As already mentioned, it's an immensely popular winter activity.

SEEING THE SIGHTS

Grizzly Discovery Center. Grizzly Park. ☎ **800/257-2570** or 406/646-7001. Fax 406/646-7004. www.grizzlydiscoveryctrcom. E-mail: info@grizzlydiscoveryctr.com. Admission $8 adults, $3.50 children 5–15. Year-round daily 8:30am–8:30pm (wildlife viewing until dusk).

For those who haven't the patience to search for and observe from a distance the free-ranging wildlife of Yellowstone, the Grizzly Discovery Center offers a closer look at the bears and wolves that inhabit the park. The interpretive center gives a well-mounted and detailed explanation of the animals' history in this country, and the controversial efforts to reintroduce them in the wild. The animals are well cared for; however, some will find it heartbreaking to see these magnificent creatures pacing the fence line of their enclosures, when the wilderness beckons nearby.

Museum of the Yellowstone. Canyon St. and Yellowstone Ave. ☎ **406/646-7814.** Admission family $18, adults $6, seniors and children $5. May–Sept daily 8am–10pm.

Since it's in the historic 1909 Union Pacific depot, this museum naturally stresses the days when luxury trains brought Victorian gents to the park. There are also displays on the Yellowstone ecosystem, including such epochal events as the 1959 earthquake that created Quake Lake, and the 1988 fires. Exhibits of Native American art and artifacts and displays on the explorations of the fur-trapping era are featured, along with a mounted grizzly bear known in his animate days as "Old Snaggletooth." Videos and films on the region's history are shown, and there are occasional "mountain man" demonstrations and lectures.

Yellowstone Imax Theater. 101 Canyon St., West Yellowstone, MT 59758. ☎ **888/854-5862** or 406/646-4100. www.yellowstoneimax.com. Admission $7.50 adults, $5.50 children 3–12. Call for show times.

This theater is attached to the Grizzly Discovery Center, which includes as well a real estate development on the park's boundary. Despite keeping such company, the IMAX concept works pretty well here—there are things an airborne camera can show you on a six-story-tall screen that you'll never see on your own two feet. Six channels of stereo Surround-Sound add to the sense of "being there." A show called *Yellowstone,* with swooping views of the canyon and falls and other sights, plays fairly often, but there are other shows as well.

WHERE TO STAY

West Yellowstone's building boom in recent years has added plenty of indistinguishable motel rooms, some put up by major chains, but you still may have to use your tent in the busy late summer months. Winter, too, with the enormous influx of snowmobilers, may require advanced reservations. The least expensive times to lodge in West Yellowstone are the fall, when there's not enough snow for winter recreation, and spring, before the summer masses arrive. Rates for rooms fluctuate considerably, depending on the season. All prices quoted in this section are for doubles, and unless noted, all these establishments are open year-round.

West Yellowstone Central Reservations handles booking for many of the hotels (☎ **888/646-7077**). Among the new hotels are the **Marriott Fairfield Inn** (☎ **800/565-6803**) at 105 S. Electric and the **Days Inn** (☎ **800/548-9551**) at 118 Electric. There are also some Best Western affiliates (the general toll-free number is ☎ **800/528-1234**), including the **Best Western Desert Inn,** 133 Canyon (☎ **406/646-7376**), the **Executive Inn,** 236 Dunraven (☎ **406/646-7681**), and the **Best Western Weston Inn,** 103 Gibbon (☎ **406/646-7373**). Doubles run from $65 to $120.

Less expensive options (doubles cost $70 to $89) include the **Brandin' Iron Motel,** 201 Canyon (☎ **800/217-4613** or 406/646-9411), and the **City Center Motel,** 214 Madison Ave. (☎ **800/742-0665** or 406/646-7337).

Firehole Ranch. 11500 Hebgen Lake Rd., West Yellowstone, MT 59758. ☎ **406/646-7294** through the summer, or 307/733-7669 year-round.

www.troutvacations.com/lodges/firehole.htm. 10 cabins, each sleeps up to 4. $225–$290 per person per day, double. Rate includes all meals, airport transfers, and activities (except guided fishing). 4-day minimum stay required. No credit cards. Kids under 12 allowed only with prior approval.

Visitors can take a boat ride to the lodge's location on a mile of private shore along Hebgen Lake, only 16 miles from Yellowstone National Park. The resort is surrounded by thousands of acres of national forest in which guests can ride horses, hike, canoe, and make use of the ranch's supply of mountain bikes. The ranch also offers fishing on Hebgen Lake and in six different streams near the park. Lodging is in 10 cabins, most suitable for two guests. The nicest units have separate living quarters, complete with wood-burning stoves, bedrooms furnished with king-size beds, and private bathrooms with tub-shower combinations. There are no television sets on the property, and telephone service is limited. Cocktails are served in a cozy nook before the serving of exquisite meals prepared by a French chef. Breakfast is buffet style, and there are box lunches at midday.

The Hibernation Station. 212 Gray Wolf Ave., West Yellowstone, MT 59758. ☎ **800/580-3557** or 406/646-4200. www.hibernationstation.com. 35 cabins (sleep up to 10). TV TEL. $99–$219 per cabin. AE, DISC, MC, V.

The Grizzly Discovery Center is part of something much bigger than a zoo—a real estate development. These luxury cabins are furnished Western style with hand-hewn log beds draped in down comforters, wall tapestries, fireplaces, and enormous bathrooms. Like a new saddle, they may need a few years to get broken in, but they're starting out with all the trimmings. Every year a few more cabins go up, and the owners say a big lodge will eventually be added. The outdoor sculptures on some of the roofs are eye-catching. You can rent a snowmobile with your room.

Stage Coach Inn. 209 Madison (corner of Dunraven), West Yellowstone, MT 59758. ☎ **800/842-2882** or 406/646-9575. 80 units. TV TEL. $55–$121 double. AE, DISC, MC, V.

The Stage Coach Inn is busy 12 months of the year, catering to both summertime park goers and snowmobilers. It's got some personality, too: The lobby is decorated with a Western flair that includes mounts of trophy animals from the American West. An enormous wooden staircase leads to second-level rooms. Guest rooms are well appointed with king and queen-size beds, modern bathrooms, and reading tables. The Coachman restaurant serves three traditional, well-prepared Western meals daily. The lounge is a popular spot, thanks to several video poker gambling machines, a large-screen TV, and a fireplace.

Three Bear Lodge. 217 Yellowstone Ave., West Yellowstone, MT 59758. ☎ **800/646-7353** or 406/646-7353. 74 units. A/C TV TEL. $73–$108 double. Snowmobile and cross-country skiing packages available in winter. DISC, MC, V.

The cozy, pine-furnished rooms of this family style inn are located fewer than 3 blocks from the park entrance. With an outdoor heated pool, indoor whirlpools, and a youth activity center, it is especially suitable for families. The inn offers snowmobile and cross-country ski packages with or without licensed guides just like every other lodging in West Yellowstone—with one difference; their snow-mobiles are brand-new. The restaurant and lounge are great spots for refueling and relaxing after a long day of playing outside.

✪ **West Yellowstone Conference Hotel Holiday Inn SunSpree Resort.** 315 Yellowstone Ave., West Yellowstone, MT 59758. ☎ **800/HOLIDAY** or 406/646-7365. www.yellowstone-conf-hotel.com. 123 units. A/C TV TEL. $79–$144 double. Snowmobile/snowcoach packages available in winter. AE, DISC, MC, V.

From its individual rooms to its restaurant, this big new resort is first-rate. Small conveniences like coffeemakers, plush carpeting, hair dryers, microwaves, a big indoor pool and laundry abound. You can arrange fishing and rafting trips, bike and ATV rentals, and chuck wagon cookouts. Snowmobilers who have been rattling around all day can relax in the Jacuzzi in the king spa suites. Rooms are spacious with bright decor, comfortable furniture, and landscape art on the walls. The Iron Horse Saloon serves regional microbrews, and the Oregon Short Line Restaurant features western cuisine. At the center of the restaurant sits the restored railroad club car that brought Victorian gents to Yellowstone a century ago. This hotel is West Yellowstone's standout offering

WHERE TO DINE

West Yellowstone can't offer the sort of fine dining you get in Jackson. Cafes, bars, and steakhouses still dominate the landscape—no fancy European bistros yet, just good fueling stations for visitors and locals who are burning calories in the woods, on the rivers and on the road. Unless we have indicated otherwise, all these places are open year-round

Apart from the choices listed below, **Jocee's Baking Company,** 29 Canyon St. (☎ **406/646-9737**), sells fresh morning pastries with coffee and espresso, and offers deli sandwiches and pizza in the afternoon. Next door at the same address is the **Arrow Leaf Ice Cream Parlor** (☎ **406/646-9776**), with 2,001 different ice cream flavors. For the best variety of coffee drinks and baked goods, visit **Cappy's** (☎ **406/646-9537**), part of the Bookpeddler, an excellent little book store in Canyon Square. At **Pete's Rocky Mountain Pizza Company,** 104 Canyon St. (☎ **406/646-7820**), you can design your own pizza. Dinner choices include traditional Italian entrees, while hamburgers and the like are served during lunch hour.

Bullwinkle's Saloon, Gambling and Eatery. 19 Madison. ☎ **406/646-7974.** Lunch entrees $5–$8; dinner entrees $9–$18. AE, DISC, MC, V. Summer daily 11am–2am (kitchen closes 11pm). AMERICAN.

Bullwinkle's is the newest restaurant in town and one of the best for traditional American food. Both the lunch and dinner menus are filled with traditional choices: burgers and salads for lunch, chicken, steaks, and ribs at dinner. The atmosphere here is lively and sometimes noisy, since the saloon also features video poker machines, but a new patio gives you a roomy outdoor alternative. You can also relax in the bar if you find yourself forced to wait during peak summer months.

The Canyon Street Grill. 22 Canyon St. ☎ **406/646-7548.** Most dishes $5–$11. No credit cards. Open daily in season 7am–7pm. TRADITIONAL.

You gotta like a restaurant whose slogan is "We are not a fast food restaurant. We are a cafe reminiscent of a by-gone era when the quality of the food meant more than how fast it could be served." This delightful, 1950s-style spot serves hearty food for breakfast, lunch, and dinner. Hamburgers and chicken sandwiches are popular, as are the milkshakes made with hard ice cream.

✪ **Elno's Tavern.** 8955 Gallatin Rd. ☎ **406/646-9344.** Reservations not accepted. Most items $4 and up. No credit cards. Daily noon–8pm. Closed first 2 weeks of Dec. AMERICAN.

Locals snowmobile out from West Yellowstone to Elno's (there's a trail that follows Highway 191) to become their own chefs at the grill here. It's a novel concept, and one that keeps people coming back to this restaurant with a fine view of Hegben Lake. At the counter order your meat—steak, teriyaki chicken, hamburger, or hot dog—and don't be surprised when it arrives raw. Go to the grill, slap it on, and stand around drink in hand shooting the breeze with other patrons until your food is exactly the way you like it. Steaks and chicken come with a baked potato or a garden salad; hamburgers come with chips. Snowmobilers can purchase gas and oil here, too.

The Outpost Restaurant. 115 Yellowstone Ave. (in the Montana Outpost Mall). ☎ **406/646-7303.** Dinner entrees $6–$15. AE, DISC, MC, V. Daily 6am–11pm. Closed Oct. 15–Apr 15. AMERICAN.

This fine restaurant tucked away in a downtown mall is hard for some visitors to find. The beef stew is typical of their family oriented, home-cooking. Also on offer are salmon, steaks, trout and an excellent salad bar. The opening of new establishments in West Yellowstone has put a dent in this restaurant's business, which may also suffer from the absence of a bar. However, it's a quiet, friendly place to feed a family.

2 Gardiner, Montana

At the north entrance to Yellowstone National Park.

At the other end of the spectrum from West Yellowstone is Gardiner, which provides the only year-round access to Yellowstone on the north. Though this tiny town (population 1,000) booms and busts with the tourist season, full-time residents manage to lead regular lives that include soccer practice, a day on the river, and a night on the town. For these folks, deer, elk, and bison meandering through the streets are no big deal. If you need additional information, contact the **Gardiner Chamber of Commerce,** 222 Park St., P.O. Box 81, Gardiner, MT 59030 (☎ **406/848-7971;** www. gardinerchamber.com; e-mail: gardinerchamber@gomontana.com).

WHERE TO STAY

Gardiner has long had funky, friendly bars and lodging—thin-walled motels with cranky TV's where if you show up late they've gone to bed and left a key in the door. These days it also has some newer, chain-affiliated lodgings, built to accommodate the ever-increasing traffic to the park. As with all the gateway towns, make your reservations early if you're coming during the peak season. The steep fall-off in the off-season leads to discounts that can be considerably less expensive than the in-season rates quoted below, so be sure to ask.

Chain motels include the new **Motel 6** (109 Hellroaring Dr., ☎ **877/266-8356** or 406/848-7520) and the virtually new **Super 8** (on U.S. 89 South, ☎ **800/800-8000** or 406/848-7401). Both are open year-round, with high season rates ranging from $80 to $100 double.

✪ **Absaroka Lodge.** U.S. 89 at the Yellowstone River Bridge. ☎ **800/755-7414** or 406/848-7414. www.yellowstonemotel.com. E-mail: ablodge@aol.com. 41 units. A/C TV TEL. $50–$100 double. AE, DC, DISC, MC, V.

Every room in this lodge has a balcony, many with nice views of the Yellowstone River. The lodge's riverbank location—with a nice slope of lawn overlooking the river gorge—is just a few blocks from the village center, and the rooms are well appointed with queen-size beds. Suites with kitchenettes cost a little more. The owners have been in business here for decades, but the building is modern and new. Like most other properties in town, the lodge has staff ready and able to assist in arrangements with outfitters for fly-fishing, rafting, and, in the fall, hunting.

Best Western by Mammoth Hot Springs. U.S. 89, P.O. Box 646, Gardiner, MT 59030. ☎ **800/828-9080** or 406/848-7311. www.bestwestern.com/ mammothhotsprings. 85 units. A/C TV TEL. Summer $94–$104 double. Winter packages available. AE, MC, V.

Though a half mile from the center of the town, the Best Western also has nicely furnished rooms with spectacular views, and is adjacent to the Mine, one of the town's better restaurants. There is also a heated pool, and an adjacent casino (Montana allows low stakes gambling.) During winter months you can rent cross-country skiing and snowmobile equipment.

Comfort Inn. 107 Hellroaring, Gardiner, MT 59030. ☎ **800/228-5150** or 406/848-7536. 80 units. Summer $90–$145 double. AE, DC, DISC, MC, V.

This log cabin–style hotel looks as though it belongs here, unlike a lot of chain operations. The centerpiece is a 3,000-square-foot rustic lobby, decorated with wild game trophies, and a large second floor balcony with views of the park and passing wildlife. Family suites that sleep six and luxurious Jacuzzi suites are available, along with a self-service Laundromat.

WHERE TO DINE

An indication that Gardiner has kept in touch with its mining town roots is the lack of fancy restaurants—instead, you'll find some steakhouse fare, hearty breakfasts, and travelers food. An espresso machine or two have shown up, but you might prefer the dish-clattering local color of the park-side coffee shops.

Bear Country Restaurant. 232 Park St. ☎ **406/848-7188.** Breakfast $2– $5; lunch entrees $5–$8; dinner entrees $9–$12. AE, DISC, MC, V. Summer daily 7am–10pm; winter daily 8am–2pm. TRADITIONAL AMERICAN.

There's nothing fancy about this pleasantly rundown, family oriented restaurant. Its location across from the park entrance, its early morning hours and its no-nonsense service are among its attractions. The American fare menu is undistinguished, but the portions are generous, and you'll be among locals.

The Chico Inn. Old Chico Road, Pray, MT. ☎ **800/HOT-WADA.** Reservations recommended. Dinner entrees $16–$27. AE, DISC. Daily 5:30–10pm summer. CONTINENTAL.

It's 30 miles north of Gardiner, but it's worth the drive for some of the best food in the Rockies, and a chance to visit the bar where Peter Fonda's *Easy Rider* motorcycle is enshrined. You'll want to linger over the food, so consider a night's stay in either the old lodge or the newer additions; you can relax and digest in the hot springs.

Outlaw's Pizza. Hwy. 89 (in the Yellowstone Outpost Mall). ☎ **406/848-7733.** Reservations not accepted. Most items $6–$15. MC, V. Daily 11am–11pm. ITALIAN.

You come here for the decent pizza (which makes it the best in town), the soups made daily, a decent salad bar, the pasta dishes, and terrific views of the mountains. Western theme art decorates the walls. You can order take-out.

The Yellowstone Mine. In the Best Western by Mammoth Hot Springs, Hwy. 89. ☎ **406/848-7336.** Reservations not accepted. Breakfast $4–$6; dinner $11–$22. AE, DISC, MC, V. Daily 6–11am and 5–9pm. AMERICAN.

The low-light old-time mining atmosphere here may not spark your appetite, but the meals come in healthy portions and the prices are reasonable. Steaks and seafood are the restaurant's specialty. There's also a lounge and casino.

3 Cooke City, Montana

Near the Northeast Entrance to Yellowstone National Park.

Mining gold and platinum and other precious metals pumped intermittent life into Cooke City for 100 years, but now there is only park tourism. Fewer than 100 residents live year-round in the town today, and Silver Gate, right next to the park entrance, is barely in the double figures. In the winter, when the cloud-scraping Beartooth Pass closes to the north, supplies for these towns have to come through the park. *My advice:* Visit in summer and take the breathtaking drive north over the pass (U.S. 212 toward Red Lodge), or south along the scenic Chief Joseph Highway (Wyo. 296).

Contact the **Colter Pass/Cooke City/Silver Gate Chamber of Commerce** at Box 1071, Cooke City, MT 59020-1071 (☎ **406/838-2395** for information and a map of hiking and snowmobiling trails in the area).

A room for the night will be less expensive than in other gateway towns, anywhere from $35 to $80 a night. The **Soda Butte Lodge** (☎ **406/838-2251**) is the biggest, newest, and poshest motel in Cooke City, and it includes the good **Prospector Restaurant** and a small casino; or you can go to the cheaper, bare-bones **Alpine Motel,** also on Main Street (☎ **406/838-2262**). For a bite to eat and a great selection of beers, try the funky **Beartooth Cafe** (☎ **406/ 838-2475**).

4 Jackson, Wyoming

Near the south entrance of Grand Teton National Park.

Of all the gateway towns to Yellowstone and Grand Teton, Jackson has managed best to reap the fruits of tourism while retaining some semblance of its original ranch-town character. There's no denying that the heart of Jackson is thick with shops and motels and tourists, but what's admirable about the town is the way it used some of its wealth to preserve open space and enhance the arts and cultural agenda of the community.

Jackson has a wealth of outdoor recreation to occupy hordes of visitors. In summer, you can play golf at world-class courses, chase trout in pristine streams or lakes, drift a river in a raft or kayak, or ride horses at one of the area's dude ranches. Come winter, you can shush down the mountain slopes, cross-country ski on the seemingly endless trails, or ride a snowmobile into the forest.

And if you're tired of the great outdoors, well, you can go shopping. Jackson has national brand-name fashion outlets, tourist curio shops, some excellent art galleries, clothing stores, antiques shops, and outdoor equipment suppliers. The retail frenzy concentrates around the town's delightful central square, a grassy park with entryways arched by tangles of elk antlers.

Oh, yeah, there are a couple of nice parks up the road, too.

ESSENTIALS

Information on air service to Jackson and rental car agencies is discussed in chapter 2 under "Getting There."

GETTING THERE If you're driving, come north from I-80 at Rock Springs on U.S. Highway 191/189, or east from I-15 at Idaho Falls on U.S. Highway 26 and either travel via Snake River Canyon on that highway or veer north over Teton Pass on Wyoming Highway 32. If you are coming south from Yellowstone National Park, you can stay on U.S. Highway 89, which runs north-south through both parks and into town. For up-to-date weather information and road conditions, contact the **Chamber of Commerce** (see below), or ☎ **888/WYO-ROAD** (in-state).

VISITOR INFORMATION   The **Jackson Hole Chamber of Commerce** is a source of information concerning just about everything in and around Jackson. Along with the U.S. Forest Service and National Park Service, representatives of the chamber can be found at the **Visitors Center** (no phone), 532 N. Cache. For information on lodging, events, and activities, contact the chamber at P.O. Box E, Jackson, WY 83001 (☎ **307/733-3316;** www. jacksonholechamber.com; e-mail: info@jacksonholechamber.com). There are a couple of fairly comprehensive booking services that operate on the Web: **Travel Wizard of Jackson Hole** (☎**800/606-0011** or 307/733-0011; www.TravelWizard.com) and **Jackson Hole Central Reservations** (☎ **800/443-6931;** www.jhsnow.com).

GETTING AROUND   Taxi service is available from **All Star Taxi** (☎ **800/378-2944** or 307/733-2888) and **Buckboard Cab** (☎ **307/733-7372**). **Alltrans, Inc.** (☎ **800/443-6133** or 307/733-3135) offers shuttle service from the airport and national park tours. Before you call a cab, remember that many of the hotels and car-rental agencies in the Jackson area offer free shuttle service to and from the airport.

You can also rely on the local mass-transit system to get around the valley. The **Southern Teton Area Rapid Transit (START)** offers bus transport from Teton Village to Jackson daily for $2 (students up to high school ride free). Winter and summer service runs about hourly between downtown and Teton Village, shutting down around 6pm in the winter, running into the evening during the summer. For specific schedule information, contact START at ☎ **307/733-4521.**

GETTING OUTSIDE

Whether you're a raw beginner, a seasoned pro, or an adrenaline addict, Jackson can make you feel at home. There's mountain biking, hiking, fishing, kayaking, and river-running in the summer, and skiing, snowmobiling, and snowboarding in the winter.

SPORTING GOODS & EQUIPMENT RENTALS   Serious climbers with serious wallets will appreciate the gear at ✪ **Teton Mountaineering,** at 170 N. Cache (☎ **800/360-3595** or 307/733-3595), a block from the square, where you can get killer

Jackson or Jackson Hole?

You'll see every kind of merchandise imaginable fashioned with an image of the Tetons and the words *Jackson Hole, Wyoming* scrawled over it. You *may* notice that on the map, the town just south of Grand Teton National Park is called Jackson. But your plane ticket says *Jackson Hole, Wyoming.* But wait a minute—the postmark just says *Jackson.* The names seem to be used interchangeably, and the reason is actually pretty simple.

Three mountain men ran a fur trapping company in these parts in the 1800s: one named David Jackson, another named Jedediah Smith, and a third named William Sublette. Mountain men in those days referred to a valley as a hole. As the story goes, Sublette (for whom the county southeast of Teton County is named) called the valley *Jackson's Hole,* since his friend and partner David Jackson spent a great deal of time in it. That name was shortened, and when the town materialized, it was also named for David Jackson. So the city itself is Jackson, Wyoming, and it lies in the great valley that runs the length of the Tetons on the east side, Jackson Hole.

Nordic skis and high-grade fleece jackets. **Adventure Sports,** at Dornan's in the town of Moose (☎ 307/733-3307), has a small selection of mountain-bike, kayak, and canoe rentals, and advice on where to go with the gear. When snowboards are put away for the summer, the **Boardroom** switches to BMX bikes and skateboards, at 225 W. Broadway (☎ 307/733-8327). The competition in Teton Village, is **Hole in the Wall Snowboard Shop** (☎ 307/739-2687). **Hoback Sports,** 40 S. Millward (☎ 307/733-5335), has a large selection of skis, boards, and summer mountain bikes for rent and sale. **Skinny Skis,** at 65 W. Deloney off Town Square (☎ 307/733-6094), is a year-round specialty sports shop and has an excellent selection of equipment and clothing. For serviceable factory seconds at steeply discounted prices, head north to the little town of Moose near the entrance to Grand Teton National Park and shop **Moosely Seconds** (☎ 307/733-7176).

SUMMER SPORTS & ACTIVITIES

FISHING   Yellowstone and Grand Teton national parks have incredible fishing in their lakes and streams; see the park sections for details.

The Snake River emerges from Jackson Lake Dam as a broad, strong river, with decent fishing from its banks in certain spots—like right below the dam—and better fishing if you float the river. Fly-fishers should ask advice at local stores on recent insect hatches and good stretches of river, or hire a guide to keep them company. Outdoor gear stores will provide all the tackle you need and more information on fishing conditions in the area than you can likely process. ♦ **High Country Flies,** 165 N. Center St. (☎ **307/733-7210**), has a vast selection of high-quality fishing gear, flies, and fly-tying supplies, along with lessons and guided trips, as well as free advice if you just want to gab about where to cast. The **Jack Dennis Outdoor Shop** on the Town Square at 50 E. Broadway (☎ **307/733-3270**) is a much bigger store with room to display some big boats, and it also offers lessons and guides. There's a smaller edition of the Dennis store in Teton Village (☎ **307/733-6838**). **Westbank Anglers,** 3670 N. Moose-Wilson Rd. (☎ **307/733-6483**), is another full-service fly shop that sells gear and organizes trips around Jackson Hole.

GOLF   The **Jackson Hole Golf and Tennis Club** (☎ **307/733-3111**), north of Jackson off U.S. 89, has an 18-hole course that's one of the best in the country. The **Teton Pines Resort,** 3450 N. Clubhouse Dr. (☎ **800/238-2223** or 307/733-1005), designed by Arnold Palmer and Ed Seay, is a challenging course; it's hard to imagine this is a cross-country ski center in winter. Both are open to the public.

HIKING   In addition to the myriad trails in Grand Teton National Park (see chapter 6), there are trails in the surrounding forest—they may be less well maintained, but they also get less use, which means more solitude for hikers. Adjacent to Grand Teton on the east and south is **Bridger-Teton National Forest;** go east and over the Continental Divide and you're in **Shoshone National Forest.** Together, these forests encompass a huge piece of mountain real estate, including glaciers, 13,000-foot peaks, and some of the best alpine fishing lakes in the world. Among the mountain ranges included in these forests are the **Absarokas,** the **Gros Ventre,** the **Wyoming,** and the **Wind River Range,** or "Winds," as they're called by locals, which stretch about 120 miles from just southeast of Jackson near Pinedale to the South Pass area and the Red Desert. A **visitor center** located in the log cabin at 340 N. Cache in downtown Jackson (☎ **307/739-5500**) provides all of the hiking and access information you'll need for Bridger-Teton, including the Gros

Ventre and Teton wilderness areas. If you want guided hikes, ask at the visitors center.

HORSEBACK RIDING   Trail rides are a staple of the Western vacation experience, and there are several companies in the area that will put you in the saddle. Some hotels, including those in Grand Teton National Park, have stables and operate trail rides for their guests. For details, contact **Jackson Hole Trail Rides** (☎ 307/733-6992), **Snow King Stables** (☎ 307/733-5781), **Spring Creek Ranch Riding Stables** (☎ 800/443-6139), or the **Mill Iron Ranch** (☎ 307/733-6390).

KAYAKING, CANOEING & SAILING   Canoeists and kayakers enjoy the upper Snake River, from Jackson Lake Dam down to Moose, and expert kayakers can ride through Snake River Canyon and Hoback white water. Beginners should be wary of the upper Snake—snags and spring currents have claimed lives, so a guide is recommended. Canoeists paddle Jenny Lake and, with a small portage or two, String and Leigh Lakes. The big lake, Jackson, attracts sailboats and sea kayaks, but beware the sudden afternoon eruptions of gusty wind and thunderstorms. If you're going on your own, you'll need a boat permit before launching in the park. Ask at the visitors center at Moose, or call the **National Park Service** at ☎ 307/739-3300 for information. Once you get outside the park, you're in the jurisdiction of the **Bridger-Teton National Forest,** offices in Jackson at 340 N. Cache (☎ 307/739-5500).

Several operators in Jackson run schools and guide services for beginners, intermediates, and advanced paddlers. The two major outfits are the **Snake River Kayak and Canoe School,** 365 N. Cache, Jackson 83001 (☎ 800/KAYAK-01), and **Rendezvous Sports,** 1035 W. Broadway (P.O. Box 3482), Jackson, WY 83001 (☎ 307/733-2471).

RAFTING   There are two parts to the Snake River—the smooth water, much of it running through Grand Teton Park north of Jackson, and the white water of the canyon, to the south and west. A rafting trip down the upper Snake, usually from Jackson Lake Dam or Pacific Creek to Moose, is not about wild water but about wildlife: Moose, bald eagles, osprey and other creatures come to the water just like we do. Several operators provide scenic float trips in the park; see chapter 6 for a list.

For the more adventurous, the most popular way to experience the Snake River is white-water rafting; these are wet, wild, white-knuckle tours. Several companies offer adrenaline-pumping day trips down the Snake, but don't plan on just being a passenger—this is a participatory sport. Contact **Barker-Ewing** (☎ 800/448-4202); **Charlie Sands Wildwater** (☎ 800/358-8184 or 307/733-4410); **Dave Hansen Whitewater** (☎ 800/732-6295); **Jackson Hole Whitewater,** P.O. Box 3695, Jackson, WY 83001 (☎ 800/648-2602); **Lewis and Clark Expeditions** (☎ 800/824-5375); or **Mad River Boat Trips** (☎ 800/458-7238 or 307/733-6203). Costs vary depending on the type and length of trip.

WINTER SPORTS & ACTIVITIES

CROSS-COUNTRY SKIING   With five Nordic centers and a couple of national parks at your feet, plus the 3.5-million-acre Bridger-Teton National Forest, cross-country skiers have plenty of choices. If you're new to cross-country skiing on any level, you might choose to start on the groomed, level trails at one of the Nordic centers. If, however, you have experience in the steep, deep powder of untracked wilderness, visit or call the National Park Service in **Grand Teton National Park** (☎ 307/739-3300) or the **Bridger-Teton National Forest** in downtown Jackson at 340 N. Cache (☎ 307/739-5500) and check in before you go.

The local ski shops are an excellent source of unofficial advice about the area's backcountry. Keep in mind that many of the trails used by cross-country skiers are also used by snowmobiles. For those seeking instruction, lessons are available at the Nordic centers, or you can check the schedule of **Teton Parks and Recreation** (☎ 307/733-5056).

The **Jackson Hole Nordic Center,** 7658 Teewinot, Teton Village (☎ 307/733-2629), on the flats just east of Teton Village, is a small part of the giant facility that includes some of the best downhill skiing around (see below).

Teton Pines Cross Country Skiing Center (☎ 307/733-1005) has 7.8 miles of groomed trails that wind over the resort's golf course. **Spring Creek Ranch Touring Center,** 1800 N. Spirit Dance Rd., Jackson (☎ 800/443-6139), maintains 8.5 miles of groomed trails, and you don't have to be a guest to enjoy them. For more information on both, see "Where to Stay," below.

At **Grand Targhee** (☎ 307/353-2304), you can rent or buy anything you need in the way of equipment and take off on the resort's 7.2 miles of groomed trails.

DOGSLEDDING   If your idea of mushing is not oatmeal but a pack of yipping dogs, you might want to try your hand at dogsledding, an enjoyable open-air way to tour the high country during the winter. **Jackson Hole Iditarod,** P.O. Box 1940, Jackson, WY 83001 (☎ **800/554-7388**), associated with Iditarod racer Frank Teasley, offers both half- and full-day trips in five-person sleds (the fifth companion is your guide) and you can take a turn in the driver's stand. The half-day ride costs $130 per person, gives the dogs an 11-mile workout, and includes a lunch of hot soup and cocoa before you head back to the kennels. For $225 a head, you can take the full-day excursion out to Granite Hot Springs, a 22-mile trip total. You get a hot lunch, plus your choice of barbecued trout or steak for dinner. Another Iditarod veteran, Bill Snodgrass, leads trips in the national forests around Togwotee Pass with his **Washakie Outfitting** (☎ **800/249-0662**). These trips book up pretty quickly, so call 3 to 4 days in advance to reserve a spot.

DOWNHILL SKIING   This is one of the premier destinations for skiers in the entire country. Despite a relatively remote location, chilly temperatures, and high percentage of black diamond trails (though still plenty of intermediate trails), skiers flock here in droves. The two largest ski resorts in the area have been expanding in recent years, putting in faster chairs, and eliminating long waits in lift lines.

✪ **Jackson Hole Ski Resort,** 7658 Teewinot, Teton Village, WY 83025 (☎ **307/733-2292** or 307/733-4005; www.jacksonhole. com), is making improvements to move into the elite international ranks; incidentally, prices are moving up too. Take the tram to the top of **Rendezvous Mountain** and plunge down Tensleep Bowl if you want to get a taste of skiing on the edge, or try the gentler, intermediate runs down the sides of **Apres Vous Mountain.**

✪ **Grand Targhee Resort,** Ski Hill Rd., Box SKI, Alta, WY 83422 (☎ **800/TARGHEE** or 307/353-2300), has the best snow in the universe: Deep, forgiving powder from November through spring (over 500 in. annually), and a more peaceful, less crowded village that provides a worthy alternative to Teton Village.

Snow King Resort, 100 E. Snow King, Jackson, WY 83001 (☎ **800/522-7669** or 307/733-5200), lights up its hill above Jackson at night; it's the smallest of the valley's resorts, with fairly steep and unvaried terrain, but it's within walking distance of downtown Jackson.

SNOWMOBILING   Though West Yellowstone is the most popular base for snowmobiling in the Yellowstone area, Jackson has a growing contingent of snowmobile aficionados and outfitters. You don't really need a guide to tour Yellowstone, where snowmobiles are required to stay on groomed roads, and you can also handle Togwotee Pass and the Granite Hot Springs area if you stick to groomed trails. Snowmobilers also head for the rugged Gros Ventre Mountains and the Greys River area, 45 miles west of Jackson. The operators who rent snowmobiles (including the necessary clothing and helmets) also have guides to take you on 1-day and multiday tours of Jackson Hole and the surrounding area. **High Country Snowmobile Tours,** at 3510 S. Hwy. 89 in Jackson (☎ **800/524-0130**), offers touring service for Jackson Hole, Yellowstone, and the Gros Ventre Mountains. **Jackson Hole Snowmobile Tours,** 1000 S. Hwy. 59 (☎ **800/633-1733**), offers 1-day trips in Yellowstone and multiday trips along the Continental Divide. In addition to renting snowmobiles, **Wyoming Adventures,** 1050 S. Hwy 89 (☎ **800/637-7147**), also takes trips along the Continental Divide as well as Grey's River. A typical 1-day outing costs from $140 to $180 with pickup and drop-off service, equipment, fuel, a continental breakfast, and lunch at Old Faithful included.

Flagg Ranch Snowmobiles (☎ **800/443-2311**) provides rentals and guided tours from the resort near the park's south gate. Elsewhere in Jackson, snowmobiles can be rented at **Leisure Sports,** 1075 S. Hwy 89 (☎ **307/733-3040**), and **BEST Adventures** (☎ **800/562-3948**).

A BIRD'S-EYE VIEW

AERIAL TOURING   For a much quicker climb to the tops of the mountains, call **Jackson Hole Aviation** (☎ **307/733-4767**), at the Jackson Hole Airport, or **Grand Valley Aviation,** Driggs Airport, Driggs, ID 83422 (☎ **800/472-6382** or 208/354-8131). You'll actually be looking down at the summits which climbers strain to top, and you'll get a new perspective on the immensity of the Grand Teton (though you won't get too close—the park has some air-space restrictions). Take your pick: Jackson Hole Aviation offers airplane trips, and Grand Valley has the Super Teton Ride, in a glider that takes you to 11,800 feet on the west side of the Grand.

BALLOONING   The folks at the **Wyoming Balloon Company,** P.O. Box 2578, Jackson, WY 83001 (☎ **307/739-0900**), like to fire up early, in the still air that cloaks the Teton Valley around 6am. Their "float trips" stay aloft for a little more than an hour, cruising over a 3,000-acre ranch with a full frontal view of the Tetons. The journey concludes with a champagne breakfast at the landing site.

AREA ATTRACTIONS

Beyond its role as a staging area for explorations of Grand Teton and Yellowstone national parks, Jackson is a place to relax, shop, play some golf, or watch a gunfight on the city square every night at six. Or simply to check out the sights.

Jackson Hole Aerial Tram Rides. At Jackson Hole Ski Resort, 7658 Teewinot, Teton Village. ☎ **307/739-2753.** $16 adults, $13 seniors, $6 children. Late May–Sept daily 9am–5pm, extended hours to 7pm mid-June–Aug. Tram runs approximately every half hour.

Here you can see the Tetons from an elevation above 10,000 feet— but don't expect a private tour. During busy summer days the tram carries 45 passengers, packed in like the skiers who take a lift in the winter. The top of Rendezvous Mountain offers a great view, but even in the middle of summer it can get pretty chilly, so bring a light coat.

National Museum of Wildlife Art. 2820 Rungius Rd. (3 miles north of town on U.S. Hwy. 89, across from the National Elk Refuge). ☎ **307/733-5771.** Admission $6 adults, $5 students and seniors, children under 6 free. Open daily 9am–5pm.

If you don't spot this museum on your way into Jackson from the north, consider that a triumph of design: It's jagged, red-sandstone facade is meant to blend into the steep hillside facing the elk refuge. Within this 50,000-square-foot castle is some of the best wildlife art in the country, as well as exhibits on the elk refuge and a 200-seat auditorium with regular slide shows and lectures on a wide range of subjects. The museum has 12 galleries displaying collections dating from the 19th century to the present. The museum also houses a repository of internationally acclaimed wildlife films, and in the winter it's the take-off point for sled tours of the elk refuge (you can also view the wildlife through spotting scopes on the balcony).

Jackson Hole Museum. 105 N. Glenwood (at the corner of Deloney). ☎ **307/733-2414.** Admission $3 adults, $2 seniors, $1 students and children. Mon–Sat 9:30am–6pm, Sun 10am–5pm. Closed Oct–May.

Dedicated local volunteers keep up this a repository of early photographs, artifacts, and other items of historical significance, and they'll guide you through the collections with care. You can browse the exhibits or go down the street to the Historical Society at Glenwood and Mercil to do some research. At the museum, you'll find collections of trade beads, antique pole furniture, pistols, and Indian artifacts.

National Elk Refuge. U.S. Hwy. 26/89, P.O. Box 510, Jackson, WY 83001. ☎ **307/733-9212.** Visitor Center open daily 8am–7pm in summer.

It's not exactly nature's way, but the U.S. Fish & Wildlife Service makes sure that the elk in this area eat well during the winter by feeding them alfalfa pellets. It keeps them out of the haystacks of area ranchers, and creates a beautiful tableau on the meadowy flats along the Gros Ventre River, where thousands of elk, some with huge antler racks, dot the snow for miles. Drivers on Hwy. 89 may also see trumpeter swans, coyotes, moose, bighorn sheep, and, lately, wolves. Though the cultivated meadows and pellets help the elk survive the winter, some biologists say this approach results in over-population and the spread of diseases like brucellosis.

Regardless, you'll seldom have such a good opportunity to see these magnificent animals up close. Each winter from mid-December until March the Fish and Wildlife Service offers **horse-drawn sleigh rides** that weave among the refuge elk. Rides early in the winter will find young, energetic bulls playing and banging heads, while late-winter visits (when the Fish and Wildlife Service begins feeding the animals) witness a more placid scene. Rides leave from the museum between 10am and 4pm on a first-come, first-served basis. Tickets for the 45-minute rides cost $10 for adults and $6 for children 6 to 12, and can be purchased at the National Museum of Wildlife Art. Ask about a combination pass for the sleigh ride and the museum.

ART GALLERIES

Collectors, tired of bighorn sheep on the crags and weather-beaten cowboys on their horses, often dismiss Western art. But while Jackson has plenty of that genre in stock, some of its two dozen galleries are more adventurous and sophisticated.

The **Martin Harris Gallery,** at 60 E. Broadway, has beautifully displayed art that sticks largely to western themes. The beauty of Tom Mangelson's wildlife photography has been somewhat diluted by its display in airports and malls, but Jackson is where he started, and at the **Images of Nature Gallery,** 170 N. Cache, you'll find some of signed and numbered works. The **Center Street Gallery,** 172 Center St., has the lock on abstract Western art in Jackson. A mile north of town, at 1975 U.S. Hwy. 89 (toward the park), the **Wilcox Gallery** showcases more than 20 painters and sculptors from across the nation.

WHERE TO STAY

The thin-walled, dimly lit motels of the past are just memories now—Jackson lodgings these days come with palatial trappings, and in some cases, prices that start at $500 a night. You'll still find a few quiet, simple hostelries on the back streets south and east of the square, but I suspect their days are numbered. Some of these new places offer excellent amenities, but could have been built anywhere, so I give them only brief mention, and move on to what is distinctly Jacksonian. Prices are generally discounted in off-season (spring/fall), but not during ski season.

Clustered together near the junction west of downtown where Hwy. 22 leaves U.S. Hwy. 26/89 and heads north to Teton Village is a colony of chain franchises **Motel 6** (600 S. Hwy. 89; ☎ **307/ 733-1620**) and the not-just-numerically superior **Super 8** (750 S. Hwy. 89; ☎ **800/800-8000** or 307/733-6833). Also in the vicinity are the more upscale and expensive **Days Inn** (350 S. Hwy. 89; ☎ **800/329-7466** or 307/733-0033), with private hot tubs and fireplaces; and the **Red Lion Inn** (90 W. Broadway; ☎ **307/ 734-0035**). High season prices for the motels range from $85 to $160. Rooms at the Red Lion start at $500 a night.

IN JACKSON

Jackson Hole Lodge. 420 W. Broadway, Jackson, WY 83001. ☎ **307/ 733-2992.** 59 units. A/C TV TEL. $80–$130 double; $150–$280 condo. AE, DC, DISC, MC, V.

Though it sits near one of the busiest intersections in Jackson, and is packed into a small space, this lodge is quiet and well designed. The pool is not just for splashing—you can swim its 40-foot length, sit in one of the whirlpools, take a sauna, or lounge on your own sundeck. If you're traveling with kids, your best bet is the condo lodgings, with two upstairs bedrooms, a full kitchen, and a living room with foldout couch.

✪ **Rusty Parrot Lodge.** 175 N. Jackson, Jackson, WY 83001. ☎ **307/733- 2000.** www.rustyparrot.com. 32 units. TV TEL. $108–$275 double. Rates include full breakfast. AE, CB, DC, DISC, MC, V.

The name sounds like an out-of-tune jungle bird, but since 1990 the Rusty Parrot has shown excellent pitch, cultivating a country lodge and spa right in the heart of busy Jackson. Located across from Miller Park, the Parrot is decorated in the new-Western style of peeled log, with an interior appointed with pine furniture and river rock fireplaces. The breakfast that comes with your room includes omelettes, fresh pastries, fruits, cereals, and freshly ground coffee.

Trapper Inn. 235 N. Cache, Jackson, WY 83001. ☎ **800/341-8000,** or 307/733-2648 for reservations. 50 units. A/C TV TEL. $98–$178 double. AE, DC, DISC, MC, V.

The employees here are some of the most helpful in Jackson. Just 2 short blocks from town square, the Trapper is hard to miss if you're walking north on Cache from the Town Square. On the left side of Cache you'll notice the crazy Trapper guy on the sign. Though the decor of the rooms is undistinguished, their spaciousness is luxurious. In the newest building, erected in 1991, many rooms come with miniature refrigerators; laundry facilities and an indoor/outdoor hot tub are also on hand.

Virginian Lodge. 750 W. Broadway, Jackson, WY 83001. ☎ **800/262-4999** or 307/733-2792. 181 units. A/C TV TEL. $95–$109 double. AE, DC, DISC, MC, V.

It's not brand-new, it's not a resort, it doesn't have a golf course, and the highway is right outside the door, but since its overhaul in 1995, the Virginian is attempting to earn its spurs as one of the better motels in Jackson. Given its location on the busy Broadway strip, that's not likely to happen, but the prices remain reasonable, and it's a busy, cheerful place to stay. There is a large outdoor pool to enjoy in summer, and you can get a room with a private Jacuzzi. Kids can romp in the arcade, families can eat in the Carriage House, and parents can relax in the Virginian Saloon.

Wort Hotel. 50 N. Glenwood, Jackson, WY 83001. ☎ **307/733-2190.** www.worthotel.com. 60 units. A/C TV TEL. $125–$174 double. AE, DISC, MC, V.

Located on Broadway just off the town square, an area constantly in flux with new buildings and new shops, the Wort's Tudor-style two-story building was largely rebuilt after a 1980 fire. Opened in the early 1940s by the wife and son of Charles Wort, an early 20th-century homesteader, it has an older style, both in the noisy and relaxed **Silver Dollar Bar** and the quiet, formal dining room (there's a more bustling coffee shop next to it). The comfortable rooms feature lodgepole pine furniture, thick carpeting, and a modern decor with Western artwork.

A warm, romantic fireplace graces the lobby; another fireplace and a huge hand-carved mural accent a mezzanine sitting area, providing a second hideaway. In the famous bar, the bar itself is inlaid with 2,032 silver dollars, the most precious piece of furniture rescued during the fire.

NEAR JACKSON

✪ **Amangani.** 1535 North East Butte Rd., Jackson, WY 83002 (on top of East Gros Ventre Butte). ☎ **877/734-7333** or 307/734-7333. 40 units. A/C TV TEL. $600–$800 double. AE, DC, DISC, MC, V.

Chopped into the side of East Gros Ventre Butte, Amangani's rough rock exterior blends in so well that the lights from its windows and pool appear to be glowing from within the mountain. The style is understated and rustic, but every detail is expensively done. Owner Adrianne Zecha has resorts like this around the world, from Bali to Hong Kong, and while the designs are tailored to the landscape, the approach is the same: personal service and luxury. Little touches include CDs in every bedroom, cashmere throws on the day beds, and slate and redwood walls. There's an outdoor pool, a health center, and an on-site restaurant.

Spring Creek Resort. P.O. Box 4780 (on top of the East Gros Ventre Butte), Jackson, WY 83001. ☎ **800/443-6139** or 307/733-8833. 106 units. A/C TV TEL. $210 double. AE, MC, V.

Atop East Gros Ventre Butte, 1,000 feet above the Snake River and minutes from the airport and downtown Jackson, this resort commands a panoramic view of the Grand Tetons and 1,500 acres of land populated by deer, moose, and the horses at its riding facility in the valley below. Though it seems a little less exclusive now that Amangani has opened next door, Spring Creek still has much going for it. The rooms are divided among four buildings with cabinlike exteriors and have fireplaces, Native American floor and wall coverings, refrigerators, coffeemakers, and balconies with views of the Tetons. Most rooms have king- or queen-size beds, and the studio units boast kitchenettes. In addition to its own rooms, the resort arranges accommodations in the privately owned condominiums that dot the butte—large, lavishly furnished, and featuring completely equipped kitchens. There is a pool, two tennis courts, and a concierge who will arrange horseback rides and fishing excursions. Winter skiing at Teton Village is only 15 miles away.

IN TETON VILLAGE

You can take advantage of the attractions of Jackson, to the south, and Grand Teton, to the north, without suffering the crowds by journeying to Teton Village, which is approximately equidistant from both. Located at the foot of the ski hill, the village and surrounding area offer several fine eating and dining establishments, and activities nearby include skiing, ballooning, and hiking in Grand Teton National Park.

During winter months, this is the center of activity in the valley. While lodging in the town of Jackson tends to be a little cheaper in the winter than the summer, at Teton Village the ratio is reversed— rooms by the ski hill get more expensive after the snow falls. Accommodations on this side of the valley run the gamut from pricey dude ranches and resorts to less expensive ski lodges that offer good value during the less hectic summer months. All establishments are open year-round unless otherwise indicated.

Alpenhof Hotel. 3255 W. McCollister Dr., Teton Village, WY 83025. ☎ **800/ 732-3244** or 307/733-3242. Fax 307/739-1516. www.alpenhof.com. E-mail: gm@alpenhoflodge.com. 42 units. A/C TV TEL. Dec–Apr $108–$408, May–Sept $78–$324, Oct $104–$114 single or double. AE, DC, DISC, MC, V. Closed Nov.

Welcome to Switzerland. This chaletlike hostelry has a prize location only 50 yards from the ski resort tram. Four stories tall, with a pitched roof and flower boxes on the balconies, the hotel combines an old-world atmosphere with excellent service. Recent upgrades include redoing the dining room and deluxe accommodations with brightly colored alpine fabrics, newly constructed handcrafted European furnishings, and tiled bathrooms with big, soft towels. Two junior suites with kitchenettes, five rooms with fireplaces, and four rooms with a shared deck—which you get to by an outside staircase—are among the outstanding features of the rooms. Economy rooms offer double or queen beds, while deluxe units are larger. Your choices for dinner include award-winning and expensive Continental fare that is served in The Alpenhof dining room, or pork, game, and pasta, which are staples in Dietrich's Bar and Bistro, a casual second-level dining area overloaded with Bavarian furniture.

Hostelx. Box 546, Teton Village, WY 83025. ☎ **307/733-3415**. www. Hostelx.com. Summer $40–$50 up to 4 people; winter $47–$60 up to 4 people. No credit cards.

If you came to Wyoming to ski, not to lie in the lap of luxury, get yourself a room at Hostelx and hit the slopes. It's a great bargain for skiers who don't need the trimmings, and it's not a dormitory, either—private rooms with king-size beds hold up to four people, and there's a coin-op laundry, a game room, a place to prep your skis, and a common room with a fireplace where ski movies run during the winter. You can walk to the Mangy Moose and other fun spots, and when you're on the slopes, nobody will be able to tell you apart from the skiers staying at the Ritz.

Jackson Hole Resort Lodging. 3200 McCollister Dr., P.O. Box 51087, Teton Village, WY 83025. ☎ **800/443-8613** or 307/733-3990. Fax 307/733-0244. E-mail: info@jhresortlodging.com. 125 units. A/C TV TEL. Winter $90–$100 double; $340 2-bdrm loft; $635–$1,440 3–5-bdrm homes. Off-season $52–$64; $126 2-bdrm loft; $190–$606 3–5-bdrm homes. Call for shoulder season rates. AE, DISC, MC, V.

The wide range of prices above is indicative of the variety of properties now under the wing of this management group. Most of them are in the Teton Village area, and they range from rooms in the relatively inexpensive and simple Crystal Springs Inn to deluxe private homes. Also available are condos at the Jackson Hole Racquet Club, 4 miles south of the ski resort at Teton Village on 550 acres along the Moose-Wilson Road. The condos are fully equipped with balconies, fireplaces, washer/dryers, and kitchens. You can comfortably fit a family in many of these loft-style condos, and the resort has amenities (some for a fee) like tennis courts, a health club, and an indoor pool. Don't expect coddling from the staff, which checks you in and lets you be.

The Resort Hotel. Box 348, Teton Village, WY 83025. ☎ **800/445-4655** or 307/733-3657. Fax 307/733-9543. www.ResortHotelJH.com. 101 units. A/C TV TEL. $169–$239 double; call for off-season rates. AE, DC, DISC, MC, V.

Major renovations were completed in 1998, and the hotel was reborn as a better facility, with prices that compare favorably to surrounding resorts. Wooden walls, stone floors, overstuffed furniture, and stone fireplaces accent the main reception area. Standard guestrooms in the main lodge provide a comfortable place to hang your hat, especially in rooms with views of either the mountains or the valley floor. Larger rooms in the mountain lodge have living areas with sofa beds and tiled combination bathrooms. Four have kitchenettes. Two restaurants are on the mezzanine level: The J. Hennesey Steak House serves steak and chicken meals family style, and the Irish Pub and Grill offers a place to unwind with simple fare, and any beer you can think of. Summer visitors can enjoy the outdoor pool and whirlpools; winter visitors can ski directly to a locker room with whirlpool or sauna, and drop their skis off for an overnight tune-up.

Teton Pines Resort. 3450 N. Clubhouse Dr., Jackson, WY 83001. ☎ **800/238-2223** or 307/733-1005. 16 suites, 2 town homes. A/C TV TEL. Summer $350–$695 suite; rest of year $125–$485 suite. AE, MC, V.

Arnold Palmer and Ed Seay designed the challenging 18-hole golf course attached to this luxury resort. Don't expect to improve your handicap, but you can expect to sooth your frustrations in the comfortable rooms, which feature his and her bathrooms, one with tub, one with shower. The resort offers a range of activities, some for a fee, including tennis, diving, and fly-fishing. The Jackson Hole Ski Resort is 5 minutes away. The dining room, The Grille at the Pines, is one of the better places to eat in Jackson, though pricey.

WHERE TO DINE

Jackson has more dining options than most of the other towns in this book combined, and they run the gamut of cuisine and price. You'll find the predictable steak and seafood and pasta menus—usually these days with a few de rigueur wild game dishes, too—but you'll also find more unusual choices. In addition to the choices reviewed below, you can get a quick bite at **The Merry Piglets,** 160 N. Cache St. (☎ **307/733-2966**), a snug Mexican restaurant that also serves Thai chicken wraps. **Harvest Bakery and Natural Food Cafe,** 130 W. Broadway (☎ **307/733-5418**), serves smoothies, vegetarian meals, and other breakfast and lunch entrees made from organic ingredients. At the other end of the spectrum is **Bubba's Bar-B-Que,** 515 W. Broadway (☎ **307/733-2288**), a late-night hangout dishing out ribs and other meats. If you need a good shot of espresso with your morning paper, stop at Pearl Street Bagel, 145 W. Pearl (☎ **703/739-1218**), or the **Betty Rock Coffee House & Cafe,** 325 W. Pearl St. (☎ **307/733-0747**), where you can sit outside on the deck.

EXPENSIVE

✪ **The Blue Lion.** 160 N. Millward. ☎ **307/733-3912.** Reservations recommended. Dinner $15–$28. AE, DC, MC, V. Daily 5:30–10pm; closed Tues. CONTINENTAL.

In the fast-moving, high-rent world of Jackson dining, the Blue Lion stays in the forefront by staying the same. On the outside, it's a two-story blue clapboard building across from the town park—it looks like a comfy family home. On the inside, it's soft light in intimate rooms and unhurried meals of elegant food, priced for people who aren't too concerned about prices. The menu features rack of lamb and the usual (in Jackson) wild game specialties, like grilled elk loin in a peppercorn sauce. Fresh fish is flown in for dishes like the wine-basted trout stuffed with Canadian snow crab. Summer diners can eat outside on the patio deck just north of the entrance.

The Cadillac Grille. 55 N. Cache. ☎ **307/733-3279.** Reservations recommended. Lunch $5–$8; dinner $15–$25. AE, MC, V. Daily 11am–3pm and 5:30–9:30pm. Closed Nov to mid-Dec. CONTINENTAL.

Neon and an eclectic menu give this restaurant a trendy air that attracts see-and-be-seen visitors more than locals. The chefs work hard on presentation, but they also know how to cook a wide-ranging variety of dishes, from fire-roasted elk tenderloins to garlic-painted Chilean sea bass. The wine list is equally long and varied. The menu in this art deco restaurant changes regularly, but the place itself is one of Jackson's longer-lived establishments.

The Granary at Spring Creek. P.O. Box 3154 (on top of the East Gros Ventre Butte). ☎ **800/443-6139** or 307/733-8833. Reservations suggested. Lunch $8–$15; dinner $15–$28. AE, DC, MC, V. Daily 11:30am–2pm and 5:50–8pm. AMERICAN.

In this restaurant perched atop Gros Ventre Butte 15 minutes from downtown Jackson, you can enjoy a fantastic view ever over a plate of roasted monkfish and Tuscan bean and lobster ragout. Across the valley lie the Tetons and below is the Spring Creek equestrian center. Lunch is especially pleasant when weather allows dining outside on a wood deck. The menu changes, but you may find elk flank fajitas at lunch and potato-encrusted red snapper at dinner.

Snake River Grill. Town Square, Jackson. ☎ **307/733-0557.** Reservations recommended. Dinner $15–$30. AE, MC, V. Daily 5:30–9pm. Closed Nov and Apr. ECLECTIC.

This is a popular drop-in spot for locals, including some of the glitterati who sojourn in the area—Harrison Ford and Uma Thurman have been spotted. It's an award-winning restaurant for both its wine list and its menu, which features regular fresh fish dishes (ahi tuna is a favorite), bourbon-marinated pork chops, and some game entrees like venison chops and Idaho trout. From a wood-burning oven come pizzas with exotic ingredients like duck sausage or eggplant with portobello mushrooms. The front-room dining area overlooks the busy Town Square, but there's a more private, romantic room in the back.

Stiegler's. Teton Village Rd. at the Aspens. ☎ **307/733-1071.** Reservations recommended. Main courses $14–$24. AE, MC, V. Tues–Sun 5:30–10pm. AUSTRIAN/CONTINENTAL.

Austrian cuisine isn't exactly lurking beyond every street corner waiting to be summoned with a Julie Andrews yodel, but in Jackson, there are two options: Steigler's Restaurant or Steigler's Bar. Since 1983, Steigler's has been confusing, astonishing, and delighting customers with such favorites as the *Bauern Schmaus* (a "farmer's feast" that includes pork and bratwurst) and the less-perplexing venison St. Hubertus. You'll recognize the desserts, at least: Apfelstrudel and Sacher torte. Tyrolean leather breeches are, of course, optional.

The Strutting Grouse. At Jackson Golf and Tennis Club, Hwy. 191 (near Kelly, WY). ☎ **307/733-7788.** Lunch $6–$14; dinner $18–$24. AE, DISC, MC, V. Summer daily 11am–2pm and 5:30–9pm; closed winter. WESTERN.

Golfers strut into this restaurant after watching how far their golf balls fly at this altitude, and sit down to excellent food, the best of it grilled over mesquite coals. A stone fireplace burns at the center of this big timber dining room overlooking the golf course. The diet-conscious can order lunch from a menu that includes several salads, as well as mesquite-grilled chicken strips and pizza with duck sausage and sun-dried tomatoes. As the sun heads lower in the sky behind the Tetons, the dinner menu appears, offering the usual choices of beef, lamb, and fish entrees, as well as a chef's special, typically a game dish.

✪ **Sweetwater Restaurant.** At the corner of King and Pearl. ☎ **307/ 733-3553.** Reservations recommended. Lunch $5–$7; dinner $13–$18. DC, MC, V. Daily 11am–3pm and 5:30–10pm, shorter hours in winter. AMERICAN.

Though this little log restaurant serves American fare, it does so in a decidedly offbeat way. The eclectic menu includes, for example, a Greek salad, a Baja chicken salad, and a cowboy grilled roast beef sandwich. An outside table is a great spot at which to enjoy a summer lunch. The dinner menu is just as quirky, and livened by nightly specials; try the unique smoked buffalo carpaccio before diving into the giant salmon fillet smoked on the Sweetwater's mesquite grill. Vegetarians will want to sample the spinach-and-feta casserole that is topped with a cheese soufflé.

Teton Pines Resort. 3450 N. Clubhouse Dr. off Teton Village Rd., Jackson. ☎ **800/238-2223** or 307/733-1005. Reservations recommended. Dinner $15–$28. AE, MC, V. Mon–Sat 11:30am–2:30pm and 6–9pm; Sun 9am–1pm. PACIFIC RIM.

This golf resort just happens to be home to what locals consider one of the finest restaurants in the valley. The Grille at the Pines overlooks a placid trout pond and Teton Pines golf course. An impressive menu includes a succulent array of well-prepared steak and veal dishes, as well as the obligatory pastas. For an appetizer, try the tempura nori roll, with tuna, Dungeness crab, and Arctic char; for a main course, lamb chops with pear and mint salsa and pistachio couscous is recommended.

MODERATE

Acadian House. 170 N. Millward. ☎ **307/739-1269.** Reservations recommended. Dinner entrees $9–$17. AE, DC, MC, V. Daily 5:30–10pm. CAJUN.

Taking over a building next to the Blue Lion puts the Acadian House in snazzy culinary company, and its Cajun dishes seem to be holding their own. The spice doesn't burn the way it does in Louisiana, but there's plenty of cayenne for Rocky Mountain taste buds. Traditional dishes like *boudin*—sausage served with red beans and rice, and crawfish etouffée make appearances with continental-style creations like Cajun pasta. If you've never treated yourself to the South's most delicious bottom-feeder, try the catfish, a delicious, blackened-to-perfection delicacy topped with almonds, pecans, and white wine.

Anthony's. 62 S. Glenwood St. ☎ **307/733-3717.** Reservations not accepted. Dinner entrees $10–$17. MC, V. Daily 5:30–9:30pm. Closed Thanksgiving and Christmas. ITALIAN.

There was a time when Anthony's was *the* Italian restaurant in Jackson, and you would stand in line for a table in an atmosphere of friendly frenzy. The menu has changed little since those days, but Anthony's is no longer top-of-the-line when it comes to Italian dining in Jackson. It's still a family favorite, and conveniently located if you're staying in town. The menu features numerous pastas like fettuccine with cream, broccoli, and mushrooms that tend toward the heavy side.

Lame Duck. 680 E. Broadway. ☎ **307/733-4311.** Dinner $8–$17. AE, MC, V. Daily 5:30–10pm. CHINESE/JAPANESE.

While Italian food seems to travel well to the Northern Rockies, to find a good Asian meal you have to search far and wide—or at least up Broadway toward the elk refuge. You may start worrying when you see the drinks menu—yes, they come with parasols—or the mix of Japanese and Chinese (and even Indonesian) items among the dinner fare, but don't be concerned: This is decent, middle-of-the-road cooking, and the sushi and sashimi are quite good. The menu includes dishes like Six Delicacies (duck, lobster, shrimp, snow peas, and mushrooms served with a secret sauce) and the spicy Fireworks Shrimp (shrimp, snow peas, and bamboo shoots in a hot sauce that warrants a "Beware" sign).

Mangy Moose. Teton Village. ☎ **307/733-4913.** Reservations for larger parties recommended. Dinner entrees $11–$20. AE, MC, V. Daily 5:30–10pm. Closed mid-Oct to Dec 1. AMERICAN

Coming off the slopes at the end of a hard day of skiing or snowboarding, you can slide right to the porch of this ski area institution. Good luck getting a seat inside, but if you like a lot of noise and laughter and tasty dishes like buffalo meat loaf, be patient—it beats getting into your car and driving elsewhere. The decor matches the pandemonium: It looks like an upscale junk shop, with bicycles, old signs, and, naturally, a moose head or two hanging from the walls and rafters. They have typical Wyoming fare (steak, seafood, and pasta), a good salad bar, and a smattering of Mexican dishes. Try the hot spinach and artichoke heart dip as an appetizer.

✪ **Nani's Genuine Pasta House.** 240 N. Glenwood. ☎ **307/733-3888.** Reservations suggested. Dinner entrees $10–$17. Open Tues–Sat 5–10pm. MC, V. ITALIAN.

At Nani's, the setting is simple but the food is extraordinary. There are two menus: a *carta classico* featuring pasta favorites like *puttanesca* (tomato, anchovy, garlic and Kalamata olives) and mussels in wine broth; and a menu that features a region of Italy, with dishes like roasted pheasant or Fontina cheese melted with eggs and cream. Your only problem with this restaurant might be finding it—it's tucked away behind a rather run-down motel.

✪ **Nora's Fish Creek Inn.** 5600 W. WY 22, Wilson. ☎ **307/733-8288.** Breakfast $5–$8; lunch entrees $4–$7; dinner entrees $12–$15. DISC, MC, V. Daily 6am–9:30pm. AMERICAN.

If you want to hang with the locals and if you like to eat a lot, Nora's is the place to go—especially at breakfast, when they have all-you-can-eat pancakes and huevos rancheros that barely stay on the huge plates. Prices are inexpensive compared to those at any of the other restaurants in town. You still get as many coffee refills as you like. Dinner is fish, fish, and more fish, like fresh Idaho trout.

Snake River Brewing Company. 265 S. Millward St. ☎ **307/739-2337.** Main dishes $7–$11. AE, MC, V. Daily noon–midnight; kitchen open until 11pm. PIZZA/BREW PUB.

Microbreweries are sprouting (and spouting) all over the country, but this one is a cut above the others, judging from the prizes it's won for lines like its pale ale and zonker stout. In a roomy, high-ceilinged new building, the brewery serves up excellent pizza cooked in a wood-fired oven—try the P.S.T. (Prosciutto, spinach, and tomato). They also have pastas, calzones, and various sandwiches. The 15 brewing vats are all around and above you, sometimes humming a bit too loudly, and you can play foozball and pool on the mezzanine. Beer lovers will appreciate the happy hour from 4 to 6pm, and occasionally there's live music.

Vista Grande. Teton Village Rd., Teton Village. ☎ **307/733-6964.** Reservations not accepted. Main courses $8–$17. AE, MC, V. Daily 5–10pm. MEXICAN.

You're not going to find terrific Mexican food in Jackson, but if you must have it this is the place to get large servings and good margaritas. Crowded and noisy, it's fun for families and just down the road from the ski area. The only problem is the fairly long wait for a table during the busy seasons. There is a little more variety on this menu than you find at run-of-the-mill Mexican joints—a jalapeño spinach chicken breast and a beef tenderloin topped with mango salsa, for example. You'll find the requisite fajitas, burritos, chimichangas, and enchiladas, but you'll also find chicken asados (grilled chicken on a bed of rice with pico de gallo), blackened tuna, and a vegetarian plate.

INEXPENSIVE

Billy's Giant Hamburgers. West side of town square. ☎ **307/733-3279.** Lunch and dinner entrees $4–$6. AE, MC, V. Daily 11:30am–10pm. Closed Nov to mid-Dec. BURGERS.

If you take a wrong turn while entering the posh Cadillac Grill (right instead of left) you find yourself in this cramped '50s-style lunch booth and counter shop—and you might just stay. Big, juicy burgers are what you'll get, cooked right in front of you. You can actually sit in here and order from the fancy Cadillac, perhaps a Maine lobster and a fine Sauvignon Blanc, or go easy on your wallet and order a giant cheeseburger with a pile of fries on the side.

✪ **The Bunnery.** 130 N. Cache St. ☎ **307/733-5474.** Breakfast $4–$7; lunch entrees $5–$7; dinner entrees (summer only) $8–$15. MC, V. Daily 7am–3pm year-round, also open daily 5–9:30pm in summer. BREAKFAST/BAKERY/SANDWICHES

A Jackson mainstay, this bakery and restaurant is a great place to have one of the famous Bunnery breakfasts—perhaps a big soft spinach omelette with sour cream and Swiss cheese, or eggs Benedict. These are cramped quarters, though, and you'll often find yourself waiting in a line that stretches down the boardwalk of the Hole-In-The-Wall Mall just off the square—that's not bad in the summer, but you won't want to wait long on a cold winter morning. Sandwiches like the grilled tuna and cheddar are reasonably priced and the portions are large. The coffee is good. You might want to pick up a baguette or some other baked goodie on your way out.

Jedediah's House of Sourdough. 135 E. Broadway. ☎ **307/733-5671.** Reservations not accepted. Breakfast $4–$6; lunch entrees $5–$6. AE, DC, MC, V. Daily 7am–2pm. AMERICAN.

You feel like you've walked into the kitchen of some sodbuster's log cabin home when you enter Jedediah's. Bring a big appetite for breakfast, and a little patience—you may have to wait for a table, then you may have to wait for food, staring at the interesting old photos on the wall. But it's worth it, especially for the rich flavor of the sourjacks, a stack of sourdough pancakes served with blueberries. The 'Diah's omelette is a big three-egg concoction stuffed with bacon, onions, and cheddar cheese and served with a side of potatoes. In summer months meals are also served outside on a patio.

JACKSON AFTER DARK

Talented musicians from well-known orchestras participate in the **Grand Teton Music Festival** (☎ 307/733-1128) held in summer in the amphitheater next to the tram lift. Tickets are usually available on short notice, especially for the weeknight chamber music performances, which are often terrific.

The **Jackson Hole Playhouse,** 145 W. Deloney (☎ 307/733-6994), and the **Grand Teton Mainstage Theatre,** 49 W. Broadway (☎ 307/733-3670), produce musicals, melodramas, and other light fare during the summer months. Tickets for all shows should be reserved.

Those less impressed with dramaturgy should head down to the **Silver Dollar Bar** at 50 N. Glenwood in the Wort Hotel for a drink with one of the real or imagined cowpokes who are bellied up to the bar. And, yes, those 1921 silver dollars are authentic. At the very famous **Million Dollar Cowboy Bar** down the street you can dance the two-step to live bands. If you want some high-octane dancing fun led by some talented local hoofers, head out to Wilson and the **Stagecoach Bar** on Wyo. 22 on a Sunday night. It's the only night they have live music in this scruffy bar and hamburger joint, and the place is jammed wall to wall.

5 Cody, Wyoming

Cody is 53 miles from the east entrance to Yellowstone.

Almost from the moment trappers first reported the unworldly marvels of Yellowstone, would-be entrepreneurs were setting up shop. However, none could match the scale of William F. "Buffalo Bill" Cody, the famed scout and showman, who in 1887 set about building a hunting resort, an irrigation project and a city on the eastern edge of the park. Today Cody is one of the most beautifully situated communities in Wyoming, near the juncture of rivers that pour from the rugged Absaroka Range. The drive from the east entrance of Yellowstone to Cody cuts through the magnificent East Yellowstone (Wapiti) Valley, a drive Theodore Roosevelt once called the most scenic 50 miles in the world.

The town fairly oozes Western charm year-round, but it's at its best during the summer; daytime skies are cloudless and the longest running rodeo in the country provides entertainment every night under the stars. Museums, a re-created Western town, and retail shops supply plenty of diversions. Cody's residents, a mostly friendly lot, preserve and promote their particular brand of Western heritage to visitors the world over. And it's not too hard a sell: Though certainly not the resort-laden mountain paradise Jackson is, Cody's Western charm seems much more authentic.

ESSENTIALS

Information on air service to Cody and rental car agencies is discussed in "Getting There" in chapter 2.

GETTING THERE   If you're driving from Cheyenne, travel north on I-25 to Casper, then west on U.S. Highway 20/26 to Shoshoni, where U.S. Highway 20 turns north to Thermopolis. From there, it's another 84 miles to Cody on Wyo. 120. From Jackson, take U.S. Highway 191 to the West Thumb Junction in Yellowstone, drive east along the northern boundary of Yellowstone Lake and continue on U.S. Highway 14/16/20 to Cody. If you enter Wyoming from the west on Interstate 80, drive north from Rock Springs on U.S. Highway 191 to Farson, Wyo. 28 to Lander, Wyo. 789 to Thermopolis, and Wyo. 120 to Cody. Call ☎ **888/ WYO-ROAD** (in-state) or 307/772-0824 for **road and travel information.**

VISITOR INFORMATION   For printed information on this area of Wyoming, contact the **Park County Travel Council,** 836 Sheridan Ave., P.O. Box 2454, Cody, WY 82414 (☎ **307/587-2777**), or the **Wyoming Business Council Travel and Tourism Division,** I-25 at College Drive, Cheyenne, WY 82002 (☎ **307/777-7777**).

GETTING OUTSIDE

Because of its close proximity to Yellowstone, the best place to get outdoors near Cody is the park itself, but be aware that the only access to Yellowstone from Cody during the winter months is by snowmobile over dizzying Sylvan Pass. Once you're outside the park,

Cody doesn't have the plethora of activities Jackson Hole does, but it's still a bustling community. **Buffalo Bill State Park,** located along the canyon and reservoir 6 miles west of Cody, is a hot spot for recreationists, with opportunities for hiking, fishing, and a variety of water sports. Its **Buffalo Bill Reservoir** is regarded as one of the premier spots for windsurfing in the United States. The park also has facilities for camping and picnicking. In the winter, cross-country and downhill skiing, ice climbing, and snowmobiling are popular in the Cody area.

If you'd rather not be your own driver in the park's heavy summer traffic, guided Yellowstone National Park day trips are available locally through **Grub Steak Expeditions,** P.O. Box 1013, Cody, WY 82414 (☎ **307/527-6316**), **Buffalo Bill's Yellowstone Country,** 1202 14th St., Cody, WY 82414 (☎ **877-640-8609** or 307/527-5988; www.yellowstonecountryres.com; e-mail: byyccr@trib.com), and **Yellowstone Expedition Services,** P.O. Box 1956, Cody, WY 82414 (☎ **888-808-7990** or 307/587-5452; e-mail: yestour@cody.wtop.net).

BIKING   If you want to explore the area on two wheels, mountain bikes and local trail information are available at **Olde Faithful Bicycles,** 1362 Sheridan Ave. (☎ **307/527-5110;** e-mail: bikecody@wyoming.com). Though there isn't a marked network of bike paths in the Cody area, you can ride on the Forest Service trails west of town off U.S. Highway 14/16/20 in the Shoshone National Forest. For specific trail information, call Olde Faithful Bicycles or the Forest Service at ☎ **307/527-6921.**

CROSS-COUNTRY SKIING   If you favor a groomed course for cross-country skiing, try the **North Fork Nordic Trails** in Shoshone National Forest near the east entrance to the park off U.S. Highway 14/16/20. You can circuit 25 kilometers of trails adjacent to the Sleeping Giant downhill area (see below) and the Pahaska Tepee resort.

DOWNHILL SKIING   Near the east entrance to the park, 50 miles west of Cody, is an inexpensive, family oriented ski area, cheap and not challenging: **Sleeping Giant Ski Area,** 349 Yellowstone Highway, Cody, WY 82414 (☎ **307/527-SNOW;** www.westwyoming.com/Sleeping Giant). *Our suggestion:* Drive north to Red Lodge, Montana, for longer, steeper runs and a bigger resort; travel time from Cody is about the same.

FISHING   Yellowstone's legendary fly-fishing waters are a short drive away, but you should try the smaller but excellent angling streams west of Cody: **The Clark's Fork of the Yellowstone, the North and South Forks of the Shoshone,** and **Sunlight Creek.** To the east, the warmer and slower **Big Horn River,** and **Big Horn Lake,** nurture catfish, walleye, and ling for boat fishers. For advice on the trout streams near Cody, ask at **North Fork Anglers,** 1438 Sheridan Ave. (☎ **307/527-7274;** e-mail: flyfish@wavecom.net), where they stock gear and clothing and also guide short day trips or longer, overnight excursions. If you like to troll or cast from a boat, **Buffalo Bill Reservoir** has produced some big Mackinaw, as well as rainbow, brown, and cutthroat trout. You have a shot at landing a rainbow over 15 pounds at **Monster Lake** (☎ **800-840-5137;** www.monsterlake.com), a private 150-acre pond on the Deseret Ranch 10 miles south of Cody. It's strictly catch-and-release for these lunker rainbows and cutthroats, and there's a hefty fee per rod.

FLOAT TRIPS One of the most popular things to do in Cody in summertime is to float along the Shoshone River, the major eastern drainage of the Yellowstone River. The mild Class I and II rapids make it an enjoyable trip for almost anyone. Contact **Wyoming River Trips** (1701 Sheridan Ave.; **800/586-6661** or 307/587-6661; www.imt.net/~wyoriver/; e-mail: wrt@wave.park.wy.us), or **River Runners,** 491 Sheridan Ave. (☎ **307/527-RAFT;** www.westwyoming.com/rafting/). Prices run from about $18 to $50, depending on the length and difficulty of the trip.

GOLF The **Olive Glenn Golf and Country Club,** 802 Meadow Lane, is an 18-hole PGA championship that is open to the public daily from 6am to 9pm. Greens fees are a modest $20 for 9 holes, $35 for 18. Call ☎ **307/587-5551** for tee times.

SNOWMOBILING The most popular Cody snowmobiling trails originate from nearby **Pahaska Teepee Resort,** located 51 miles from Cody on U.S. Highway 14/16/20 (see "Where to Stay," below). Don't take the Pahaska Tepee Trail over 8,541-foot Sylvan Pass if you're afraid of heights; but if you're not, it connects to the Yellowstone National Park trails and the lengthy Continental Divide Snowmobile Trail, and offers breathtaking views including Avalanche Peak (10,566 ft.) and Cody Peak (10,267 ft.). The Sunlight trail system is located 36 miles north of Cody, and winds through the wilds to a stunning view of the Beartooth Mountains. Sledders start from a parking area at the junction of Wyo. 296 and U.S. Highway 212 and follow the Beartooth Scenic Byway east for 16 miles to a warming hut. To the east, there are 70 miles of snowmobile routes in the Bighorn Mountains. Snowmobiles can be rented at **Pahaska Tepee Resort** and in Cody at **Mountain Valley Engine Service,** 422 W. Yellowstone Ave. (☎ **307/587-6218**).

WINDSURFING   According to *Outside* magazine, the 8-mile-long, 4-mile-wide Buffalo Bill Reservoir, which receives wind from three mountain gorges, is one of the top-10 windsurfing destinations in the continental United States. It's best experienced in the warmer months of June to September. There is a boat ramp near the campground on the north side of the reservoir just off U.S. Highway 14/16/20. There are no places to rent a windsurf board in the vicinity.

SPECIAL EVENTS

The Buffalo Bill Historical Center is a tremendous resource for unique events in Cody. The April festival of **Cowboy Songs and Range Ballads** features storytelling, poetry, and some fine yodeling and balladry. In mid-June, the **Plains Indian Powwow** brings the Robbie Powwow Garden on the south end of the Buffalo Bill Historical Center parking lot alive with whirling color. Traditional dance competitions are coupled with craft shows and Native American food, and non-Indians are welcomed into round dances. Call the **Buffalo Bill Historical Center** (☎ **307/587-4771**) for exact dates of these and other events and special exhibits.

Every July 1 to July 4, during the **Cody Stampede,** the streets are filled with parades, rodeos, fireworks, street dances, barbecues, and entertainment, capped by a top-notch rodeo. Call ☎ **800/207-0744** or 307/587-5155 for tickets. For 2 days in July, the cool rhythms of jazz and the brassy sound of big-band and swing music take over the lawn of the Elks Club at 1202 Beck Ave. (next to the Cody Convention Center) during the **Yellowstone Jazz Festival.** Featured musicians come from afar, playing varieties of jazz from 11am until dark. Call ☎ **307/587-3898** for additional information.

Late in August, the Buffalo Bill Historical Center (see above) stages the **Buffalo Bill Celebrity Shootout,** where celebrities and local shooters test their skills in trap, skeet, sporting clays, and silhouette shooting. It's a more serious test of marksmanship than the melodramatic shoot-out staged every summer evening at 6pm in front of the Irma Hotel.

SEEING THE SIGHTS

✪ **Buffalo Bill Historical Center.** 720 Sheridan Ave. ☎ **307/587-4771.** Admission $10 adults, $6 students (18 and over), $4 ages 6–17. Admission is good for 2 consecutive days. Group tour rates available by request. Open daily, call for seasonal hours.

This extraordinarily valuable museum casts a scholarly eye on the relics of the West's young history while offering some flash and entertainment for tourists. The complex actually houses four different museums in 237,000 square feet of space: the Buffalo Bill Museum, the Whitney Gallery of Western Art, the Plains Indian Museum, and the Cody Firearms Museum.

The **Buffalo Bill Museum** is a monument to one of the earliest manifestations of America's celebrity culture, displaying the wares that turned a frontier scout and buffalo hunter into a renowned showman. Posters trumpet his world-famous Wild West shows featuring "Custer's Last Rally" and "Cossack of the Caucasus," and there are some grainy film clips of the show itself. **The Whitney Gallery** showcases work by the adventurous artists who carried their pallets to the frontier to record firsthand the wilderness beauty, the proud Indian cultures and the lives of trappers and cowboys in the 19th century. Bygone artists like Frederic Remington, George Catlin, Charlie Russell, Albert Bierstadt, and Alfred Jacob Miller share exhibition space with modern western artists like Jim Bama and Harry Jackson. **The Plains Indian Museum** is devoted to the history of plains tribes including the Blackfeet, Cheyenne, Crow, Gros Ventre, Shoshone, and Sioux. Exhibits lucidly explain the migrations and customs of the tribes, and display art and artifacts including cradle boards, ceremonial dresses and robes, pipes, and beadwork. **The Cody Firearms Museum** displays weaponry dating from 16th-century Europe in its collection of more than 4,000 pieces.

Every year the center features special exhibitions, and a wide variety of educational programs run throughout the year. Late September's annual Plains Indian Seminar brings in scholars and students for an in-depth examination of Native American issues. The Harold McCracken Research Library is an excellent resource for historic photographs, an archive of cowboy music and thousands of books and manuscripts.

Tecumseh's Old West Miniature Village and Museum. 142 W. Yellowstone Ave. ☎ **307/587-5362.** Admission $3. Open June–Aug daily 8am–8pm; call for winter hours.

You have to pass through a trading post of ordinary Western tourist plunder to get to this finely detailed miniature diorama of Western history. It depicts everything from fur trappers floating the rivers to Custer's last moments at Little Big Horn. There is also a small museum of Indian and pioneer artifacts.

✪ **Cody Nite Rodeo.** Stampede Park. ☎ **800/207-0744.** Admission $10 adults, $4 ages 7–12 years. June–Aug nightly 8:30pm.

If you want to see a rodeo in Wyoming, Cody offers a sure thing: a nightly dust-up between bulls, broncs, and cowboys, as well as roping, cutting, and kids' events like the "calf scramble." Pay an extra two bucks and you get a seat just above the chutes in the Buzzard's Roost. The 6,000-seat stadium sits out on an open terrace above the river west of town—not a bad place to be on a cool Wyoming evening beneath the stars. Once a year some of the nation's top rodeo competitors show up for the Fourth of July Cody Stampede (see "Special Events," above).

Old Trail Town. 1831 Demaris Dr. ☎ **307/587-5302.** Admission $4. May 15–Sept 15, daily 8am–7pm.

Walking the creaky boardwalks here, you'll pass by gray storefronts and clapboard cabins gathered from ghost towns around the region and assembled on the original town site of Cody City, a short jog from the rodeo grounds. Archaeologist Bob Edgar hasn't wasted any paint on these relics, which include a cabin from Kaycee where Butch Cassidy and the Sundance Kid once conspired, and what must be the largest collection of worn-out buckboard carriages in the United States. On the west end of the "town" are the relocated graves of a number of Western notables, including John "Liver-eating" Johnson, Robert Redford's model for *Jeremiah Johnson.*

The Buffalo Bill Reservoir. 6 miles west of Cody on U.S. Highway 14/16/20 at the top of Shoshone Canyon. ☎ **307/527-6076** visitors center. Free admission. May–Sept daily 8am–8pm.

The **Buffalo Bill Dam** drops like a slim concrete knife 328 feet into the gorge carved by the Shoshone River west of Cody. You can walk out atop the dam and look down the steep canyon or back across the deep blue water of the reservoir. Several workers died building it, and when it was completed in 1910, it was the tallest dam in the world. The lake behind it serves anglers, boaters and windsurfers, while providing irrigation water to farmers downstream. An octagonal visitors center perched next to the dam provides exhibits on the reservoir, wildlife, and area recreation.

There is a boat launch along the north lakeshore off U.S. Highway 14/16/20 and a clean, spacious campground that lacks only adequate shade.

Cody Wildlife Exhibit. 433 Yellowstone Ave. ☎ **307/587-2804.** Admission $4 adults, $2 children over 6. Group rates available. May–Oct, daily 9am–8pm.

Trophy hunters will be envious of this collection of more than 400 mounted animals from all over the world, displayed in simulated habitats. Others will skip it and head for the park: While there are no elephants, stuffed or otherwise, 53 miles west in Yellowstone, there are plenty of other interesting species, all of them breathing.

WHERE TO STAY

If you want to book lodging before you arrive, contact **Cody Area Central Reservations** (☎ **888/468-6996**).

Buffalo Bill Village Resort: Comfort Inn, Holiday Inn & Buffalo Bill Village Historic Cabins. 17th and Sheridan Ave., Cody, WY 82414. ☎ **800/527-5544.** Fax 307-587-2795. Email: jblair@wavecom.net. **Comfort Inn:** 75 units. A/C TV TEL. $75–$130 double. **Holiday Inn:** 190 units. A/C TV TEL. $75–$130 double. **Buffalo Bill Village Historic Cabins:** 83 units. TV TEL. $50–$130 double. AE, CB, DC, DISC, MC, V. Buffalo Bill Village is open only from May–Sept.

This is not exactly a "resort" but an oddly matched cluster of lodgings with a convenient downtown location. The Holiday and Comfort Inns are similar to their chain brethren elsewhere, but the village of aged cabins provides a rustic exterior with a more Western feel, and modern conveniences inside. Family units have two bedrooms. There is also a brief "Old West" boardwalk where you can shop for curios or sign up for tours and river trips, an outdoor heated pool, and several restaurants.

The Comfort Inn and Holiday Inn are priced identically, and have similar amenities (the rooms at the Comfort Inn, built in 1993, are slightly newer, and breakfast is included in the rate). The rooms at Buffalo Bill Village are simply equipped and less expensive.

✪ **Cody's Guest Houses.** 1525 Beck Ave., Cody, WY 82414. ☎ **307/587-6000.** Fax 307/587-8048. www.wtp.net/cghouses. E-mail: cghouses@cody.wtp.net. 10 units consisting of 1- to 3-bdrm houses (sleep up to 11) and suites. June–Sept $80 double, $450 3-bdrm house; Oct–May $60 double, $335 3-bdrm house. AE, DISC, MC, V.

Finely restored older properties located in residential neighborhoods allow guests to feel as if they're "home"—and they are nice homes indeed, some of them with two-person spas, honeymoon suites, kitchens and washer/dryer, antique furniture, and Victorian decor. You can pick among cozy cottages, executive suites, the Victorian

Mayor's Inn (where tea is served), and the big Western lodge, which comfortably sleeps eight.

✪ **Double Diamond X Ranch.** 3453 Southfork Rd., Cody, WY 82414. ☎ **800/833-RANCH.** Fax 307/587-2708. www.ddxranch.com. E-mail: ddx@cody.wtp.net. 5 cabins, one 7-unit lodge. $1,460 per adult per week, $1,020 per child. Rates include meals and activities. Ask about seasonal discounts. MC, V.

Ranches along the South Fork of the Shoshone River don't have the kind of traffic that streams along the North Fork into Yellowstone, but they do have the same kind of scenery: green horse pastures, volcanic rock spires, tumbling rivers, and snow-capped peaks. Guests visit the Double Diamond X to ride, fish, view wildlife, and just relax. Guests are coddled with bounteous meals, a pool, Jacuzzis, children's programs, and live evening entertainment.

The Irma Hotel. 1192 Sheridan Ave., Cody, WY 82414. ☎ **800/745-4762** or 307/587-4221. www.irmahotel.com. E-mail: irma@cody.wtp.net. 40 units. A/C TV TEL. $75–$102 double. AE, DC, DISC, MC, V.

Buffalo Bill's entrepreneurial gusto may have left him virtually penniless, but it left us this charming old hotel in the heart of town. Cody hoped to corral tourists who got off the train on their way to Yellowstone, and one of his lures was an elaborate cherrywood bar, a gift from straight-laced Queen Victoria. You can still hoist a jar on Her Royal Majesty's slab in the Silver Saddle Saloon, or spend the night in a renovated room that may have once housed a president or prince. The hotel is named for Cody's daughter Irma, and built in part with locally quarried sandstone and river rock. The large restaurant—a bit dark when you come in out of the summer sunlight—serves excellent prime rib and a summer breakfast buffet. Every summer night except Monday a gang of mustachioed gunfighters draw crowds as they fire blanks at each other on the porch along 11th Street. Suites are named after local characters from the town's early days: The Irma Suite, on the corner of the building, has a queen-size bed, writing table, a vanity in the bedroom area, a small sitting area with TV, and an old-fashioned bathroom with a tub-shower combination.

Pahaska Tepee Resort. 183 Yellowstone Hwy., Cody, WY 82414. ☎ **800/628-7791** or 307/527-7701. Fax 307/527-4019. 48 units. Mid-June to Aug $96–$105 double; Sept–Oct, Dec–Mar and May $60–$85. DISC, MC, V. Closed Nov and Apr.

Buffalo Bill's hunting lodge, only a mile from the east entrance to Yellowstone, was given his Lakota name, "Pahaska" (long-hair), when it opened in 1905. Near the top of the beautiful Wapiti Valley along U.S. Highway 14/16/20, Pahaska is a popular roost winter and summer for people visiting Yellowstone and its environs. Far from town and close to the park, the neighborhood often boasts moose and elk sightings. It's also useful to have a grocery store, gas station and gift shop, in addition to a dining room with lodgepole beams, a big fireplace and a good view. However, the rooms seem thin-walled, particularly in the winter, and the spare furnishings have begun to show signs of age. The Tepee Tavern features Molesworth fixtures.

WHERE TO DINE

For its size, Cody may have more good restaurants than any of the gateways, especially considering that the town virtually shuts down from November to May. The town's finest restaurants aren't all meat-and-potatoes operations, either, though there's no shortage of good prime rib. Note that all the restaurants listed in this section are open year-round.

If you need something less than a formal meal, like a plateful of fuel food or a jolt of caffeine for a busy day, Cody has a good supply of familiar fast-food joints and a few informal, inexpensive places. **Peter's Cafe Bakery,** at 1191 Sheridan Ave. (☎ **307/527-5040**), across the street from The Irma, serves a full breakfast starting at 7am, with fresh-baked bagels, pastries, and espresso. **Maxwell's Bakery,** 937 Sheridan Ave. (☎ **307/527-7749**) (see Maxwell's Restaurant, below), offers croissants and other fragrant bakery items, along with coffee drinks, in the early hours before the adjacent restaurant opens. There is also the **Cody Coffee Co. & Eatery,** 1702 Sheridan Ave. (☎ **307/527-7879**), for coffee drinks, fresh-made pastries, soups, and sandwiches. One of the best places to get a beer and burger is the **Proud Cut Saloon** (☎ **307/527-6905**), 1227 Sheridan Ave. Finally, there's a sports bar with a full menu of ribs and pastas and Greek food attached to the **Black Sheep Restaurant,** 1901 Mt. View Dr. (☎ **307/527-5253**).

Cassie's Supper Club. 214 Yellowstone Ave. ☎ **307/527-5500.** Dinner entrees $13–$25. AE, DISC, MC, V. Mon–Sat 11am–2pm and 5–10pm, Sun 5–10pm. TRADITIONAL WESTERN.

Cassie's is the sort of place you might expect of the West: big platters of beef, four bars serving drinks, and lots of people in a restaurant that can hold over 400. Located along the highway west of town in what was once a "House of Ill Fame," Cassie's is now very respectable and very busy. In the Buffalo Bar, a 20-foot mural depicts horses, cowboys and shoot-outs, and there is local artwork throughout the club. Hesitant dancers are lured on the floor by free Western swing lessons several evenings a week. Live music nightly.

✪ **Franca's Italian Dining.** 1421 Rumsey Ave. ☎ **888/806-5354** or 307/ 587-5354. Reservations recommended. Main courses $14.50–$26. No credit cards. Wed–Sun 6–10pm. Open May 15–Oct 15. ITALIAN.

Franca Facchetti uses her mother's old-world recipes to cook four-course meals that will transport you from the sagebrush hills of Wyoming to the grapevined hills of northern Italy. Italian cuisine is the one exotic cuisine that seems to take root in this state; you have only to taste Franca's loin of veal in tuna sauce to be convinced. Try the ravioli, or the popular tortellini—or if you're lucky, maybe you'll show up on a night that Franca cooks fresh salmon stuffed with sole mousse and pistachios. The small restaurant is in a turn-of-the-century home a block off Sheridan Avenue, and nicely decorated by Franca's artist-husband. There's an impressive wine cellar.

La Comida. 1385 Sheridan Ave. ☎ **307/587-9556.** E-mail: cajun@ wavecom.net. Dinner entrees $5–$11. AE, DISC, MC, V. Daily 11am–10pm. MEXICAN.

The cheerfully lit wood patio of La Comida invites you and your family to sit outside and watch the passing scene on Sheridan Avenue. Favorites include pechuga over rice (tasty bites of chicken breast baked in cream with green chiles and Swiss cheese) and a quesadilla filled with shaved rib-eye steak and green chiles. Like most Mexican fare in this region, the spices are mild, just like the night air on fair summer nights on La Comida's casual porch.

Maxwell's Restaurant. 937 Sheridan Ave. ☎ **307/527-7749.** Lunch entrees $7–$10; dinner entrees $8.75–$16.50. DISC, MC, V. Mon–Sat 11am–9pm. ECLECTIC AMERICAN.

A family restaurant, in which *family* does not translate to *bland,* Maxwell's has some spicy chicken and pasta dishes to go with its salads, seafood, and beef. The wine list is respectable, and you can order a Philly steak, uncommon in Wyoming. The low-backed booths and varnished wood tables are sometimes packed and noisy, but it's a friendly crowd.

Silver Dollar Bar & Grill. 1313 Sheridan Ave. ☎ **307/587-3554.** Reservations not accepted. Most items $5–$8. No credit cards. Grill open Mon–Sat 11am–10pm, Thurs 11am–7pm, Sun noon–10pm. BURGERS/PUB GRUB.

Visitors expect music, loud voices, and hearty food in Wyoming bars, and the Silver Dollar has offered all of these for decades. The building was once the town's post office, and like a post office, it's a good place to mingle with locals. The burgers are touted as Wyoming's best.

Stefan's Restaurant. 1367 Sheridan Ave. ☎ **307/587-8511.** Lunch entrees $5–$7; dinner entrees $10–$23. AE, DISC, MC, V. Summer daily 8am–10pm; off-season Mon–Sat 11am–9pm. ECLECTIC.

Stefan is a restless chef, so the menu of his restaurant today is almost completely different from what he began with a few years ago. Among the entree survivors is a local favorite, a filet mignon stuffed with Gorgonzola, sun-dried tomatoes, and portobellos. The Southwestern interior might lead you to expect an enchilada or two, but you can't tell a restaurant by its decor—you're just as likely to find a swordfish in an avocado and mango sauce. Experimentation has kept Stefan's menu deliciously spry. There are separate lunch and Sunday brunch menus and a "little bites" menu with $3 children's meals.

9

A Yellowstone & Grand Teton Nature Guide

*T*hough they are often linked in peoples' minds, Yellowstone and Grant Teton national parks couldn't be more different. One is an immense wilderness plateau that sits atop a caldera seething with molten lava; the other is a striking set of peaks rising from a broad river plain. One encloses some of the most remote backcountry in the Lower 48, and provides crucial habitat for rare species like grizzly bears and wolves; the other is only a bike ride away from a busy resort town, and includes an airport and grazing cattle in its mix of activities.

What they *do* share is the affection of millions of visitors who come here annually to renew their ties to the natural beauty of the northern Rockies. Many Americans make the pilgrimage to see these shining mountains, alpine lakes, majestic elk, and astonishing geysers.

Unfortunately, mineral development, logging, and housing developments have diminished the wildlands, often called the **Greater Yellowstone Ecosystem,** that once surrounded the parks. The ecosystem is an interdependent system of watersheds, mountain ranges, wildlife habitat, and other components that scientists say extends beyond the two parks to include seven national forests, an Indian reservation, three national wildlife refuges, and nearly a million acres of private land. To put it into an imaginable perspective: The 18 million acres that comprise the ecosystem span an area that is as big as Connecticut, Rhode Island, and Delaware combined. It is one of the earth's largest intact temperate ecosystems.

It's also a massive and important watershed. Water from west of the Continental Divide runs for 27 miles through Yellowstone before draining into the Snake River, travels through Grand Teton National Park and Idaho before running into the Columbia River, and then wends it way west through Oregon where it drains into the Pacific Ocean.

Water on the eastern slopes of the Divide runs through Yellowstone to form the Madison and Gallatin Rivers, which meet the Jefferson River west of Bozeman, Montana, and form the Missouri. Then, as the song lyrics tell us, the Mighty Mo runs "down the Mississippi to Gulf of Mexico."

As if that weren't enough, the headwaters of the Yellowstone River are in the remote Thorofare country south of Yellowstone Lake. After running north the length of the park, the Yellowstone winds across Montana as the longest undammed river in America to a meeting point with the Missouri in North Dakota.

1 The Parks Today

It has long been difficult for park managers to both provide the citizenry with a good vacation and protect the natural wonders of the parks. One challenge is that the parks must be made accessible to 3 million annual visitors—many of whom have different, even contradictory, expectations of a wilderness vacation. This means new facilities under construction and catching up on much-needed road repair after decades of neglect. At the same time, the parks are wild preserves, and the Park Service must cope with the impact of 6 million feet on the forests, meadows, and thermal areas, as well as on the day-to-day lives of the millions of animals that inhabit the area.

It's a tough balancing act. Some of the pivotal issues in the parks today include: the impact of snowmobiles; the reintroduced wolves and the livestock losses of ranchers in and around the parks; the inadequacy of the park's infrastructure—sewage is the latest problem—to cope with 3 million annual human visitors; increased winter use despite no studies of the impacts on wildlife; the reduction of habitat surrounding the parks, coupled with a growing population of elk and bison seeking forage beyond park boundaries and possibly infecting domestic animals with a disease called brucellosis. And that's the short list.

Often, possible solutions are a case of too little, too late, layering complex management strategies on an ecosystem that might do better if it were simply allowed to work things out naturally. The problem is, Grand Teton and Yellowstone have already been altered significantly by humans, so "natural" becomes a relative concept.

A good example is the reintroduction of wolves, a natural predator of the overpopulated elk, which were eliminated in the 1920s. These days, though, there are ranches all around the parks, and the Defenders of Wildlife offers payments to anyone who loses a calf to a canine—and they do, because wolves haven't read the management plan. When wolves wander down to Grand Teton, park officials put out roadkill carcasses to keep them well fed and away from cattle, which are legally allowed to graze in the park. It's no picnic for park managers, though it is one for the wolves—literally.

These artificial boundaries also cause problems for bison. The state of Montana now allows hunters to shoot bison when they stray outside the park. Ranchers fear bison because of brucellosis, a disease that, when transmitted to cattle, causes cows to abort fetuses. Now there is talk of mass vaccinations of elk and bison, though, so far, there is no evidence that either species has ever infected livestock.

As for the proliferation of snowmobiles and cars, most agree there will have to be changes as visitation continues to grow. Snowmobilers arrive in the park in flocks as soon as the snow starts falling and remain until late February. While the popularity of the sport has had a positive affect on the tourism industry in the gateways of West Yellowstone, Jackson, and Gardiner, park officials are studying the long-term environmental impact of the machines. In their opinion, the snowmobiles create their own types of problems. First, the machines are noisy. Second, they share the same narrow trails as wildlife during months when the animals' energy levels are depleted by bad weather and a lack of food. Third, engine emissions create air pollution, which some say presents a health hazard. Finally, snowmobilers tend to drive the crowded paths at high speed, which can lead to accidents. As a consequence, the future of snowmobiles in the park is under study.

Then there's the traffic issue. Park roads are narrow and twisty, so the intrusion of 30-foot-long motor homes and pickup trucks towing trailers creates congestion, especially during the peak summer months. There have been studies of transportation alternatives to unclog park roadways, even a monorail that would wind through Yellowstone, but no decisive action.

As the world awakens to the accelerating loss of vital species in shrinking wild habitat, the value of an ecosystem like this is heightened, and it become ever more imperative to find ways in which to preserve it. Recently, park scientists have battled to protect the Yellowstone cutthroat trout in Yellowstone Lake from the impact of lake trout introduced by man. They have also recognized the enormous value of the microbes evolving in Yellowstone's superhot thermal areas, and have signed a unique agreement with a private company giving it exclusive rights to collect and market microbes from the park, with a royalty to be paid to American taxpayers. That agreement is now on hold because of a court challenge.

2   Landscape & Geology

The Yellowstone and Grand Teton region is one of the most dynamic seismic areas in the world—racked by earthquakes, riven by cracks where water boils to the surface, and littered with the detritus of previous volcanic eruptions. Today, the cauldron of the Yellowstone caldera is again filling with magma. The record in the rock shows that for the last 2 million years the plateau has blown its top every 600,000 years or so—and the last explosion was about 600,000 years ago. That means a titanic blow—bigger than anything seen in recorded history—could happen, well, any century now. The geological time frame is a long one, by human standards.

As you'll learn when you visit the exhibits on the park's geology at Moose, Mammoth, and the various geothermal areas, what you see on the surface—great layers of ash, and the core of volcanic vents, like Mount Washburn and Bunsen Peak—is only a fraction of the story of Yellowstone and Grand Teton.

Situated on 2.2 million acres, Yellowstone is significantly larger than its sister to the south. Encompassing 3,472 square miles, Yellowstone boasts 370 miles of paved roads and 1,200 miles of trails, and is home to more geysers and hot springs than the combined total in the rest of the world.

Though it can't match Yellowstone's size, Grand Teton National Park is nothing to sneeze at. It has towering mountain spires reaching almost 14,000 feet skyward that have been compared to the cathedral towers of Chartres, picturesque glacial lakes, and a great deal of interesting topography. The 485 square miles of Grand Teton contain 159 miles of paved roads and 230 miles of hiking trails.

THE FACES OF YELLOWSTONE NATIONAL PARK

By the completion of the 1872 Hayden expedition, explorers had identified several distinct areas in the park, each with its own physical characteristics. Less spectacular than the craggy mountain scenery of Grand Teton and less imposing that the vast expanses of the Grand Canyon of Arizona, Yellowstone's beauty is subtle, reflecting the changes it has undergone during its explosive past.

Though Yellowstone has its share of mountains, much of the park is a high mountain plateau. The environment changes dramatically as you move vertically up the mountain slopes from the foothill zones in the valleys—the elevation at the entrance at West

Geysers, Hot Springs, Mud Pots & Fumaroles: What's the Difference?

Here's a way to identify the four most common types of thermal attractions in Yellowstone.

Geysers, the most prominent and spectacular of the thermal features in the park, are formed by the marriage of three elements: heat in the center (mantle) of the earth, water, and pressure-resistant rock. Here's how they work together: First, there has to be a water source, which, in this area, comes in the form of snow-melt that sinks into the earth, reaching depths of 10,000 feet—that's 2 miles, but remember, thermal areas in Yellowstone are that close to the surface. The second element is heat, which is still there, as are cauldrons of magma. When water moves toward the center of the earth, it is converted to boiling water by the heat and begins a trip back towards the surface, often carrying minerals with it. But that's not all that happens: The third element, pressure-resistant rock, acts like a geologic traffic cop by guiding the water towards the surface. Since the geyser's plumbing system does not have a way to diffuse energy, pressure builds, the boiling water is converted to steam, and voilà! It is spewed forth from vents in the earth's surface. Following the eruptions, silica that once was a component of the magma—which may not have reached the surface—returns down the pathway to form a lining through which more snowmelt will travel, and the process repeats itself.

Hot springs are closely related to geysers but don't display the same eruptions because they don't develop the same subsurface pressures. Their colorful appearance is created by different minerals, algae, the absorption of light by colloidal particles—tiny, suspended particles of liquid—and reflections.

Mud pots are hot springs on the earth's surface that are formed as heated water mixes with clay and undissolved minerals. Some are very colorful, others unsightly and smelly.

Fumaroles are steam vents called "dry geysers," from which gases rush into the air; they are considered hot springs, which lack a liquid component.

Yellowstone is 6,600 feet, for example, compared to 5,300 at the Gardiner Entrance. Since the park lies about halfway between the equator and the north pole, its summers consist of long, warm days that stimulate plant growth at the lower elevations.

As you walk the park trails, you'll find that plant distribution changes as the elevation changes. At the lowest elevations, down around 5,000 feet above sea level, you'll find **grassy flats** and sagebrush growing on dry, porous souls, with creeks and rivers cutting through to form wildlife-rich **riparian zones.** Next up are the **foothills,** sloping upward toward peaks, sometimes humped by deposits of glacial moraine. Douglas fir, pine, and other confers clad these slopes, as well as aspen, and sometimes there are marshes and ponds. Shrubs like huckleberry and flowers like columbine favor such wet and shady spots.

Then comes the **mountain zone** (from 6,000 to 7,600 ft.), thickening forests with more lodgepole pine, broken by meadow areas where wildlife often grazes. The transition area between the highest forest and the bare surface above treeline is known as the **subalpine zone** (between 7,600 and 11,300 ft. of elevation). Finally, we come to the bare rock at the top of the continent (breathing heavily yet?), where small, hardy plants like glacier lilies and sky pilot bloom briefly and close to the ground after snow melt.

Though the park is most famous for its geysers, visitors can choose among very different environments, reflections of the long-term effect of geologic activity and weather.

The limestone terraces at **Mammoth Hot Springs** give testimony to the subsurface volcanic activity throughout the region. The park sits atop a rare geologic hot spot where molten rock still rises to within 2 miles of the earth's surface, heating the water in a plumbing system that still mystifies scientists.

The **northern section of the park,** between Mammoth Hot Springs and the Tower-Roosevelt area, is a high plains area that is primarily defined by mountainous regions, forests, and broad expanses of river valleys that were created by ice movements.

The road between the Tower-Roosevelt junction and the Northeast Entrance winds through the **Lamar Valley,** an area that has been covered by glaciers three times, most recently during an ice age that began 25,000 years ago and continued for 10,000 years. In geologic terms, that was yesterday. Because this area was a favorite spot of Theodore Roosevelt, it is often referred to as "Roosevelt Country." The beautiful valley, where elk, bison and wolves interact, is still dotted with glacial ponds and strewn with boulders deposited by moving ice.

Further south are **Pelican** and **Hayden Valleys,** the two largest, most prominent, ancient lakebeds in the park. They feature large, open meadows with abundant plant life that provides food for a population of bison and elk.

In the warm months, you'll enjoy the contrast between the lush green valleys and **Canyon Country,** the largest region, in the center of the park. Canyon Country is defined by the Grand Canyon of the Yellowstone, a colorful, 1,000-foot-deep, 20-mile-long gorge—a miniaturized version of its granddaddy in Arizona. The Yellowstone River cuts through the valley, in some places moving 64,000 cubic feet of water per second, creating two waterfalls in the process, one of which is more than twice the height of Niagara Falls.

When you arrive at the **southern geyser basins,** you may feel that you've been transported through a geologic time warp. The cratered landscapes here are unlike any other in the park. Here you will find the largest collections of thermal areas in the world—there are perhaps 600 geysers and 10,000 geothermal features in the park—and the largest geysers in the park. The result: boiling water that is catapulted skyward, and barren patches of sterile dirt; hot, bubbling pools that are unimaginably colorful; and of course, the star of this show, Old Faithful geyser. Plan on spending at least 79 minutes here, because that's the typical period between eruptions that send thousands of gallons of boiling water through the sky at a speed exceeding 100 miles per hour.

You'll see the park's volcanic activity on a 17-mile journey east to the **lake area,** the scene of three volcanic eruptions that took place more than 600,000 years ago. When the final eruption blasted more than 1,000 square miles of the Rocky Mountains into the stratosphere, it created the Yellowstone caldera, a massive depression measuring 28 by 47 miles, and Yellowstone Lake basin, some 20 miles long, 14 miles wide, and reaching depths of 390 feet. You'll notice as you travel the roads here that the landscape consists of flat plateaus of lava that are hundreds of feet thick.

THE SPIRES OF GRAND TETON NATIONAL PARK

Your first sight of the towering spires of the **Cathedral Group**—the *trois tetons* (three breasts), as the French trappers called them—will create an indelible impression. A bit of history makes them even more interesting.

Their formation began more than 2.5 billion years ago when sand and volcanic debris settled in an ancient ocean that covered this entire area. Scientists estimate roughly 40 to 80 million years ago, a compression of the earth's surface caused an uplift of the entire Rocky Mountain chain from Mexico to Canada. This was just the first step in an ongoing series of events that included several periods during which the area was covered by a miles-thick crust of ice.

Then, 6 million to 9 million years ago (that's like yesterday, in geologic time), the shifting of the earth's plates caused movement along the north-south Teton fault that produced a tremendous uplift. The result: The rock from which the mountains you see today were carved was moved to its present site from a position 20,000 to 30,000 feet *below* what is today the floor of the valley.

The west block of rock tipped upward to create the **Teton Range,** and the eastern block swung downward to form the valley that is now called **Jackson Hole**—kind of like a pair of horizontal swinging doors that moved the earth 5 miles.

At this conclusion of the upheaval, and after eons of erosion and glaciation, the **Grand Teton peak,** centerpiece of this 40-mile-long fault area, towered 13,770 foot above sea level, more than a mile above the visitor's center at Moose Junction. It is surrounded by seven other peaks more than 12,000 feet high, in conditions that support mountain glaciers. As you gaze upward at this magnificent range, you will notice that many of the cliffs are more than half a mile high.

During geologic explorations of **Mount Moran** (elevation 12,605 ft.), which gets less attention than it deserves, it was discovered that erosion has removed some 3,000 feet of material from its summit, so it once must have been more than 15,000 feet high. Equally remarkable is the fact that the thin layer of Flathead sandstone on the top of this peak is found in the valley below, buried at least 24,000 feet below the surface—further evidence of the upthrust of the mountains.

Though this is the youngest range in the Rockies, in yet another geologic anomaly the rocks here are some of the oldest in North America, consisting of granitic gneisses and schists, which are the hardest and least porous rocks known to geologists.

The Teton area experienced a cooling trend about 150,000 years ago, during which time glaciers more than 2,000 feet thick flowed from higher elevations and an ice sheet covered Jackson Hole. When it melted for the final time, some 60,000 to 80,000 years ago, it gouged a 386-foot-deep, 16-mile-long depression that is now known as **Jackson Lake.**

The receding layers of ice also left other calling cards. Several beautiful **glacial lakes** were created, including Phelps, Taggart, Bradley, Jenny, String, and Leigh. The sides of **Cascade Canyon** were polished by receding ice. Glacial lakes called **cirque lakes** were carved at the heads of canyons, and the peaks of the mountains were honed to their present jagged edges. Five glaciers have survived on Mt. Moran. The best trail for glacial views is the Cascade Trail, which leads to the Schoolroom Glacier. But you shouldn't walk on the Mt. Moran glaciers unless you are experienced; it's very dangerous.

3 Plant Life in the Parks

When it comes to the variety of plants in the two parks, the only limiting factor is the high altitude—otherwise, the diversity of terrain, weather and soils permits a fairly wide range of vegetation. Estimates vary, but in the ecosystem known as Greater Yellowstone, there are more than 1,500 plant varieties. In an area larger than many of our states on the eastern seaboard—more than 3,900 square miles between the two parks—there's plenty of room for them to stretch their roots and branches. Because of the diverse terrain, some species are found living on the dry valley beds in hostile soil, in close proximity to other species that predominate in lush meadows and riverbeds. Some thrive in thermal areas, while others do well in alpine areas, near mountain lakes, and in cirques near glaciers.

The history of the parks' plant life makes for interesting reading. Examination of plant fossils indicates that life began during the Eocene epoch, approximately 58 million years ago, and continued for 25 million years. The inspection of petrified tree stumps in Yellowstone's Lamar Valley led to the identification of 27 distinct layers of forests, one atop the other.

Climatic conditions during the Eocene period were similar to those in the southeastern and south-central United States. Difficult as it may be to imagine, the area was once a warm temperate zone in which rainfall may have averaged 50 to 60 inches per year at what was then an elevation of 3,000 feet above sea level.

These days, the elevation ranges from 5,000 to 13,000 feet, the average low temperature is approximately 30°, and hundreds of inches of snow fall each year. Plants have adapted to a growing season that is merely 60 days in duration. As a consequence, forests once populated with hardwoods, like maple, magnolia, and sycamore, are now filled with conifers, the most common of which are pine, spruce, and fir. A smattering of cottonwood and aspen thrive in the cool park temperatures.

Some experts speculate that during the glacial periods the tallest mountains in the Lamar Valley of Yellowstone were islands amid a sea of ice, thus providing refuge for some species of plant life.

The parks have several growing zones. Above 10,000 feet in the alpine zone, plants adapt to wind, snow, and lack of soil by growing close to the ground, flowering soon after the snows melt—you'll find them on trails near Dunraven Pass in Yellowstone and in Cascade Canyon in Grand Teton.

In Yellowstone, the Canyon and subalpine regions, at 7,000 to 10,000 feet, are known for **conifer forests** and open meadows of **wildflowers.** As elevation increases, wildflowers are abundant and healthy, while trees become stunted or shrublike.

In the valley in Grand Teton, at 6,400 to 7,000 feet, the porous valley soil supports plants that are capable of tolerating hot and dry summertime conditions. **Sagebrush, wildflowers,** and **grasses** thrive and predominate. Plants bloom in a pageant of colors from early June until early July.

Identifying the plants described below does not require a degree in botany. However, a copy of Richard J. Shaw's book *Plants of Yellowstone and Grand Teton National Park* (Wheelright Press; 1836 Sunnyside Ave., Salt Lake City, UT 84108), which is well illustrated with color photos, will simplify the task, as will Earl Jensen's videotape *Wildflowers of Yellowstone,* which is available at many bookstores. If you can't find these at your local bookstore, then they can be purchased by mail from the Yellowstone Association (its complete address and telephone number are given in chapter 2, "Planning Your Trip to Yellowstone & Grand Teton National Parks."

TREES

Coniferous trees are most common in the parks, because of the high altitude and short growing season, but there are some hardy deciduous trees as well, such as cottonwood and aspen. The most common cone-bearing trees in the parks are lodgepole pines, which cover as much as 80 percent of Yellowstone, and Douglas fir, subalpine fir, Engelmann spruce, blue spruce, and whitebark pine. The key to identification is the trees' basic shape, the shape of their needles, and their cones.

LODGEPOLE PINE   This familiar tree grows tall and slender, bare trunk at the bottom and needles near the top, so that dense stands look like the spears of a closely ranked army. The needles of the lodgepole are clustered in pairs, typically around 3 inches long. You'll see logs from this tree supporting teepees and in the construction of cabins.

Lodgepole Pine   *Douglas Fir*

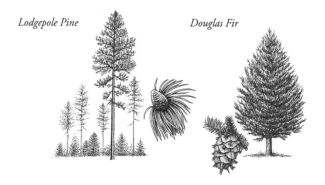

DOUGLAS FIR   "Doug fir" is actually a member of the pine family, with prickly cones and dark, deeply etched bark. This tree has flat, flexible, single needles that grow around the branch, giving the tree the appearance of fullness. Another giveaway is that its cones hang downward, and they do not disintegrate aloft, but litter the forest floor. These trees like the north-facing side of the mountain.

SUBALPINE FIR   You can usually distinguish firs by their needles, which sprout individually from branches instead of in clusters, like a pine; and by their cones, which grow upright on the branch until they dry out and blow away. Look for the slender, conical crown of this tree. When heavy snows weigh the lower branches down, they often become rooted, forming a circle of smaller trees called a snow mat. You'll find Subalpine Fir up high near the treeline.

Subalpine Fir

ENGELMANN SPRUCE   This tree also likes the higher elevations, growing in shaded ravines and in the canyons of the Teton range above 6,800 feet, and sometimes much higher. Look for it near Kepler Cascades, Spring Creek, and the South Entrance of Yellowstone National Park. It is distinguished by single needles that are square and sharp to the touch, and cones with papery scales that are approximately 1.5 inches long.

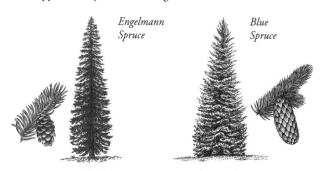

Engelmann Spruce

Blue Spruce

BLUE SPRUCE   The Englemann Spruce's cousin, this is most commonly found along the Snake River near Jackson. True to its name, it is most easily identified by its bluish appearance, rather stiff, sharp needles, and cones that are twice the size of the Englemann.

OTHER PLANTS

Here's a brief listing of some of the most common and interesting plants found in the ecosystem.

Glacier Lily

Indian Paintbrush

GLACIER LILY   A member of the Lily family with a nodding flower on a 6- to 12-inch stem, this bright yellow spring flower is found in abundance in both parks at elevations of more than 7,500 feet. Also known as the Fawn Lily, Trout Lily, and Adders Tongue, it is especially common near Sylvan Pass and on Dunraven Pass.

Photo Tip

To successfully record your discovery of the parks' flora, consider adding to your arsenal of camera gear a microlens that will allow you to focus within 6 inches of blossoms. A 200 ISO film speed will add to the chances of properly exposing the film, even on cloudy days.

INDIAN PAINTBRUSH   This is the Wyoming state flower. It exhibits a distinctive narrow, brightly colored, scarlet bloom that is most commonly found from mid-June to early September in the Snake River bottom land. Other species are white, yellow, orange, and pink.

PLAINS PRICKLY PEAR   This member of the cactus family is only one of two species found in the park, most frequently in the Mammoth area and near the Snake River. It is distinguished by thick, flat green stems armed with spines and a conspicuous yellow flower with numerous petals that you'll see during midsummer. Indians, who recognized prickly pear's medicinal qualities, treated warts by lacerating them, then applying juice from the plant.

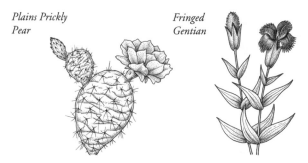

Plains Prickly Pear

Fringed Gentian

FRINGED GENTIAN   This member of the Gentian family is the official flower of Yellowstone Park, where it is common and blooms throughout the summer. The purple petals are fused into a 2-inch-long corolla and sit atop 1- to 3-foot-tall stems. It is also found between Jackson Lake Dam and the Jackson Lake Lodge.

ROUNDLEAF HAREBELL   This delicate, herbaceous perennial is abundant in the forests and along roadsides, primarily in July and August. Perched atop 1-foot-tall stems, its roundish, heart-shaped basal leaves are conspicuous, since buds grow erect but the purple blossoms droop or are horizontal, nature's way of protecting pollen from rainfall.

Roundleaf
Harebell

Silky
Phacelia

SILKY PHACELIA   Silky is one of the most photogenic and easily recognized species in the parks. Growing in purple clumps alongside the road at Dunraven Pass, the flower derives its name from the silvery pubescence that covers stems and leaves. The best time for photographing this star is July and August.

SHOOTING STAR   The shooting star is characterized by pinkish 0.5- to 1-inch long flowers that dangle earthward like meteorites from a 12-inch stem; they bloom in June. It is commonly found near thermal areas, streambeds, and Yellowstone Lake.

Shooting
Star

Yellow Monkey-
Flower

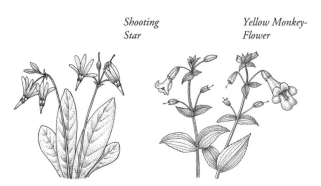

YELLOW MONKEY-FLOWER   The monkey-flower exhibits a bright yellow petal that, together with orange spots, attracts insect pollinators near stream beds at elevations of 7,000 to 9,000 feet all summer. It is also commonly found near thermal areas and Yellowstone Lake.

FAIRYSLIPPER (also known as the **Calypso Orchid**)   Finding this beautiful orchid may require some supersleuthing, but the challenge and the payoff are worth the effort. It is one of 15 orchid species found in the parks, and considered by many to be the most beautiful and striking. Found parkwide during May and June, it usually has one small, green leaf and a red-pink flower that resembles a small lady's slipper, hence the name. It is found in cool, deep-shaded areas and is becoming rare because its habitat is disappearing.

*Fairyslipper
(a.k.a. Calypso
Orchid)*   *Bitterroot*

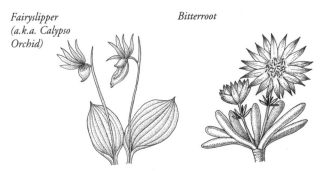

BITTERROOT   The state flower of Montana, the bitterroot, with its fleshy rose and white petals, which extend to 1 inch in length, makes its first appearance in early June in dry, open, sometimes stony soil and in grassy meadows. It was a source of food for Indians, who introduced it to Captain Lewis of Lewis and Clark fame, hence its botanical name.

*Columbia
Monkshood*

COLUMBIA MONKSHOOD   This is a purple, irregularly shaped flower with a hood-shaped structure that has two sepals at its side and two below (these make up the calyx, the leafy parts that surround the flower). Its stem varies in height from 2 to 5 feet; you'll find them in wet meadows and on stream banks from June through August. It is commonly found near thermal areas, stream beds, and Yellowstone Lake.

4 Wildlife in the Parks

For many, the primary reason for a visit to these parks is the wild-life: bighorn sheep, bison, elk, bald eagles, river otters, and moose all wandering free, often within roadside view of travelers. Yellowstone and Grand Teton parks are home to the largest concentration of free-roaming wildlife in the Lower 48. This includes one of the largest herds of elk in North America, the largest free-roaming herd of bison in the Lower 48, and the only significant population of grizzly bears in the Lower 48 located a sizable distance south of the Canadian border.

But it doesn't stop there. Also in Yellowstone/Grand Teton are eight species of ungulates (hoofed mammals), black and grizzly bears, three species of wild cats, as well as coyotes, wolverines, pine martens, 70 smaller species of mammals, and 290 species of birds. Add to that the wolves reintroduced in 1995—and now reproducing prolifically—and you have a rich array of wildlife intermingling throughout the parks. Most of these creatures will ignore or shy away from humans. But humans, never shy, want to get ever closer to the animals, and that can cause problems. Unlike the critters that inhabit petting zoos, the animals in the Greater Yellowstone Ecosystem are wild and pose a constant threat to the safety of visitors.

There may be shocks, too, for tourists not familiar with animals in the wild. In 1998, wolves in Slough Creek set upon a coyote that wandered into their new territory, sending a message to coyotes—and to people with spotting scopes on the hill across the creek—that this would now be a coyote-free zone. It was not a pretty death. But death is a day-to-day affair in the parks. In the spring, you'll see carcasses of elk that died during the long winter, and often you'll see predators feeding. That's part of the picture when you vow to interfere as little as possible with nature's way.

Park naturalists generally agree that every major vertebrate wildlife species thought to have been present since the ice age over

Photo Tip

Photographers need to be armed with a telephoto lens, preferably a zoom, to get good shots of wildlife. Even the bigger animals in the park present minimal risks to humans, unless you move in for a close-up of a grazing bison or a grizzly bear. Invest in a 300-millimeter lens, or 100- to 300-millimeter zoom, and you should get some good shots, without disturbing the wildlife or putting yourself at risk.

10,000 years ago is a resident of the parks today, as are several rare or endangered species, the most notable being the grizzly bear and bald eagle.

MAMMALS

BEAR (BLACK & GRIZZLY)   In recent years, grizzly bears have been quite visible, including a pair that foraged daily in a meadow just off the road over Dunraven Pass while dozens of photographers clicked away. That's unusual. Unless you have the patience to spend weeks outdoors in bear country like the Lamar or Hayden Valleys, your chances of seeing a grizzly in Yellowstone or Grand Teton aren't that good—you may have to go to the grizzly zoo in West Yellowstone. But it's the bears that tourists are always asking to see, and they've made a comeback after nearly dying off after park garbage dumps were closed in the early 1970s.

Estimates vary, but there are probably more than 500 grizzly bears in the Greater Yellowstone Ecosystem today, and an equal or greater number of black bears.

Rangers say you're most likely to spot the black bears, especially during spring months after they emerge with new cubs from their winter dens. But I must confess that in years of visiting Yellowstone I've seen half a dozen grizzlies and not a single black bear. Neither type of bear sits along park roads the way they once did, begging for food, or wrestling over park lodge garbage while tourists sat watching on bleachers. Bears who get a taste for human food, or get too comfortable around human campsites, are relocated to the backcountry. Black bears are most commonly sighted in the Canyon-Tower and Madison–Old Faithful areas where they feed on green grass, herbs, berries, ants, and carrion.

Grizzly bears are most commonly seen in the northeast area of the park, in the meadows on the hillsides of the Lamar Valley, or wandering the Hayden Valley north of Yellowstone Lake. They also feed on trout spawning in Yellowstone Lake tributaries during the late spring (campgrounds by these streams are closed during spawning times). They are most active in the spring, when they emerge from hibernation hungry, and in the fall, fattening up for winter.

Grizzly bears can do you the most damage, particularly when their cubs are around, or when they think you're after their food.

BIGHORN SHEEP   If there's a hint of a foothold, a bighorn sheep will find it. Its hooves are hard and durable on the outside but soft and grippy underneath, a perfect design for steep, rocky terrain.

Black Bear or Grizzly?

Since a black bear may be black, brown, or cinnamon, here are some identifiers. The griz is the larger of the two, typically, 3.5 feet at the shoulder with a dish-faced profile and a pronounced hump between the shoulders. The black's ears are rounder, just like those you see on stuffed animals. The grizzly's color is typically more yellowish-brown, but the coat is sometimes recognized by its cinnamon color, often highlighted by silver tips.

Caution: Park rangers attempt to keep track of the griz to avoid human/bear incidents. However, since the grizzlies don't follow prescribed pathways, it is best to assume they are always in the area; always make noise when traveling off the beaten pathway.

Black Bear

Grizzly Bear

You'll often hear them clattering before you spot their stocky, gray-brown bodies and white rumps. Six feet long, the males weigh up to 300 pounds. Their horns are coiled; the females' straight. The Greater Yellowstone Ecosystem probably contains the largest concentration of bighorns in the United States. Look for them on Mount Washburn, along Specimen Ridge, and in the Gallatin Range in Yellowstone; they are also seen occasionally in the Heart Mountain area in southern Yellowstone. In Grand Teton, smaller herds are found in the Gros Ventre valley, as well as the western slopes of the Tetons. East of the Tetons, in the Wind River Range, a large herd of bighorn sheep congregates in the winter south of the town of Dubois in Whiskey Basin.

BISON Bison (or buffalo) seem pretty indifferent to humans as they wander the roads and go about their grazing, but don't think for a minute they're docile. Their prodigious size, their cute calves (which look like cattle calves) and their lack of fear ensure that bison are key attractions. On ballerina-thin ankles, these burly brown

Bighorn Sheep   *Bison*

animals carry as much as 2,000 pounds in their thick shoulders and massive chests. Those big heads helps them clear snow for winter browsing, but during harsh winters they instinctively migrate to lower elevations (some biologists insist that both grizzlies and bison were driven up on the plateau from their natural home on the prairie). If their wanderings take them into Montana, they're in trouble; ranchers are legally allowed to shoot them in order to protect their livestock from brucellosis. Bison are much in evidence in the summer; you'll see them munching grass and rolling in dust pits in Hayden Valley, Pelican Valley, the Madison River area, and the geyser areas near the Firehole River. In the winter, snowmobilers often have to make way for the shaggy beasts, who take advantage of the snowpacked roads to travel around.

COYOTE   The wily coyote is the predator most often spotted by park visitors. Looking something like a small, lanky shepherd dog with grizzled, gray-brown coat, the coyotes number around 450, living in 65 packs that make their homes in burrows and caves. Numbers have dropped some since wolf reintroduction, but coyotes are very adaptable. Active hunters year-round, they feast on small animals such as squirrels and rabbits, as well as the carcasses of animals that died naturally or were killed by larger carnivores, like bears and wolves. They are seen near most park roads, in the meadows and the sagebrush. Coyote pups are considered a delicacy by great horned owls, eagles, cougars, and bears.

WOLF   In a controversial move, gray wolves were reintroduced to Yellowstone in 1995 for the first time since the 1920s, when they were eliminated by hunters operating under a federal predator control program designed to protect cattle herds. The population of Canadian gray wolves is thriving in its new environment, well over 100 animals have spread from Montana down to Grand Teton,

Wolf or Coyote?

Wolves and coyotes both bear a striking resemblance to large dogs. Here are some ways to distinguish them.

- Coyotes are the more delicate-looking; wolves are sturdy, almost massive.
- Coyotes grow to a height of 20 inches; wolves often grow to 34 inches.
- Coyotes have long, pointed ears; wolf ears are rounded and relatively short.
- Coyotes have thin, delicate legs, similar to those of a fox; wolves' legs are thick and long.

Coyote   *Wolf*

where they're now denning in the Gros Ventre and the valley. They are high-profile occupants of the Lamar Valley and are under constant observation by visitors with binoculars or spotting scopes who travel the area.

ELK   It is estimated that 63,000 elk (wapiti) populate the Ecosystem, 40 percent of which live in Yellowstone or Grand Teton. The most common large animal in the parks, elk are rather sociable and travel in small bands. Males are easily identifiable by a massive set of antlers. Though they shed them every spring, by early summer bulls are beginning to display prodigious racks that, by year end, are the envy of their cousins in the deer family. Their grayish-brown bodies, which typically weigh as much as 900 pounds, are accented by chestnut brown heads and necks, a shaggy mane, a short tail, and a distinctive tan patch on their rumps.

One herd can usually be located in the vicinity of Mammoth Hot Springs, often on the lawn of the main square. Others are found throughout each park. During winter months, the northern Yellowstone herd heads to a winter grazing area near Gardiner, while their cousins in Grand Teton head for the National Elk Refuge in nearby Jackson where food is more plentiful.

MOOSE   Perhaps because of their size, their homely appearance, or the palmate antler racks that can grow to 6 feet across, moose sightings provide park visitors with unequaled excitement. The largest member of the deer family, a typical adult male weighs 1,000 pounds and is most easily recognizable by a broad, pendulous muzzle and fleshy dewlap that hangs beneath his neck like a bell.

Elk   *Moose*

Moose sightings are most frequent on the edges of ponds and in damp, lush valley bottoms where they feed on willows and water plants, especially along the Moose-Wilson Road and near the Jackson Lake Lodge in Grand Teton.

The plodding, nibbling moose in a meadow is not to be approached—and is not likely to budge if you do. Though it appears ungainly, a moose is capable of traveling at 30 miles per hour; cows will charge any perceived threat to a calf, and bulls become particularly ornery in the fall, so giving them a wide berth is recommended.

MULE DEER   Not to be outnumbered by their larger cousins, an estimated 120,000 mule deer live in the ecosystem, thousands of them within the park boundaries. They are most often spotted near forest boundaries or in areas covered with grass and sagebrush. Their most distinguishing characteristics are their huge ears and a black tip on their tail that contrasts with their white rump. When they run, they bounce, all four legs in the air. Fawns, often in pairs, are typically born in late spring.

PRONGHORN ANTELOPE   The often-sighted pronghorn graze near the North Entrance to Yellowstone and on the valley floors of Grand Teton, but they are shy and difficult to approach or

Antlers or Horns?

Most of the larger, four-legged animals roaming the parks have lavish headpieces that are either horns or antlers. But what's the difference?

Antlers are shed every year; horns last a lifetime.

Male deer, elk, and moose shed their *antlers* every spring, so they are as bald as Ping-Pong balls when the parks open. By early June, though, new, velvet-covered protuberances are making their appearance.

In comparison, both sexes of bison and pronghorn grow one set of horns during their lifetimes.

photograph because of their excellent vision and speed. Often mistakenly referred to as *just* an antelope, the Pronghorn is identified by its short, black horns, tan and white bodies, and black accent stripes. They can run 45 miles per hour, but they can't clear fences.

Mule Deer

Pronghorn Antelope

5 Birds in the Parks

The skies above the parks are filled with predators on the wing, including eagles and 27 species of hawks, not to mention ospreys, falcons, and owls. Here are descriptions of some of the birds you might want to look for.

BALD EAGLE   The bald eagle holds a position in the pecking order that parallels that of the grizzly. Of all the birds in the park, visitors are most interested in spotting this endangered species, once almost wiped out by the pesticide DDT. The Yellowstone/Grand Teton area is now home to one of largest populations of eagles in

---

Birding Tip

Take a picnic lunch, or plan a relaxing break at the Oxbow Bend overlook in Grand Teton. Weather permitting, you can soak up some sunshine and observe the great blue herons, osprey, pelicans, cormorants, and, just maybe, a bald eagle. Though a popular spot, there's always room for one more vehicle.

---

the Continental United States; more than 200 of these magnificent birds make their homes in the parks. Bald eagles are most recognizable by their striking white head, tail feathers, and wingspans up to 7 feet. They typically live within 2 miles of water, so the Yellowstone Plateau, Snake River, Yellowstone Lake, and headwaters of Madison River are prime spotting areas for this spectacular bird.

GOLDEN EAGLE The bald eagle's cousin, the golden eagle, is similar in appearance, though smaller, and it does not have a white head—sometimes it is confused with an immature bald. The golden eagle goes after small mammals like jackrabbits and prairie dogs. It works out in the open country; sometimes you'll find them feeding on roadkill.

Bald Eagle

Golden Eagle

OSPREY The osprey, which is nicknamed the "fish eagle" (on account of its diet), is a smaller version of the eagle, growing from 21 to 24 inches and with a white underbody and brown topsides. It is recognizable by a whistling sound it makes while hunting. Ospreys tend to create large nests made of twigs and branches that are found on the tops of trees and power poles. Look for this handsome, interesting bird in the Snake River area and the Grand Canyon of the Yellowstone River, a popular nesting area.

TRUMPETER SWAN   The trumpeter swan, one of the largest birds on the continent, has chosen the ecosystem as a sanctuary. Easily recognizable by their long, curved necks, snowy white bodies, and black bills, they are found in marshes and on lakes and rivers. Odds of a sighting are excellent on the Madison River near the West Yellowstone Entrance, and on Christian Pond, Swan Lake, and Cygnet Pond in Grand Teton.

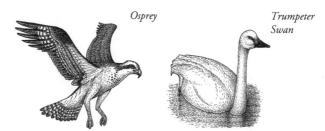

Osprey

Trumpeter Swan

OTHER RAPTORS   American Kestrels, Prairie Falcons, and **Red-Tailed Hawks** are seen on Antelope Flats–Kelly Road in Grand Teton, most often over hay fields, where they search for small rodents.

American Kestrel

Prairie Falcon

Red-Tailed Hawk

OTHER AQUATIC BIRDS   The **Great Blue Heron,** a skinny, long-legged wading bird, is found in wetlands and rocky outcrops, especially near the end of Jackson Lake. Yellowstone Lake is a prime viewing area for the best fishers in the park, the **American White Pelicans** that capture fish in their long, yellow pouched bill. The **American Dipper,** the only aquatic songbird in North America, revels in cold, fast-flowing mountain streams. The slate-gray dipper is tiny, only 7 to 8 inches tall, and is recognized by its long bill and stubby tail.

*Great Blue
Heron*

*American White
Pelican*

*American
Dipper*

Index

See also separate Accommodations and Restaurants indexes, below.

RESTAURANTS

FROMMER'S® COMPLETE TRAVEL GUIDES

Alaska
Amsterdam
Arizona
Atlanta
Australia
Austria
Bahamas
Barcelona, Madrid & Seville
Beijing
Belgium, Holland & Luxembourg
Bermuda
Boston
Budapest & the Best of Hungary
California
Canada
Cancún, Cozumel &
  the Yucatán
Cape Cod, Nantucket & Martha's Vineyard
Caribbean
Caribbean Cruises & Ports of Call
Caribbean Ports of Call
Carolinas & Georgia
Chicago
China
Colorado
Costa Rica
Denmark
Denver, Boulder & Colorado Springs
England
Europe
Florida
France
Germany
Greece
Greek Islands
Hawaii
Hong Kong
Honolulu, Waikiki & Oahu
Ireland
Israel
Italy
Jamaica & Barbados
Japan
Las Vegas
London
Los Angeles
Maryland & Delaware
Maui
Mexico
Miami & the Keys

Montana & Wyoming
Montréal & Québec City
Munich & the Bavarian Alps
Nashville & Memphis
Nepal
New England
New Mexico
New Orleans
New York City
Nova Scotia, New Brunswick &
  Prince Edward Island
Oregon
Paris
Philadelphia & the
  Amish Country
Portugal
Prague & the Best of the Czech Republic
Provence & the Riviera
Puerto Rico
Rome
San Antonio & Austin
San Diego
San Francisco
Santa Fe, Taos &
  Albuquerque
Scandinavia
Scotland
Seattle & Portland
Singapore & Malaysia
South Africa
Southeast Asia
South Pacific
Spain
Sweden
Switzerland
Thailand
Tokyo
Toronto
Tuscany & Umbria
USA
Utah
Vancouver & Victoria
Vermont, New Hampshire
  & Maine
Vienna & the Danube Valley
Virgin Islands
Virginia
Walt Disney World & Orlando
Washington, D.C.
Washington State

FROMMER'S® DOLLAR-A-DAY GUIDES

Australia from $50 a Day
California from $60 a Day
Caribbean from $70 a Day
England from $70 a Day
Europe from $60 a Day
Florida from $60 a Day

Hawaii from $70 a Day
Ireland from $50 a Day
Israel from $45 a Day
Italy from $70 a Day
London from $85 a Day
New York from $80 a Day

New Zealand from $50 a Day
Paris from $85 a Day
San Francisco from $60 a Day
Washington, D.C.,
   from $60 a Day

FROMMER'S® PORTABLE GUIDES

Acapulco, Ixtapa &
   Zihuatanejo
Alaska Cruises & Ports of Call
Bahamas
Baja & Los Cabos
Berlin
California Wine Country
Charleston & Savannah
Chicago

Dublin
Hawaii: The Big Island
Las Vegas
London
Maine Coast
Maui
New Orleans
New York City
Paris

Puerto Vallarta, Manzanillo
   & Guadalajara
San Diego
San Francisco
Sydney
Tampa & St. Petersburg
Venice
Washington, D.C.

FROMMER'S® NATIONAL PARK GUIDES

Family Vacations in the
   National Parks
Grand Canyon

National Parks of the
   American West
Rocky Mountain

Yellowstone & Grand Teton
Yosemite & Sequoia/
   Kings Canyon
Zion & Bryce Canyon

FROMMER'S® GREAT OUTDOOR GUIDES

New England
Northern California

Southern California & Baja
Washington & Oregon

FROMMER'S® MEMORABLE WALKS

Chicago
London

New York
Paris

San Francisco
Washington D.C.

FROMMER'S® IRREVERENT GUIDES

Amsterdam
Boston
Chicago
Las Vegas

London
Los Angeles
Manhattan

New Orleans
Paris
San Francisco

Seattle & Portland
Vancouver
Walt Disney World
Washington, D.C.

FROMMER'S® BEST-LOVED DRIVING TOURS

America
Britain
California

Florida
France
Germany

Ireland
Italy
New England

Scotland
Spain
Western Europe

THE COMPLETE IDIOT'S TRAVEL GUIDES

Boston
Chicago
Cruise Vacations
Planning Your Trip to Europe
Florida
Hawaii

Ireland
Las Vegas
London
Mexico's Beach Resorts
New Orleans
New York City

Paris
San Francisco
Spain
Walt Disney World
Washington, D.C.

THE UNOFFICIAL GUIDES®

Bed & Breakfast in
New England
Bed & Breakfast in
the Northwest
Beyond Disney
Branson, Missouri
California with Kids
Chicago

Cruises
Florida with Kids
The Great Smoky &
Blue Ridge
Mountains
Inside Disney
Las Vegas

London
Miami & the Keys
Mini Las Vegas
Mini-Mickey
New Orleans
New York City
Paris

San Francisco
Skiing in the West
Walt Disney World
Walt Disney World
for Grown-ups
Walt Disney World
for Kids
Washington, D.C.

SPECIAL-INTEREST TITLES

Born to Shop: France
Born to Shop: Hong Kong
Born to Shop: Italy
Born to Shop: New York
Born to Shop: Paris
Frommer's Britain's Best Bike Rides
The Civil War Trust's Official Guide
to the Civil War Discovery Trail
Frommer's Caribbean Hideaways
Frommer's Europe's Greatest Driving Tours
Frommer's Food Lover's Companion to France
Frommer's Food Lover's Companion to Italy
Frommer's Gay & Lesbian Europe
Israel Past & Present
Monks' Guide to California

Monks' Guide to New York City
The Moon
New York City with Kids
Unforgettable Weekends
Outside Magazine's Guide
to Family Vacations
Places Rated Almanac
Retirement Places Rated
Road Atlas Britain
Road Atlas Europe
Washington, D.C., with Kids
Wonderful Weekends from Boston
Wonderful Weekends from New York City
Wonderful Weekends from San Francisco
Wonderful Weekends from Los Angeles

Next time, make your *own* hotel arrangements.

Yahoo! Travel